THE·GREATEST·LITTLE MOTOR·BOAT·AFLOAT

THE LEGENDARY DISAPPEARING PROPELLER BOAT

DISAPPEARING PROPELLER BOAT COMPANY

Garth is much to honorable to break his word and he has promised me not to.

WE are well and trust you are. Best to Uncle Billy and Yourself in haste

Clair

New Devices put them in all boats from now on How do they look to you?

New starter looks and acts like a real job.

New timer according to your reports does also, also reports from shop here.

I will say we are going to have some boat this year what say You?

Excerpt from the handwritten letter dated March 2, 1922:
Clair Hodgson (President) to W. J. Johnston Jr. (Factory Manager).

THE·GREATEST·LITTLE
MOTOR·BOAT·AFLOAT

THE LEGENDARY DISAPPEARING PROPELLER BOAT

DODINGTON · FOSSEY · GOCKEL · OGILVIE · SMITH

Foreword by Ron Hill

A BOSTON MILLS PRESS BOOK

The Greatest Little Motor Boat Afloat
ISBN 0-919783-89-9

Published in 1994 by
Stoddart Publishing Co. Limited
34 Lesmill Road
Toronto, Canada
M3B 2T6
(416)445-3333

A BOSTON MILLS PRESS BOOK
The Boston Mills Press
132 Main Street
Erin, Ontario
N0B 1T0

Design by John Denison
Cover design by Gillian Stead
Typeset by Speed River Graphics
Printed in Canada

The publisher gratefully acknowledges the support of the Canada
Council, the Ontario Ministry of Culture and Communications,
Ontario Arts Council, and the Ontario Publishing Centre in the
development of writing and publishing in Canada

Contents

Foreword 7
Acknowledgements 10

PORT CARLING & NORTH TONAWANDA
GENESIS TO 1926

Chapter One
    Boatbuilding in the Port Carling Area
    Before the Dispro.................... 13
Chapter Two
    The Invention of "Johnston's Patent
    Disappearing Propeller" 23
Chapter Three
    The Formative Years, 1915-1918 37
Chapter Four
    The Good Years, 1919-1922 47
Chapter Five
    Life in the D.P. Factory 71
Chapter Six
    The United States Venture 85
Chapter Seven
    The Decline and Fall of the Disappearing
    Propeller Boat Company 91
Chapter Eight
    The D.P.'s Last Brief Appearance in Port
    Carling 103

LINDSAY, 1927-1936

Chapter Nine
    The Lindsay Boat Company 113

GRAVENHURST, 1936-1958

Chapter Ten
    The Dispro Returns to Muskoka........ 125

Memories of a Dispro Salesman 143
Dippy Anecdotes & Apocryphal Tales 149
Epilogue 155
Appendices 160
Bibliography 166

Paul Dodington's WHARERAH.

Foreword

There aren't many left now, perhaps a hundred or so kept running and shining by their proud owners, a few scattered across Canada and overseas, a few in marine museums, some rotting, bereft of their beautiful brass fittings, abandoned in the woods behind the cottage or filled with stones and sent ignominiously to the bottom of the lake. But the memories — these are plentiful, as vivid as yesterday and much more colourful. How many times have we heard at boat shows or club regattas, or while going through locks on the Trent Canal System or in Port Carling, "My God! An old Dispro — my father had one at the cottage for years." Then the stories would come — the storms they survived, how stable they were even with the mother-in-law, several kids and a big picnic basket on board, the little tricks to keep the confounded engine running, how that heartwarming "put-put-put" could be heard from far off through the evening haze by expectant children at the island dock, how perfect they were for trolling and for cruising in shallow water. Stories of exasperation, pride, annoyance and devotion but never any serious complaints...always fondly told with more than a trace of longing for the lazy, lovely never ending summers in which they were popular.

It was the outboard motor, of course, that did them in. Noisy, but fast and efficient, stuck on the back of a plastic "Tupperware" runabout. Noise and speed were what the 50s generation wanted. The Dispro became a symbol of a slower, more tranquil era. Nostalgia? Certainly; "a song of innocence written in the light of experience," as Malcolm Muggeridge wrote, and that's what this book is all about. It is the story of the evolution of an oversized rowboat with a little engine and an ingenious contraption that allows the propeller to come up into a housing within the boat even while the engine is running, thus protecting the propeller from damage. This is the Dispro, which captured the hearts and affections of thousands of happy owners. It is written by five men uniquely qualified to share their knowledge and experience with all those who knew the "Greatest Little Motor Boat Afloat" and with those who want to know the facinating history of an early Canadian industry.

Paul Dodington is the only one of the five whose family had a Dispro. His earliest memories of summer centre on his aunt's *Wharerah*; he showed such interest in the little boat that she allowed him to run it solo at the tender age of 11. But he remembers many other Dispros, too, as his summer home was just around the bay from where the first Dispro's keel hit the water at Johnston's Port Carling factory in 1915.

Paul, who is a genius at anything mechanical, put himself through Victoria College, University of Toronto, by repairing power lawnmowers and chainsaws at Eaton's. He had expected to teach history after graduating from the Faculty of Education but was asked by the Ontario Department of Education to set up a course of study on small engines and to teach that subject at the newly opened Castle Frank High School in 1963.

All through the 60s Paul's fascination with the Dispro grew and he began researching the D.P. story seriously, interviewing Billy Johnston and many of his factory employees, salesmen and office managers. Much of this material was tape-recorded. He has built up a substantial collection of original catalogues, advertisements, photographs and patents, many of which are reproduced in this book.

In 1976, the year of the Metro Toronto teachers' strike, Paul resigned from Castle Frank and moved to Port Carling permanently with his wife Nora and their three year-old daughter, Vicky; their second daughter, Amy, was born in 1977. Vicky is the fourth generation of Dodingtons to run *Wharerah*. Toronto lost a consummate teacher but the Dispro enthusiasts were lucky. Paul is devoting his talents full time to the restoration of the ever-increasing number of Dispro boats and engines that awakened interest has revealed.

It is interesting to note that three out of the five authors are actively involved with antique car clubs. The love of old and beautiful cars and the desire to bring them back to life is easily transferred to vintage boats. Paul Gockel, the youngest of the five, met Paul Dodington at an antique car show. One fine August evening in 1968 Mr. and Mrs. Gockel brought their 15 year-old son from their summer home in Port Sandfield to see the Dodington collection of antique cars. It wasn't long before they were all out for a Dispro ride and heading into the Muskoka sunset. The boy was smitten and soon had a Dispro of his own. Paul was so enamoured of this wonderful little boat that he set about searching the area for abandoned Dispro hulls and motors to renovate. Since Paul is an American, from Cleveland, Ohio, where he received his B.A. and M.A. in History, it seemed logical that he should research and write about the American subsidiary company in North Tonawanda; he also contributed the chapter on "Plant Life".

In any loosely formed group of people with a common interest it usually requires the leadership and determination of one individual to organize everybody to form a club. For the Dispro lovers that person was Joe Fossey. With the assistance of Jim Smith, Joe got the club underway. Without his drive and sustained efforts there would have been no club. He served as president for its first two years with Jim as his able secretary.

Joe has had a lifelong interest in boats. Soon after his marriage to Irene 34 years ago, he built his first craft, only 12 feet in length, made of wood and powered by a little 2½ outboard. The success of this venture whetted his appetite for more power and speed. Later he built a hydroplane with a 5 h.p. engine and with this project became a charter member of the Toronto Hydroplane Club. While his house was being constructed Joe built a 16-foot Canada One Design boat in the uncompleted living room; fortunately the picture window was large enough to allow its removal. After much tinkering with the Ford engine he had produced a boat, the *Miss Highland*, good enough to become the National High Point Champion for 1958 and 1959. Later Joe built a Corvette-powered, rear-engine California V-drive ski boat and introduced this fast-growing class of racing boat to eastern Canada.

In 1965 Chrysler Outboard, after hearing of Joe's achievements, asked him to become its service representative for Ontario and Western Canada. He was also asked to be crew chief of the Yellowbird racing project, which later captured the U-2 National High Points for 1967-69. After nine years with Chrysler, Joe moved to Bayliner Marine and later to J. Craft Performance Boats. At present he is Plant Manager of Dixon Valve and Coupling in Barrie, Ontario.

It seems strange that after a lifelong love affair with the building and competitive driving of fast racing boats Joe should now be so keen on one of the slowest motor boats ever made. His early wooden boat building experience had a lasting influence on him and he yearned to own one of the finely crafted wooden launches of the Muskokas. He couldn't afford an expensive Ditchburn or Minett but five years ago he was offered a Greavette Dispro. Like our other authors Joe became intrigued with the history of this remarkable craft. He subsequently bought two more Greavettes and in his travels has amassed a formidable collection of brochures, catalogues and photographs, some of which you will see in Part 3 on the Greavette Dispro.

Dr. James L. Smith, a Toronto dentist, is the careful and popular secretary-treasurer of the association that he helped Joe Fossey to establish. His is one of the more unusual boats in the club, a Lindsay Sport Special, which took him four summers of painstaking labour to renovate. At the 1982 regatta we were all glad to see him finally in the captain's seat of his lovely boat, surging ahead of us all.

Jim is interested in other antiques, too. He is a member of the Studebaker Drivers Club and owns four Studebakers which he maintains in showroom condition. An authority on outboard motors, Jim is Special Features Editor of *Antique Outboard*. He has contributed over 30 articles to this journal and he owns more than 200 motors. He is a charter member of the Antique Outboard Motor Club of America. As though these interests were not enough Jim is a pilot with 23 years experience and is a part-time flight instructor and a keen member of the Canadian Aviation Historical Society.

Bill Ogilvie, born in 1899, has the distinction to be the only one of our five authors to ride in a *brand new* Dippy. Beginning, in the spring of 1921, with a 1500 mile journey down the Mackenzie River in a sixteen foot Water-ford model Dispro, Bill was so impressed with the little boat he took a job as salesman working out of the D.P. Head Office in Toronto. By 1926 Bill was not only chief salesman but factory manager as well. He personally went to Detroit and hand-picked the 20,000 board feet of cypress used that year. Three years later Bill started his own successful yacht brokerage company (now Ogilvie Bloss Ltd.). Retiring to Lakefield after fifty years in the boat business, Bill began to pursue his second career, that of writer. Last year his First World War memoirs *Umty-Iddy-Umty* were published, also by The Boston Mills Press.

These, then, are the authors. We hope that you will enjoy reading their collected histories and reminiscences and will come to see why they consider the old Dispro "The Greatest Little Motor Boat Afloat".

Ron Hill
President,
Dispro Owners Assoc.

Acknowledgements

PORT CARLING

We would like to thank the following individuals and institutions for their invaluable assistance, patience, and encouragement:

Betty Amey; Leonard Amey; Charles F. Amey; Archives of Ontario; Bruce Clarke; Janet Clark; Cleveland Public Library; Lloyd Conrad, Lunenberg Foundry and Engineering Co.; the late Russell Cope; the late E. Buell Cox; William Croucher; Dispro Owners' Association; John Dixon; the late Annie Louise Dodington; the late James L. Dodington; Evelyn Dodington; James E. Domm; Audrey Duke; Dorothy Duke; Roger Dyment; Jack Dymond; D.A. Eisenhauer, Atlantic Bridge Co. Ltd., Lunenburg, N.S.; Ardath Fairhall; Gordon Fairhall; the late Weston Farmer, C.W. Farrar; Joe Fossey; Lloyd Foster; Rev. Stephen Gilbert, Bill Gray; Larry Healey; Ron and Jane W. Hill; Alan Howard; Bert Hurst; the late W.J. Johnston Jr.; the late Mae Johnston; Helen Langevin; Hugh MacLennan, Sr.; C.J. McCulley; the late Cameron Milner; the late Douglas Milner; Edith Moogk; Museum of the Tonawandas; William G. Ogilvie; Ontario Department of Provincial Secretary; Osgoode Hall; Port Carling Pioneer Museum; Port Carling Public Library; Bert Riddiford; Stuart Robinson; Parry Schreiber; Wayne Scott; Dr. J.L. Smith; Eric Stephen; the late Reginald Stephen; Marguerite Stimpson; the late J.S.G. Tassie; Kitty Tassie; Eleanor Thompson; Toronto City Archives ; Ian Turnbull; Stephanie Vanderburg; Tom Wood.

We would also like to thank the family of Harry Symons, author and publisher of *Ojibway Melody*, 1946, for permission to quote from that delightful book.

Our thanks also to James Woodruff, who did most of the photography.

Special thanks to Nora Dodington, who not only typed and retyped the manuscript for Part I, but who for years encouraged and patiently endured the agonizing gestation of all those elusive shreds of evidence and reminiscences into a comprehensive account of the early history of the Dispro.

Paul Dodington
Paul Gockel

LINDSAY

Mrs. S. Botting, Pat Saunders, Lloyd Eberts, Lloyd and Norma Foster, Paul Gockel.

Jim Smith

GRAVENHURST

Dedicated to my wife Irene, a research companion without whose help and understanding this writing could not have taken place. Her patience and ability to decipher the scribbled notes and hieroglyphics of this antique boat nut are appreciated. A further dedication is made to the memory of Mr. Tom Greavette and the superb craftsmen, both past and present, from Greavette Boats.

I would also like to acknowledge the following people for supplying information, assistance or encouragement in this work: James G. Perrin; Dr. Jim Smith; Paul and Nora Dodington; Paul Gockel; Bert and Jessie Hurst; Bruce L. Wilson, Greavette Boats Inc.; Ronald MacNab; Peter Lapey; Peter Moran, Simcoe County Archivist; Audrey H. Duke; Charles Amey; Alf Mortimer; Pete Miller; Jim Thrift; Dempsey Barnes; Douglas Van Patten; Weston Farmer; Gary Johnston; James E. Domm; Ron Hill; Donald Caunter; William G. Ogilvie; David Eastman, Motorboat Historical Society; Mrs. Sam Botting; Roger and Betty Dyment; Lloyd Conrad, Lunenburg Foundry; George Powell; Ed Skinner, Duke Marine Service; Jim and Linda Potter, Manotick Classic Boat Club; Peter and Diane Elliott; The Muskoka Sun; The Barrie Banner; The Barrie Examiner; Jon Wilson, Woodenboat Magazine; Peter Spectre, Woodenboat Magazine.

Joe Fossey

GENERAL

The authors would be remiss not to acknowledge the superb and special contributions made by Jim Domm of Toronto and Oro Station, Ontario, in co-ordinating and guiding the authors in the production of the book. Jim's business approach from concept to finished book kept us on track and on time. Were it not for Jim's efforts, this book could well still be in the form of a partially finished manuscript.

Benjamin Hardcastle Johnston, Postmaster of Port Carling, with his sons, about 1875. William Joseph Johnston, considered to be the founder of the commercial boatbuilding industry in Muskoka is at lower left. Behind him is Robert, the father of W.J. Johnston Jr. who later patented the Disappearing Propeller. (Courtesy Eleanor Thompson)

PORT CARLING
NORTH TONAWANDA
Genesis to 1926

Boatbuilding in the Port Carling Area Before the Dispro

by Paul Dodington

The origins of small-craft construction in the Muskoka Lakes date back to the year 1868. Prior to this time of course, the local Indians had built their bark canoes and the earliest white tourists and settlers, who first arrived in the area in the 1860s, had brought the occasional boat into Muskoka. William Holditch of Bracebridge is known to have built a large flat boat propelled by a horse and treadmill about 1864, but the propelling arrangement proved to be a failure, and it was soon abandoned.[1]

A couple of sailing vessels and a large rowboat also made brief appearances but the first really successful craft to ply the Muskoka Lakes was an 82-foot paddle steamer called the *Wenonah*, which in Ojibway means *First-Born Daughter*. She was built in Gravenhurst in 1866 and was the first of a magnificent fleet of steamers which plied the Muskoka Lakes for almost 100 years.

In 1868, Benjamin Hardcastle Johnston, a pioneer who had recently moved to the Muskoka wilderness from London, Ontario with his four sons, acquired some land at the south end of Lake Rosseau, between Brackenrig and Arthurlie Bays. Here he built a home, one of the first tourist establishments, which he named "Wild Goose Lodge". It was here in a small barn that his sons first experimented with making dugouts by cutting out and shaping the centre sections of pine logs.

Johnston also built a house in 1868 beside the Baisong Rapids in the Indian River and was in the same year appointed postmaster of "Obajawanung" or Indian Village, a position which he held until his death in 1897. He foresaw the coming development of the beautiful Muskoka Lakes as one of Canada's foremost tourist attractions and joined forces with a number of other Muskoka settlers, particularly A.P. Cockburn, MPP, the owner of the steamer *Wenonah*, in petitioning the Ontario legislature in December, 1868, to build a set of locks around the Baisong Rapids in the Indian River.[2] The proposed lock would enable the steamer *Wenonah*, which was already plying the waters of Lake Muskoka, to navigate the waters of Lakes Rosseau and Joseph as well and thereby open up the surrounding area to development. Although the efforts of the petitioners were dismissed by many of the politicians in the legislature as an attempt to link up "a couple of frog ponds,"

---

[1] Florence B. Murray, *Muskoka and Haliburton 1615 — 1875* (Toronto: University of Toronto Press, 1963), XCIX.
[2] Ibid, P. 340

Port Carling in 1879 as sketched by Mr. S.R.G. Penson.

the project in fact did go ahead and the locks were completed by 1871. In reward for his efforts on behalf of the canal and lock, Benjamin Hardcastle Johnston was given the privilege of renaming the fledgling Indian Village. He called it Port Carling in honour of Sir John Carling, MP for London, Ontario, a friend and supporter, who was on a fishing trip in the village at the time.[3]

Subsequently Muskoka developed rapidly as a tourist area and a great many hotels and cottages were built, some of which still stand. This influx of vacationers created a demand for small craft and the Johnstons immediately became involved in the building of rowboats.

Exactly when and where the first Johnston rowing skiff was manufactured is in some doubt. Garth Tassie, who was actively involved in the boatbuilding business in Port Carling from 1920 until the 1940s, maintained that W.J. Johnston Sr.,[4] the eldest son of Benjamin Hardcastle Johnston, decided in 1868 to build a rowboat. "At this time," says Tassie, "the nearest place that one could be purchased was in Barrie, a good distance away. So without any previous knowledge and never having seen a boat constructed, Mr. Johnston built a rowboat which was a real success and such an advancement over the previously-owned dugouts and birchbark canoes."[5]

If this statement is true the Johnstons must have been a busy family indeed in the year 1868. It seems more logical to assume that if they were building dugouts in 1868, and had never seen a rowboat constructed, the first real rowing skiff was probably not built until later.

Even the location of the building of the first skiff is in doubt. One local history declares that it was built in 1868 by W.J. Johnston Sr. in a workshop underneath his father's post office in Port Carling.[6] Another local legend has it that it was built in a small barn still in existence, behind Wild Goose Lodge, on Lake Rosseau.

Whatever the actual circumstances surrounding the building of the first rowboat, it is evident that Johnston correctly foresaw a tremendous demand for watercraft of this type.

[3] Leila M. Cope, *A History of the Village of Port Carling* (Bracebridge, Ont.: Herald-Gazette Press, 1956), 7.

[4] Wm. Joseph Johnston Sr., 1851-1935, is believed to have been the first commercial boatbuilder in the Muskoka area.

[5] J.S.G. Tassie, *A Sketch of the Boat Building Industry at Port Carling*, circa 1938 (Document in author's collection).

[6] Leila M. Cope, Op. cit., 64.

The rocky Muskoka terrain discouraged travel overland so settlers and tourists alike depended almost exclusively on the many waterways of the area for transportation, a situation existing until well into the 1920s.

By the early 1870s W.J. Johnston had moved to Port Carling and built a shop on the riverbank just below the present bridge. Here, with the assistance of his brother-in-law, Jack Trouten, he built large numbers of rowboats for sale and for rent. Additional boat liveries were set up at Windermere, about three miles away, and at Port Sandfield, about six miles away, and by the turn of the century these three enterprises provided over 300 rowboats for the summer tourist trade.[7]

W.J. Johnston had now become a man of considerable importance in the village of Port Carling and in view of his status in the community, he bought himself a swallow-tail coat, which he wore daily along with his sea-captain's cap. He soon became known around the village as "Uncle Billy Wagtail".[8]

[7] Leila M. Cope, Ibid, 64
[8] Eleanor Thompson, Port Carling, (niece of W.J. Johnston Jr.)

W. J. JOHNSON

Near the docks and bridge are boat houses, where a fleet of skiffs of all sizes nod and dance at anchor. Furnishing boats to tourists in quite an industry here in the summer, quite apart from the numbers used by the residents. Every one rows here as a matter of course, and it would not be very surprising if from these home-trained oarsmen some of the record makers of future races may come.

The resident boat builder here is Mr. W. J. Johnson. His boat house and shops adjoin the locks upon the upper side, and are very convenient to all hotels. He builds a good variety of boats upon light, easy-running models, and of sizes to suit the requirements of all customers. It is needless for tourists coming from a distance, or for a short stay, to encumber themselves with boats, as they can be rented from Mr. Johnson by the trip, day, or week. They can be engaged by mail or ordered by post card from any of the lake hotels, and will be promptly forwarded by steamer to any point desired. Mr. Johnson has just erected a handsome three-storey dwelling, just below the bridge, on the south side of the river, where he may be found when not at the boat house.

Address: W. J. JOHNSON, Port Carling.

The earliest known advertisement for W.J. Johnston's Boat Livery. (From Guide to the Northern Lakes of Canada, Williamson Co., Toronto, 1888. Courtesy Port Carling Pioneer Museum)

The Johnston brothers — Robert (father of W.J. Johnston Jr.), W.J. Johnston Sr., (wearing his swallow-tail coat) and Garry.

15

The Robert Johnston family, circa 1895. W.J. Johnston Jr., is standing at left. (Courtesy Janet Clark)

W.J. Johnston Sr. and John Matheson in front of Registry Office, Bracebridge, around 1900. (Courtesy John Dixon)

In 1892 he engaged John Matheson, a boatbuilder from Toronto, to assist him in the business. Matheson, the son of a shipbuilder, had been born in Caithness, Scotland. At age 12 he had run away to sea and spent a few years on a four-master, running herring to Russia. Upon his return, he apprenticed with his father and others, learning the boatbuilding trade which was to occupy him the rest of his life. Emigrating to Canada in the 1880s, he built rowboats and sailboats in a shop at the foot of York Street in Toronto. He subsequently found his way to Muskoka and a year or so later joined the Johnston enterprise where his particular abilities were much in demand.[9] During his 14-year association with the Johnstons many beautiful sailing yachts and dinghies were built and it is believed that he influenced considerably the design of the Johnston rowing skiff.[10]

In the year 1900, W.J. Johnston for the first time employed his 19-year-old nephew, W.J. Johnston Jr., to look after the newly-established Port Sandfield boat livery during the summer and to work at the boat factory in Port Carling the rest of the year. (Henceforth, they will be referred to as W.J. Johnston Sr. or Jr. to avoid confusion. To the villagers, of course, they were known simply as "Uncle Billy" and "Young Billy".)[11]

In 1904, they built their first gasoline-powered motorboats, which they named *Dreadnaught* and *Fearnaught*. The craft were about 27 feet long and are believed to have been equipped with Ferro engines. This date marks the genesis of the powerboat building industry in Muskoka.

In 1906, W.J. Johnston Jr. built a fast 30 foot motor launch while attending to his duties at Port Sandfield. This boat was named the *Humming Bird* and it proved so successful that a second was also constructed. Soon afterwards, a well-to-do local cottager, Mr. J.R.C. Hodgson, who hailed from Syracuse, New York, had Johnston build him a similar craft, which was known as *Humming Bird III*. This appears to be the beginning of an association which later culminated in the formation of the Disappearing Propeller Boat Company.

At about this time a personal conflict developed between Matheson and the elder Johnston. Matheson severed his connection with the Johnstons to set up a shop on his own directly across the Indian River.

On November 22, 1910, Uncle Billy formally granted his nephew an equal partnership in the Port Sandfield agency. In return Young Billy agreed to manage that agency during the boating season and to build boats with his uncle in Port Carling the rest of the year. Subsequently, they built several more launches and sailboats, in addition to rowboats. By 1914, the boat liveries were booming enterprises and the Port Sandfield agency in particular was doing considerable business with the motorboating "carriage trade", as well as providing rowboats for guests at the numerous summer hotels which had recently been established in the vicinity.

At this time W.J. Johnston Jr. sensed an increasing demand for a small lightweight, gasoline-powered craft, about the size of a rowboat, which could be pulled up on the beach or the dock with relative ease, without damaging the propeller or shafting.[12] He may also have foreseen a dim future for the hundreds of existing Johnston rowboats unless something were done to keep them relevant in the fast-approaching motor age. So, during the summer of 1914, Young Billy Johnston turned his energies to the design of a power-driven rowboat which could be beached without damage to the propeller and which could be used either as a rowboat or a powerboat.

[9] John Dixon, Port Carling (Grandson of J. Matheson), interview with author, January 1983.
[10] Parry Schreiber, Port Carling, (Matheson & Johnston built the sailboat, *Frayia* for the Schreibers in 1896.) Interview with author, 1982.
[11] William James Johnston, Jr., 1881-1968, son of Robert Johnston.
[12] W.J. Johnston Jr. (Interview with author, July 1967)

A Matheson skiff photographed in the late 1880s in front of Matheson's boat shop in Toronto. L. to R.: Johnina Matheson, Unknown, John Matheson. (Courtesy John Dixon)

This is the earliest known photograph of Johnston's boat livery, which was located on the government dock above the Port Carling locks, opposite the island. Photo circa 1891. (Turnbull Collection)

Building one of the first gasoline-powered motorboats in the Johnston Boat Works, Port Carling, circa 1905. L. to R.: John Matheson, W.J. Johnston Jr., W.J. Johnston Sr., Alf Gage. (Courtesy Janet Clark)

The newer Johnston and Ditchburn boat liveries at the same location, as they appeared around 1900, viewed from the island. (Courtesy Port Carling Pioneer Museum)

Around 1907, the Johnston and Ditchburn Boat Liveries were moved across the lock channel to the Island. After the advent of the D.P., Johnston's livery was replaced by Temple's Moving-Picture Theatre. Note the carbide gas lamp on the dock in front of Johnston's. (Turnbull Collection)

The HUMMING BIRD at Port Sandfield, moments after its launching. The late date (1910) on the photograph would indicate that the craft is probably HUMMING BIRD III, built for J.R.C. Hodgson, who was later instrumental in establishing the Disappearing Propeller Boat Company.

Windermere, Lake Rosseau, about 1905. John Matheson was Manager of Johnston's Boat Livery here, which was located in the two buildings on the shore, at left. Windermere House, in the background, had recently been enlarged by an extensive addition onto the left side of the original building and Johnston's business increased accordingly. (Turnbull Collection)

A fleet of Johnston rowing skiffs at the Elgin House dock, Port Sandfield, circa 1910.

Advertisement in 1915 Muskoka Lakes Blue Book Directory for Rogers Bros., who provided the first Waterman Marine engine for the prototype Dispro. (Courtesy Port Carling Pioneer Museum)

Rear Quarter View
Exhaust Side Model K-1.

Waterman 2 h.p. engine.

The Waterman PORTO MOTOR, introduced in 1906, served as the inspiration for the copper-jacketed inboard engines later used in the Dispro.

22

The Invention of
"Johnston's Patent Disappearing Propeller"
by Paul Dodington

By the summer of 1914, a few small gasoline-powered boats were beginning to appear on the Muskoka Lakes. This was due in part to the recent development of smaller light-weight gasoline engines of the two-stroke variety and various technical improvements in ignition and carburetion, which provided a modicum of dependability combined with low cost.

The lightest by far of this new breed of small inboard engines was the two-horsepower Waterman, the brainchild of Mr. Cameron Waterman of Detroit, Michigan. Waterman, who is perhaps best remembered for his successful fountain pen, may actually be credited as well with the concept and early development of the outboard motor, in 1905.

By 1906, the Waterman "Porto Motor" was in commercial production, and by 1908, the Waterman Motor Co. of Detroit was also marketing its 2 h.p. K-1 model. This was an inboard engine which owed much of its efficiency and light weight to lessons learned in the early outboard experimentation: such things as the use of aluminum castings, spun copper water jackets and highly-stressed undersized parts. Lightweight pistons and connecting rods coupled with short-stroke design permitted engine r.p.m.'s much in excess of conventional standards of the day.

It is likely that W.J. Johnston Jr. first became exposed to these ultra-lightweight engines some years later, when the Rogers Brothers of Port Sandfield became Waterman agents.[1]

Unquestionably, Johnston could have had no thought of putting a gasoline engine in a rowing skiff previous to this introduction to the Waterman, as a well-known maxim of the time to describe weight-to-power ratio for typical marine gas engines was "One hundred pounds weight per horsepower".[2]

The rapidly expanding popularity of such lightweight marine engines spawned a number of gimmicks to make them adaptable to small craft operating in shallow waters. In an article in a 1913 issue of *Popular Mechanics* magazine, for instance, Clifford W. Johnston,

[1] An advertisement in *Muskoka Lakes Blue Book Directory and Chart*, Captain John Rogers, Publisher, Port Sandfield, Muskoka, 1915, lists the Rogers as agents for Waterman engines.
[2] The famous Lozier marine engines built in Buffalo, New York, weighed approximately 100 lb. per horsepower.

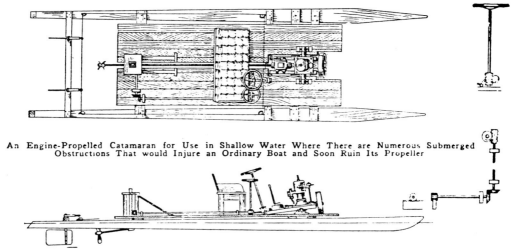

An Engine-Propelled Catamaran for Use in Shallow Water Where There are Numerous Submerged Obstructions That would Injure an Ordinary Boat and Soon Ruin Its Propeller

Clifford W. Johnston of Parry Sound designed this power-driven catamaran about 1912 or 1913. (Courtesy Wayne Scott)

of Parry Sound, Ontario submitted drawings of a power-driven catamaran, "For use in shallow water where there are numerous submerged obstructions that would injure an ordinary boat and soon ruin its propeller". This design involved mounting the engine on a half-gimbal arrangement which allowed the engine to tilt as the operator raised or lowered the propeller by means of a hand-wheel and gear set. There was no universal joint involved nor was the propeller protected from unseen underwater obstructions.

Universal joints, however, were in common use by that time, particularly in the automotive field, where they were a well-known means of transmitting power between shafts of varying angles. In fact, the legendary "Alligators", those steam-driven amphibious craft used in early lumbering operations in northern Ontario, used this concept. While the few surviving examples of Alligators are paddle-driven, it is known that twin-screw versions were made as well by West and Peachie of Simcoe, Ontario and that the propellers and shafts could be raised completely out of the water by means of universal joints. This feature would permit the craft to winch itself overland from one lake to another without sustaining propeller damage.

An ALLIGATOR showing the propeller haul-up feature.

24

"Tunnel King" Motor Boats
The Safe Boat With Protected Propellor

Note the long graceful lines of the "Standard Model."

To be fully satisfactory a boat should not only be reliable and seaworthy. It should also present an appearance on the water of which its owner can feel justly proud.

In this respect, as in all others, the Tunnel-King is exactly right. There is no other motor boat at its price which can equal it in appearance. Its lines are the lines of a real power cruiser. Its sharply pointed bow, square stern and mahogany deck, fore and aft, give it a beauty that is pleasant to look upon.

And the Tunnel-King is roomy. She is designed primarily to carry six passengers, but many more can be taken along if desired, for the Tunnel-King rides the water like a swan, owing to her real ship lines. Nothing "tubby" about the Tunnel-King—no, Sir! She's a beauty to look at as well as to sail in.

By investing in a Tunnel-King you will get continuous dividends of healthy pleasure throughout the entire boating season, wherever you may be, on salt water or fresh—sea or lake or river. The world cannot show an equal of the Tunnel-King at anywhere near the price.

■**Through weeds, snags and over rocks.**—You are bound to get there in a Tunnel-King, if there is sufficient water to float the hull. Eight inches of water is all that is required so that the hitherto inaccessible fishing grounds are now awaiting you—to try your skill against the wily big fellows.

When you do arrive at your destination, there is no need to leave your motor boat in the water to get damaged, or possibly lost, because you can, with little effort, haul it ashore like a row boat. This will not injure the boat, owing to its close-ribbed, light-planked carvel lap, or smooth hull construction, which combines lightness and strength.

This carvel lap construction also means that should the hull get damaged, the simple operation of caulking will set the matter right, quickly and inexpensively, which is not so in the case of the row boat type. The reliable water-tight carvel lap construction is used on yachts and big launches. That's why we selected it for the Tunnel-King—because it is the best.

A comfortably wide beam and a square stern design give the Tunnel-King a surprising amount of seaworthiness and stability. It is the safe boat—the one you can trust your family in even when you are not with them. The snappy, launch-like appearance of the Tunnel-King you can best judge for yourself from the illustrations.

Write for Illustrated Booklet and Prices

The TUNNEL KING, built in Toronto by Walter Dean, was another Canadian design which later provided considerable competition for the Dispro. (Courtesy Ron Hill)

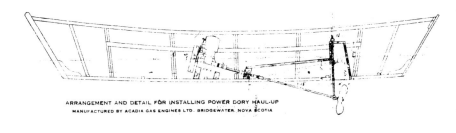

ARRANGEMENT AND DETAIL FOR INSTALLING POWER DORY HAUL-UP
MANUFACTURED BY ACADIA GAS ENGINES LTD. BRIDGEWATER, NOVA SCOTIA

Dory Shaft Haul-Up units were introduced in Nova Scotia at about the same time that Johnston's Patent Disappearing Propeller was invented but unlike Johnston's device, these units did not include the housing. In most respects, however, they bore an uncanny resemblance. (Courtesy Atlantic Bridge Co., Lunenburg, N.S.)

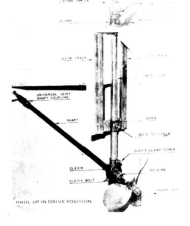

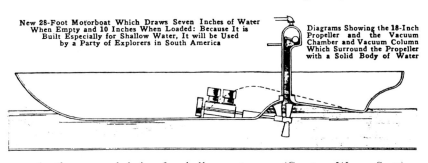

New 28-Foot Motorboat Which Draws Seven Inches of Water When Empty and 10 Inches When Loaded: Because It is Built Especially for Shallow Water, It will be Used by a Party of Explorers in South America

Diagrams Showing the 18-Inch Propeller and the Vacuum Chamber and Vacuum Column Which Surround the Propeller with a Solid Body of Water

Another unusual design for shallow water use. (Courtesy Wayne Scott)

According to the late Weston Farmer, noted American marine historian, propeller haul-up devices involving the use of universal joints were described in *Rudder* magazine as early as 1907. A.E. Luders at the Electric Launch Co., in Connecticut is said to have conducted the earliest experiments with such units.[3]

In Canada, both Lunenburg Foundry Co. Ltd. and Acadia Engine Co. Ltd., of Nova Scotia have been long-time manufacturers of propeller haul-up mechanisms for use in fishing dories. These "dory shaft haul-up" units are said to have been in production well before World War I and were originally designed to permit the craft to nestle safely on bottom at low tide or to be pulled up on slipways.

A number of other designs involved enclosing the propeller and shaft in a sort of tunnel built into the hull, including one unique arrangement in which the propeller was located at the normal waterline of the craft. When the boat was underway an engine-driven vacuum pump would draw water up a standpipe located above the propeller, thereby keeping the propeller submerged. This boat was said to draw only ten inches of water when carrying 15 passengers.

It seems unlikely that W.J. Johnston Jr. was aware of such developments, however, due to the relative geographic isolation of Port Carling in those days, coupled with his lack of formal education. Exactly how the idea of a flexible propeller shaft which could be drawn up into a housing inside a boat out of harm's way came to him will never be known but an apocryphal tale in circulation in the early 1920s explains it graphically:

"One day, the inventor got an idea while watching a large lake turtle. When there was no sign of danger, the turtle carried on his business as a peace-loving turtle should do; but in case of danger, legs and head were drawn into the shell, and the turtle was secure from harm, and, just as King Bruce got inspiration from a spider, and went out and won freedom for Scotland, so in the case of the inventor of this boat, the turtle furnished the idea of the disappearing propeller."[4]

Although W.J. Johnston Jr. has always been officially credited as the inventor of the D.P. device, considerable evidence suggests that the matter may not be quite that simple. While the apocryphal "turtle" story may have some basis in fact, and while Johnston was admittedly an excellent boatbuilder, he was not a mechanical designer or a machinist, or even a mechanic for that matter.

Edwin Rogers[5], who was well known around Port Sandfield as a mechanical wizard, operated a machine shop known variously as Muskoka Lakes Machinery & Supply Co., and Rogers Bros., in a building located immediately beside the Johnston Boat Livery. It is not known whether Rogers and Johnston were partners at this time but it is accepted that Rogers looked after most of the mechanical repairs and engine installations for Billy Johnston and it is believed that in this capacity he was actively involved in the design and manufacture of the original prototype device.

In fact some of the oldtime Muskoka boatbuilders, who were naturally very much aware of all developments on the local boatbuilding scene, maintained that the unit was

[3] Letter dated April 21, 1981, Farmer to Fossey. (Courtesy Joe Fossey)
[4] *1921 Port Carling Ripple*, (originally published by Port Carling Young People's Union. Reprinted by Port Carling Pioneer Museum 1979) p. 29
[5] Edwin Rogers, 1884-1946, son of Captain John Rogers of Port Sandfield, was a First Class Stationary Engineer. He was involved in racing boats in the early days before the D.P. and his personal craft, *Moonbird*, took first prize in an official speedboat race on at least one occasion. During the 'teens he is known to have built an experimental airboat driven by an aircraft engine and propeller. He also designed a small working model boat, driven by a jet of water from a hydraulic pump powered by a gasoline engine. In later years he developed an arrangement of built-in jacks attached to automobile axles which could be instantly activated from above in the event of a flat tire. Although he was of an inventive nature, he apparently lost interest in each of his many inventions once the technical problems had been overcome. He sold out his interest in the Muskoka Lakes Supply & Machine Co. to the Disappearing Propeller Boat Co. about 1920 for the sum of $2,900, and was never again involved with the Dispro.

The birthplace of the Disappearing Propeller at Port Sandfield. This building, located beside Johnston's Boat Livery, housed the Muskoka Lakes Supply & Machine Co., as well as Rogers Brothers. The photograph was taken in 1947, just as workmen began to remove the upper storey from the old building. The small building in front is the oil house. (Courtesy Stuart Robinson)

Edwin Rogers, his wife and daughters on the steps leading down to his machine shop at Port Sandfield. Photograph taken in 1914, the year of the invention of the D.P. Device. (Courtesy Marguerite Stimpson)

originally conceived and built by Rogers, who discarded it after a short period of experimentation. Johnston, when he saw Rogers' experimental haul-up device lying forgotten in an upstairs corner of his machine shop, apparently realized the possibilities of the retractable propeller and subsequently made arrangements to have it patented.

While the controversy may never be satisfactorily resolved, the very existence of these alternative theories concerning the origin of the Disappearing Propeller is an indication that the accepted version of the invention was found inadequate by some of those who knew both Johnston and Rogers on a personal basis.

It is not the purpose here to discredit Johnston in any way but rather to point out the fact that the Disappearing Propeller device, like most of the world's great inventions, was really the product of individuals of diverse talents pursuing a common goal. In fairness to both men, it can be stated that each made an essential contribution to the initial invention and promotion of the device, regardless of who conceived the idea first.

It appears that Edwin Rogers' unique mechanical skills and talents were necessary to convert that idea into a practical working piece of machinery. And Johnston's contribution is equally important. Had he not seen the commercial potential of a retractable propeller unit, and actively sought financial support for its initial development and production, there would have been no Disappearing Propeller Boat.

The Johnston Skiff

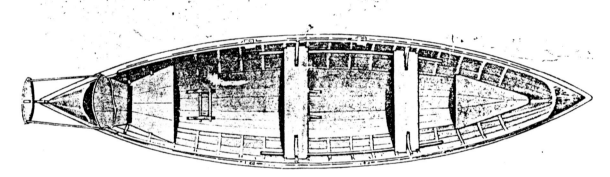

Length 14' 10"—Beam 3' 8"—Depth 16"

Johnston Skiffs were made in two sizes. This one, and the longer 16'6" model.

The initial experimentation is believed to have taken place during the summer of 1914. A wooden prototype device housing was built into a 16½ foot Johnston rowboat and a propeller shaft, universal joint and haul-up mechanism made up and installed along with a 2 h.p. Waterman K-1 engine. Rumour has it that this very first D.P. boat ignominiously rotted away many years later in a backwater near Port Sandfield.[6]

---

[6] It is thought by some that Billy's mechanically-inclined brother, Johnny, was also involved in some way in the original experimentation.

On October 23, 1914 specifications for a patent application were notarized at Bracebridge and on November 2 the formal application was received by the Canadian Patent Office in the Department of Agriculture for a "Propulsion Device for Boats".

The application was financed by R.A. Shields of New York City, who owned a summer cottage at Redwood, on Lake Joseph, about three miles from Port Sandfield, to whom W.J. Johnston Jr., named as the inventor, assigned undivided half interest. This patent was granted on March 16, 1915 and it remained the fundamental patent for its 18 year duration. A similar patent was taken out in the United States.[7] In subsequent years additional domestic and foreign patents were applied for, and granted, which provided patent protection until 1940.

Why the original patent was granted by the Canadian and U.S. patent offices is not immediately obvious, particularly in view of the fact that the general principles of its operation and layout had been previously anticipated by others. Like many of the world's greatest inventions no important engineering breakthrough was involved, but rather the D.P. device was simply a novel combination of previously existing concepts. The patentable feature of the Johnston device was that the articulating shaft and retractable propeller mechanism were combined into a special housing which, in its entirety, formed a distinct unit.[8]

Upon examination of the specifications of the original patent it is easy to see that this early device was quite unlike the devices produced afterward by the Disappearing Propeller Boat Company. Contrary to popular opinion, the purpose of the contrivance was not absolute propeller protection against underwater obstructions. Johnston states in the specification:

"...the object of the invention is to devise means whereby a screw propeller and driving shaft may be raised clear of the boat bottom so as to present no obstruction to the drawing of the boat either on to or off the run-ways and yet such a means as will allow of the propeller being moved quickly to the operative position when desired...".

He then sums up his claim with this statement:

"From this description, it will be seen that I have devised a very simple means whereby a screw propeller may be adaptable for use in small boats such as rowboats, and *in such a way that it will not interfere with the easy launching or landing of the boat..*"

In fact, when "Johnston's Patent Disappearing Propeller" was first offered for commercial sale in the summer of 1915, it was touted as a means of converting a rowboat to a motorboat. The housing, rather than being the wooden box affair used in the prototype and shown in the patent drawings, was now made of cast aluminum, combining light weight and strength.

Just how many of these units were sold during 1915 will probably never be known, but the number must necessarily have been small. Only one incomplete housing is known to have survived to the present day.

The choice of the term "Disappearing Propeller" for the contraption was clever indeed. It is a most intriguing name which immediately attracts attention and provokes curiosity as to how a propeller can possibly be made to disappear.

To raise the propeller in boats fitted with these early devices it was first necessary to stop the engine and align the two bladed propeller horizontally (a painted mark on the engine flywheel indicated the position of the propeller blades) so that it could then be raised into

[7] This date appeared on all D.P. devices until after World War II, long after the patent had expired. This original Canadian Patent was No. 161292. United States Patent No. 1,151,107 was filed on Nov. 4, 1914, and granted on Aug. 24, 1915.

[8] The wooden housing shown in the remarkably similar "Dory Shaft Haul-Up" illustrated on Page 25 was not sold as part of the unit but had to be specially constructed by the individual boat-builder.

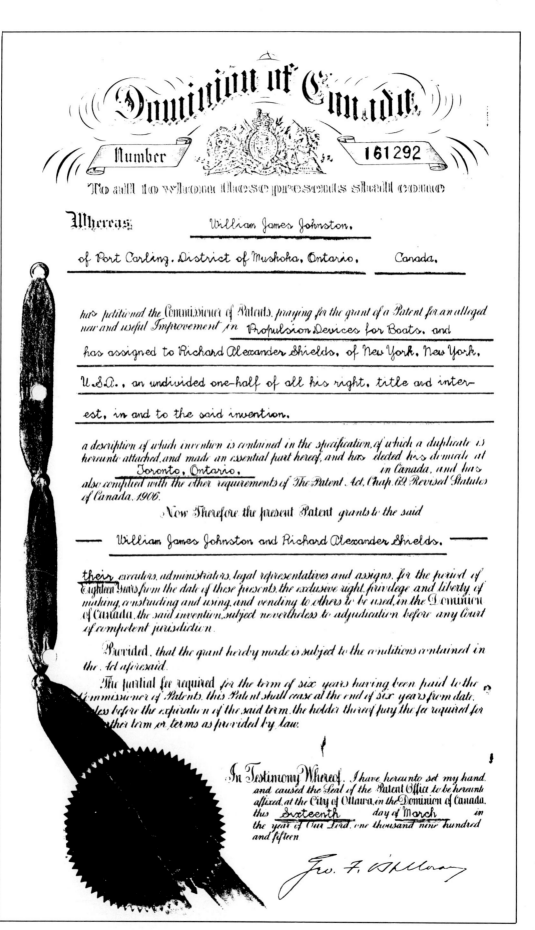

Front cover of the original Canadian D.P. Patent, No. 161292, March 16, 1915.

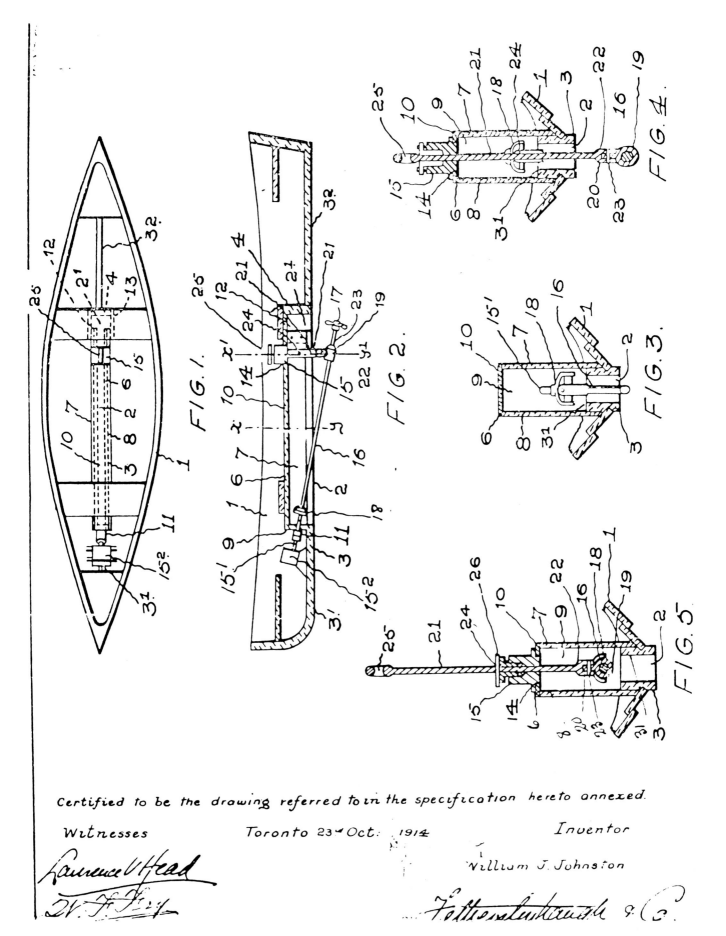

Drawing of the original device, annexed to Patent #161292. Note the wooden housing and the lack of propeller protection.

This incomplete aluminum device housing is the only known surviving example of Johnston's Patent Disappearing Propeller. (Courtesy R. Dyment)

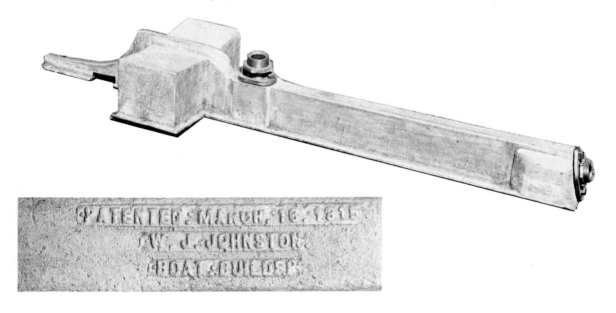

The only photograph known to exist of a Johnston skiff with Waterman engine and Johnston's Patent Disappearing Propeller installed. The splash boards were a later addition. (Courtesy C.W. Farrar)

the rather squat propeller housing. This housing in turn was designed to fit under one of the low midship seats of the Johnston rowboat. The propeller shaft, which was fitted with a universal joint located just behind the stuffing box, could be raised or lowered by means of a pull bar protruding through another stuffing box in the top of the cast aluminum housing and locked in place in the raised position by means of a pin. There was no access to the propeller without removing the boat from the water, nor could the engine be operated when the propeller was hauled up. Imagine the consequences of accidentally striking an underwater obstruction, or raising the propeller with the engine running!

The marketing of these first devices is significant in that prospective purchasers were advised that they could convert existing rowboats into motorboats with the unit. The concept of a Disappearing Propeller Boat as a complete entity had not yet developed. Advertising is believed to have been confined to the Muskoka area only.

The Model K-1 Waterman engine, which was destined to start the Dispro off on its forty-odd-year career was a very pretty little two-horsepower "one-lunger"; copper-jacketed, two stroke, using a mixture of oil and gas for fuel. Water pump, priming cock, drain cock, carburetor and timer were all of polished bronze. It had a top speed of about 800 r.p.m., and weighed only about 40 lb. complete with cast aluminum muffler. A contemporary catalogue stated, "We do not believe in selling ballast to our customers at engine prices".[9] Ignition was by vibrator coil and dry cell battery and fuel consumption was meagre indeed.

Model K-1—2 H.P.—36 Pounds.

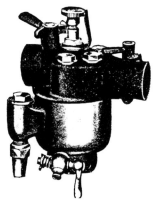

The great point in favor of this carburetor is that it is made carefully and when once adjusted—as it is before it leaves our factory—it requires no attention. With it the motor will start cold and give perfect satisfaction on a mixture of 20% gasoline and 80% kerosene as well as on alcohol, distillates, straight gasoline, benzine, etc. Our motors do not require the more expensive high test gasoline.

The Kingston Model "E" carburetor, which was factory equipment on thousands of copper-jacketed engines and small Carons.

By the end of the summer of 1915 the shortcomings of this first device must have become woefully apparent, but so must its potential have emerged. Late that summer Johnston became involved with another local cottager, John Robinson Clair Hodgson, a businessman, promoter and entrepreneur from Syracuse, New York, who saw the tremendous market potential for an improved device. Here was a man who could provide the much-needed capital and business acumen to exploit the invention properly.[10]

[9] Arrow Motor & Machine Co. Catalogue, 1917. (This concern acquired the Waterman patents and production rights in 1917.)

[10] J.R.C. Hodgson owned a cottage at Calypso Point near Gregory on Lake Joseph. Repeated efforts have failed to unearth any biographical information about this most important figure in the story of the Dispro. His address is never revealed in any existing correspondence, although in the patent applications his address is given as "Gregory". In the list of Board of Directors, however, he is listed as living in Toronto. At the time of the liquidation of the Disappearing Propeller Boat Co. in 1925, the sheriff apparently couldn't locate him either!

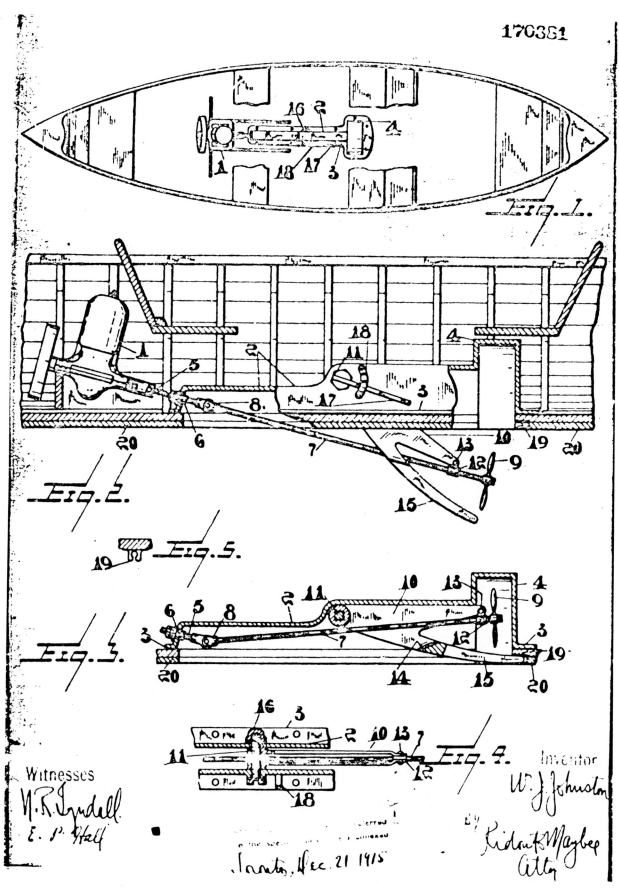

Patent drawings of the "improved device" of 1916. Note the radical design changes from the first patent. Of particular interest is the clip, no. 19, shown in Figures 2, 3 and 5, which was intended to hold the propeller and skeg in the raised position.

The earliest known advertisement for Johnston's Patent Disappearing Propeller as printed in John Roger's Muskoka Lakes Blue Book Directory, 1915. (Courtesy Port Carling Pioneer Museum)

The circumstances surrounding R.A. Shields' withdrawal from further active interest in the invention are not clear. It is believed that he probably sold his half interest in the original patent to J.R.C. Hodgson after a disagreement with Hodgson and Johnston over the rapidity with which the invention should be exploited. He is alleged to have advised Johnston at this time not to become involved with Hodgson.

On December 21, 1915 a second Canadian device patent was applied for, but this time it was called a "motor attachment for boats". Again Johnston was named as the inventor, but this time he assigned half interest to J.R.C. Hodgson. Whether or not Johnston or Rogers can actually be credited in any way with the radical conceptual and design changes that appear in this second patent will probably never be known. This improved device received its Canadian Letters Patent on June 27, 1916 and a similar application which had been filed in the U.S. Patent Office was granted on May 8, 1917. It became the standard unit of production with only one major change right through until the last Dispros were built in 1958.[11]

The basic conceptual difference between this new device and the preceding model was the provision for propeller protection from underwater hazards provided by a hollow articulating bronze skeg. The propeller and shaft could be held in any desired position from full up to full down by means of a ratchet and quadrant located beside the hand lever. The shaft itself was supported at the propeller end by a pivoting bearing fastened to the skeg, and the skeg could be raised or lowered by moving a handle inside the boat. Automatic propeller protection was also provided by the movable skeg which was designed to fold the whole contraption up into the cast-iron housing should it encounter a shoal or deadhead. The housing itself was redesigned to accommodate a rotating propeller in the "up" position, and inspection covers were installed to provide access to propeller, rock shaft and universal joint from within the boat. In theory at least, the device now appeared to be foolproof.

It was made abundantly clear in this second patent specification that the housing itself formed an integral part of the unit and was quite distinct from the hull of the boat, and that the whole device could be manufactured and sold as "an attachment for motor boats". Disappearing Propeller devices were in actual practice advertised and sold separately for many years by the Disappearing Propeller Boat Co. for installation in various types of craft. The design of the Dispro hull itself was never covered by patents of any kind.

This explains why, today, the occasional vintage hull is discovered which has a D.P. device installed but is otherwise quite unlike anything ever produced by the Disappearing Propeller Boat Company.

[11] Canadian Patent #170381. U.S Patent #1,225,252. U.K. Patent #104,178, Jan. 3, 1918.

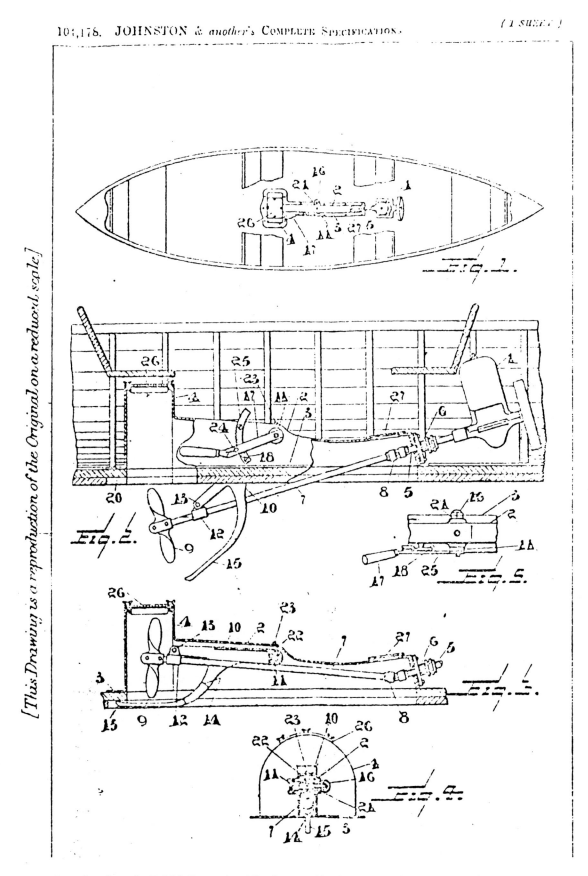

[This Drawing is a reproduction of the Original on a reduced scale.]

Drawing from the British Patent Specification: application date, February 12, 1917; acceptance date, January 3, 1918. Note the changes from the Canadian patent of one year earlier.

The Formative Years, 1915-1918

by Paul Dodington

THE ESTABLISHMENT OF THE DISAPPEARING PROPELLER BOAT
COMPANY LIMITED

In 1915, probably during the late summer or early fall, negotiations took place between J.R.C. Hodgson and W.J. Johnston Jr. which resulted in the formation of a company to facilitate production and distribution of "Disappearing Propeller Boats". It was at this time that Johnston agreed to assign to Hodgson a half interest in the invention and patent rights in return for which Hodgson agreed to finance the acquisition of a patent on the improved device and then to promote and organize a company to capitalize on the invention.[1]

In addition, Johnston gave Hodgson power of attorney having to do with all matters and transactions pertaining to inventions or patent rights. This agreement soon resulted in Hodgson's obtaining complete control over the patents. Why Johnston ever agreed to such a proposition in the first place seems in retrospect to be difficult to understand. Hodgson was probably reluctant to waste his money and his considerable entrepreneurial talents on an unknown quantity unless he was assured absolute control over its direction. And Johnston, who knew nothing about the world of business and finance, would have been delighted to turn over the business end of the enterprise to the more experienced Hodgson and to get down to the real business of building boats.

As a result of these negotiations, Clair Hodgson financed the patent application on the "improved device", and took steps to form the new company, to be named, "The Disappearing Propeller Boat Company Limited". Letters Patent were applied for in March 1916 and the company received its Ontario Charter on May 2, 1916.

The officers of the new company were:

    J.R.C. Hodgson — President
    Neil H. Wilson — Secretary
    Harry Minchinton — Treasurer
    Frank Erichsen-Brown — Director
    Vera Aull — Director

All of the above were said to reside in Toronto.[2]

---

[1] Statement of Defense, *Johnston vs. Hodgson*, Supreme Court of Ontario, #578-25.

[2] J.R.C. Hodgson is believed to have taken up permanent residence in Toronto at this time, possibly staying in the King Edward Hotel on King Street East. While no trace of him can be found in old Toronto city directories, his commitment to the promotion of the D.P. over the next few years is thought to have occupied him on a full time basis.

The original Johnston home (centre) and Boat Works (right) at Port Carling as they appeared about 1915. This factory, located just below the locks (visible in the foreground), is where the first production Dispro boats were made until the larger D.P. factory was built further downstream about 1917. The building in the background (at left) is the livery stable, later known as the Port Carling garage, where the prototype "Johnston Special" was designed and built during the summer of 1925. (Turnbull Collection)

On April 17, 1916 J.R.C. Hodgson, through his power of attorney, had purchased Johnston's half interest in the Canadian patent rights for the D.P. device for $2,500 paid stock in the new company and $1,000 cash. Hodgson, being sole owner of Canadian Patent No. 161292, now sold it on May 2, to the D.P. Boat Company for $3,000 cash and 2,000 paid shares in the new organization.

The company now began to exercise its rights under its new charter, namely, "To manufacture, repair, buy, sell and deal in boats, etc.". It was capitalized at $45,000 divided into 450 shares of $100 each.

During the next two years, both Uncle Billy and Young Billy transferred to the new company all assets owned or controlled by them, namely the machine shop and boathouse at Port Sandfield and a factory and equipment and boats at Port Carling, in return for capital stock worth $17,130.[3]

At this time, W.J. Johnston Sr., who was now 65 years of age, retired from active participation in the boatbuilding business but because of the 1910 agreement mentioned earlier, he did become a shareholder in the new company. Thereafter, he spent his retirement years until 1924 making spoon oars for the D.P. Boat Company. It is said that he could often be found in the D.P. factory lying sound asleep in the pile of shavings underneath his bench.[4]

W.J. Johnston Jr. had sold all his rights to Canadian Patent No. 161292 a short time before the D.P. Boat Company was formed. He subsequently sold all his other Canadian and foreign rights to Hodgson in a similar manner and remained a shareholder in the company, although he was never a member of the Board of Directors.

For the next nine years Johnston's influence on company policy was confined to his position as Factory Manager in Port Carling and it is likely that few, if any, of the future developments of the Dispro are attributable to him. Although W.J. Johnston Jr.'s influence on the business affairs of the company was insignificant after this time, nonetheless, a great deal of credit is due him for the effort he put into his job as Factory Manager. It is largely due to his hard work and persistence in this capacity that the factory was able to produce boats in such large quantities as the enterprise grew.

The scenario was now in place for the bitter wrangling over the ownership of patent rights which was to take place in less than a decade. Hodgson's power of attorney over Johnston in all matters concerning the disposition of the latter's half interest in the patents, plus his subsequent purchase of Johnston's half interest, eventually led to an atmosphere of mutual mistrust and bitterness which was to come to a head when the company began to experience serious financial difficulties in 1923 and 1924.

[3] Statement of Defense, *Johnston vs. Hodgson*, op. cit. and File #23792, op. cit.
[4] Bert Riddiford, Port Carling, Interview with author, December 1981.

Another view of the first D.P. factory. The steamer MEDORA is just entering the locks.

For the present moment, however, the agreements entered into by Johnston and Hodgson were undoubtedly sensible ones. Johnston's invention would probably never have become more than another "Rube Goldberg" gimmick without the special entrepreneurial talents and untiring promotional efforts of J.R.C. Hodgson. And, of course, Hodgson needed not only Billy Johnston's patent rights, but also his fine boatbuilding skills, facilities, and employees. It was a kind of symbiotic relationship which was destined to achieve success. After the unfortunate severing of these ties nine years later, any attempts by others to revive the Dispro, to even a shadow of its former glory and popularity, were doomed to frustration and eventual failure.

THE FIRST PRODUCTION DISPRO BOATS — 1916

In a handwritten letter dated March 8, 1916, to Billy Johnston, Clair Hodgson writes from his room at the King Edward Hotel in Toronto:

> "Am trying to do 7000 things at once.... . I have ordered cap for exhaust, also stopper for tank.... . I had a casting made in grey iron, weight, 70 lbs. I am trying to arrange to get it down to 45, am also having one made up in sheet iron.... . I hope to have literature soon within a day or so. Don't slacken on your boat building we will need them.... . Eaton's boat does not have to be ready until April 15th as they have no space until that time.... . When we can get a boat complete just as it will be, I will be glad to have it, but not before."[5]

Certainly there were many wrinkles to be ironed out in those first hectic months of production. From this letter, it appears, incidentally, that the T. Eaton Co. of Toronto may possibly have been the first sales agency.[6]

When the first Disappearing Propeller boats made their debut in the spring of 1916, they were considerably changed indeed from the old Johnston rowboat. At first glance the new hull looked like an overgrown version of the older boat. It was still of lapstrake construction with planking, keel, skyboards and seats of Ontario cedar, while the stem, sternpost and ribs were white oak. Length was 16½ feet with a 3 foot 9 inch beam and a depth of 17 inches. But the new "improved" cast iron device housing, which had been made considerably taller in order to accommodate a rotating propeller in the raised position, necessitated several corresponding changes to the old Johnston rowboat.

The midship seats had to be raised several inches to accommodate this taller device consequently, an extra ninth round of planking was added at the gunwales, which incidentally provided better freeboard and a drier ride. The midship seats were doubled in width and were for the first time provided with removable back rests.

Steering could be accomplished from any position in the boat except the bow seat by means of a tiller rope running under the inside gunwales. A 3½ gallon triangular gas tank snuggled into the bow, just behind the forward seat-back, while a cast bronze serial number plate graced the forward skyboard, just aft of the gasoline tank cap. A Waterman K-1 engine provided the power as before.

The starting of these early models manufactured before pull-starters were introduced in 1922 demanded considerable skill and daring on the part of the operator. He would first seat himself comfortably facing aft in the bow seat. This would cause the rudder to rise

---

[5] Letter, Hodgson to Johnston, March 8, 1916, (Author's Collection).
[6] The Eaton family had long been Muskoka cottagers at Windermere, the location of the third Johnston boat livery. Also, the 1927 Eaton's Spring & Summer Catalogue lists all three models of Dispro for sale.

completely out of the water, and any oily water in the bilge to flow around his feet. The cylinder would thereupon be primed through a special priming cup using a small oil can full of gas. The timer would be set to fire at the proper position, the carburetor mixture needle opened slightly and finally the knife blade ignition switch to the vibrator coil would be closed. A heavy iron hand crank would be shoved onto the end of the crankshaft and the engine given a "short, sharp turn to the right". The instruction book made it all sound so easy.

Usually the engine started in a forward direction, throwing the crank back rather suddenly at the astonished operator. Sometimes, however, the engine would start in reverse and the crank would be violently spun around with ever-increasing velocity until it finally parted company with the crankshaft and took off into the water like some projectile.[7] Stories are legion of people receiving broken jaws, or worse, from being so unfortunate as to be in the trajectory of these cranks and it was not long before most owners realized the distinct advantage of flipping the rim of the flywheel by hand and the pleasure of consigning the hand crank to the deep.

The next hazard to be faced by the operator was that he was now under way with absolutely no steering control over the boat.[8] It was thus of paramount importance to advance the spark and adjust the carburetor immediately before the engine took it upon itself to backfire and die ignominiously, whereupon the entire starting procedure would have to be repeated. The very best Dispro operators developed remarkable skills in this regard. They became adept at making all the required adjustments in a split second, and after leaping over the seat back, would then take their steering position triumphantly in the third seat from the bow, whence could be exerted at least partial control over the craft.

On more than one occasion, Dispro operators have been known to go through this entire exercise, only to find to their dismay that the engine had mysteriously reversed itself, and that the boat was heading inexorably backwards towards the rocks!

There was no control whatsoever provided over the engine once the craft was under way and the operator was sitting at the helm, other than a long string attached to the knife-blade ignition switch, which would simply shut the engine off entirely. It was soon discovered by practical experience, however, that the D.P. device was capable of many more wonderful tricks than were claimed for it in the patent specification and these made up in good measure for the lack of control over the engine.

It was found, for instance, that when the propeller was pulled all the way up into the housing, the resulting turbulence not only acted as a brake on the engine, slowing it right down, but that the boat would then travel in a sideways direction (to port of course!) and sometimes even in a slow reverse. So, while the Dispro might appear on paper to be a rather unmanoeuverable craft, particularly since its propeller was located far ahead of the rudder, a good operator could soon learn to compensate for this apparent lack of manoeuverability by judicious raising and lowering of the propeller. Of course, the operator could control the engine by abandoning the steering briefly and leaning into the forward engine compartment, but only for a moment! The transfer of the operator's weight forward would lift the rudder clear of the water and the boat would immediately veer off course, sometimes with disastrous results. So unless an extra hand happened to be

[7] Most of these early 2-cycle engines would operate just as happily in either a clockwise or counterclockwise direction, depending on the timing of the spark. The slightest variation in the position of the spark advance lever would do the trick. In fact, many operators developed great skill in using this feature to provide a sudden reverse when making a landing. The many twisted crankshafts and cracked flywheel hubs seen today testify to this common practice.

[8] In spite of instruction book warnings to always "Be sure D.P. Device Lever is fully up" most operators found Dispros of early vintage much more difficult to start with the propeller raised, due to the excessive drag caused by the housing.

Instructions for hand starting the early models (from the instruction book supplied with each new boat).

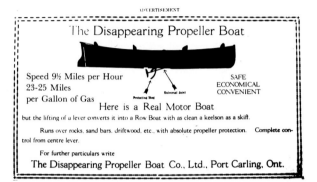
Advertisement appearing in John Rogers Muskoka Lakes Blue Book Directory, 1918. (Courtesy Port Carling Pioneer Museum)

This reproduction of a page from the catalogue of the Arrow Motor & Machine Co. 1917 shows a cockpit view of one of the earliest 1916 production models in the 100 series. Note the straight control lever and the lack of engine hood and splash boards. (Courtesy Larry Healey, Toronto)

Engine Starting Instructions

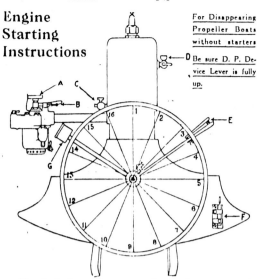

For Disappearing Propeller Boats without starters
D Be sure D. P. Device Lever is fully up.

We find the engine starts best when timer (E) and needle valve of carburetor (A) are set as shown on this chart. Use only good grade of medium gasoline engine oil. Mix thoroughly one quart to five gallons gasoline. Grease cups (G), as shown, should be kept well filled and turned down before and after each run.

Timer (E) should be set at No. 4. Turn needle valve (A) to right until closed, open to left until scratch is a ½ turn open, fill priming cup (D) with gasoline open priming cup, move flywheel slightly to take in charge, close again, put on switch (F), give flywheel short, sharp turn to right, raise timer (E) for more speed, lower for less speed. In about one-half minute close needle (A) slightly until best running results are attained.

When you become familiar with the perfect lever control of the Disappearing Propeller Device it will be unnecessary to run the engine backwards. However, same may be done by putting timer slightly to right of point 2, shown on chart. Short sharp turn of flywheel to the left; to increase speed move timer down.

20

ARROW DETACHABLE AND INBOARD MARINE MOTORS   15

It will no doubt be interesting to the reader to know that after extensive and very severe tests, covering a period of over two years, The Disappearing Propeller Boat Co. of Toronto, Ont. has decided exclusively in favor of the Model K engines. They are recommending them for installation in connection with their **Disappearing Propeller Device,** cuts of which are shown opposite.

The Disappearing Propeller Boat Co. naturally can purchase cheaper engines. It is, however, to their advantage to furnish with their device power plants which will give maximum and continuous service. They are also anxious to use an engine developing the greatest power possible, with elimination of weight. These features are all combined in the little Model K engines.

As a result of the service obtained we might mention that each year the number of engines ordered by the above mentioned concern has more than doubled. We have therefore extended to The Disappearing Propeller Boat Co. the exclusive selling rights for the Province of Ontario.

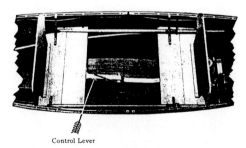

Control Lever

Above illustration shows small space occupied by Model K-1 installed in connection with DISAPPEARING PROPELLER. DEVICE manufactured by The Disappearing Propeller Boat Co., 33 Melinda St., Toronto, Ont.

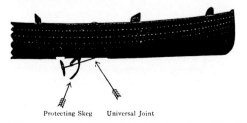

Protecting Skeg   Universal Joint

aboard to take over steering (and incidentally add ballast) most operators preferred to control speed by means of raising or lowering the propeller.

This unique feature was by no means overlooked in promotional literature for the Dispro boat. As early as 1917 it was claimed that "any speed from standing still to 9½ miles an hour can be had by raising or depressing control lever. It is not necessary to touch the engine."[9]

Despite, or perhaps as a result of, the many personality quirks exhibited by these craft, they soon made a hit with the boating fraternity in Muskoka. An ever-expanding market seemed assured for these little "putters" at $225.00 f.o.b. Port Carling.[10]

Production gradually increased and by early 1917 it became necessary to increase the capitalization to $100,000 in order to build a larger, more up-to-date factory in Port Carling, about 200 feet downstream from the original Johnston Boatworks below the bridge. This new building was expanded several times as production increased during the next few years and all Dispros built from about late 1917 to 1926 were constructed here.

More foreign patents were applied for and granted, but because of Canada's wartime involvement, neither the skilled workmen nor the potential buyers for the product existed on a scale sufficient to permit enormous expansion. In addition to the Canadian (1916) and U.S. (1917) patents, the "improved" Disappearing Propeller Device had been patented through Hodgson's efforts, in "England, Newfoundland, Australia, Holland, and all foreign countries" by 1917.[11]

Johnston subsequently transferred to Hodgson his half interest in all of these patents in return for paid stock in the company, so that by 1920 the latter had gained control of the rights worldwide to the D.P. device. At various times during the following years Hodgson sold these patent rights to the Disappearing Propeller Boat Co. as they were required and as the company could afford the purchase price.

THE INTRODUCTION OF THE JOHN BULL AND UNCLE SAM MODELS

Toward the end of 1917 a new model was added, and because of its exceptionally broad beam, it was aptly named the "John Bull". This new 16½ foot craft was designed to carry more passengers and payload with its 4 foot 11 inch beam and to be more stable than the standard models.

The origins of the design are somewhat unclear. Douglas Milner, a D.P. factory planker, indicated in an interview shortly before his death that he had been sent to Halifax and had made some plans from a Nova Scotia fishing dory. This design, he said, had been adapted to the existing Dispro hull. Garth Tassie, who joined the company in 1919, maintained, on the other hand, that the design had been taken from a lifeboat on one of the steamers of the Muskoka Lakes Navigation and Hotel Company.

While the new model was remarkably stable and would carry enormous loads, it was also rather slow because of its broad beam and it soon became known as the "workboat" of the Dispro fleet. For this reason it never achieved the popularity of the other models offered. It proved to be exceptionally difficult to build and workmen are alleged to have booked off sick whenever a "Bull" was to be built. The matter was eventually resolved when management offered to pay on the basis of an hourly rate rather than piecework to any workman willing to plank one.[12] The last John Bulls to be built on a regular basis were produced in 1924 and they thus became the shortest-lived of the three original models.[13]

---

[9] From the very beginning the speed capabilities of the craft were wildly exaggerated. These early models were capable of only about 5 m.p.h., and later 3 h.p. versions might do 6 to 6½ m.p.h.
[10] Price, 1917, Ad in *Canadian Motorboat* magazine, August, 1917.
[11] Statement of Defense, *Johnston vs. Hodgson*, op. cit.

It was becoming apparent by this time that in spite of the extra round of planking, Dispros were wet boats. Removable splashboards of 7/8 inch by 4 inch spruce were produced as accessories in an effort to alleviate the problem. These were attached horizontally out from the gunwales by means of iron brackets, and they turned out to be very effective for the purpose. They were, nevertheless, susceptible to damage against docks and were occasionally known to lift right off the boat and float away in heavy seas.[14]

By 1918 they had been redesigned as permanent extensions built out from the sheer planks and from this time on they were made of alternating light and dark 3/8 inch strips of wood having a spray-deflecting curve on the underside. These new splashboards enhanced the appearance of the craft as well and became an identifying feature of the Dispro for many years. Many older models were returned by their owners to the factory for a "retrofit" of these permanent splashboards.

In an attempt to provide some protection for the engine from the weather, a steam-bent cover was now attached to the forward side of the engine seat-back. This engine hood served better to protect the occupants of the boat from the live spark plug protruding from the top of the engine and all models built from 1917 to 1920 were so equipped.

It was now becoming evident that there was insufficient Ontario white cedar available to feed the maws of the steam-driven saws and planers in the new Port Carling factory and this shortage led to the adoption of Tidewater red cypress from Florida, Georgia and Louisiana as the standard material for planking, floorboards and seats. All but a handful of the Dispros built from 1917 until the Depression years were planked in this material. It is largely due to the remarkable staying powers of cypress that so many of these early boats have managed to survive to the present day in spite of decades of gross neglect.

The model which was soon to become the archetypal Dispro was introduced sometime in 1918 and it was an unqualified success. Many of the problems inherent in the two previous models were reduced or eliminated. Known as the "Uncle Sam", this new model was 18 feet 3 inches long with an intermediate 4 foot 8 inch beam and thus it had much of the room and stability of the John Bull without any sacrifice in speed. The extra length was added at the forward end, making the craft somewhat less bow-heavy when underway and, incidentally, providing a much drier ride.

The most striking feature of this new model was a special strip-planked foredeck. The alternating ½ inch light and dark strips blended well with the splashboards and added considerable visual appeal to the already pleasing lines of the craft.

Engines for the first time, were supplied by a Canadian concern, the A.D. Fisher Manufacturing Company of Toronto Ltd., who apparently had secured the Canadian rights to build the 2 h.p. K-1 Waterman engine, virtually unchanged, under their own name. This was known as the Model A-1 Kingfisher engine. Otherwise, the machinery in the Dispro remained similar to 1916 production.

In order to differentiate it from the other two models, the original 16½ footer which had been introduced in 1916 was now being referred to in magazine advertising as the "Water-Ford", as it was the lowest priced of the three. This marks the beginning of an advertising campaign of several years' duration in which the company attempted to hitch the Dispro to the rising fortunes of the Model T Ford car.

[12] Bert Riddiford, Port Carling, Interview with author 1981.
[13] The "John Bull" (later known as the "Utility" model) disappears from all catalogues and literature after 1924. However, six were apparently built at Lindsay about 1927 on special order for the Duquesne Hunting & Fishing Club. Eaton's 1927 Spring and Summer Catalogue mentions the availability of "Utility" models, although they may have been made up only on special order. The Duquesne boats are believed to be the last built. (Eric Stephen, Port Carling, Interview with author, 1982).
[14] Parry Schreiber, Port Carling, Interview with author, 1982. Parry's father purchased a 1916 Dispro which was later returned to the factory where these removable splashboards were fitted.

44

It seems that the directors of the company optimistically began to believe that the phenomenal success of the Ford car on the roads of North America might be duplicated to a large extent by the Dispro on the waterways and that the D.P. boat was the marine equivalent of the Ford car.[15] There were unquestionably many parallels between the Ford and the Dispro. Ford advertising for several years had stressed the car's low cost, simplicity, universality and durability, as well as its unique ability to climb hills and go places where other more expensive cars simply would have bogged down to their axles. Dispro advertising now began to stress similar virtues, particularly the boat's unique ability to navigate waters normally inaccessible to other motorboats. From this time on the Dispro became established as a rather utilitarian low-cost craft in the mind of the boat-buying public, a concept which proved virtually impossible to alter in later years.

In a subsequent chapter the adoption of several mass production techniques at the D.P factory in an attempt to increase efficiency and productivity will be covered in greater detail. However, it did not become apparent for several years that this analogy between the Ford and the Dispro was a gross oversimplification of the facts. Not only could the Dispro never hope to enjoy the universal acceptance of the Model T, but also the nature of wooden boatbuilding is such that it does not lend itself to moving assembly-line construction; nor does it permit the transfer of human skills and labour to machines, which was the essential feature of Ford's automotive mass-production system.

While these differences may appear to be self-evident today it is understandable that they may not have been perceived at the time by Clair Hodgson and the Board of Directors of the company. After all, the boats were selling like hotcakes, and in spite of the war there seemed to be an insatiable demand for them on the Muskoka Lakes alone. Surely it would be just a matter of continually enlarging production facilities so that "Dippies" could be built in ever-increasing numbers, like Ford cars.

This policy was undeniably a major factor in the subsequent meteoric rise of the Dispro to worldwide prominence but it led to disastrous consequences within a few short years. In retrospect, to paraphrase Schumacher, small might have been more beautiful in the long run.

By the end of 1918 then, the company was producing three models: the 16½ foot, "Water-Ford"; the 16½ foot, "John Bull"; and the 18 foot 3 inch, "Uncle Sam". The "war to end all wars" was just drawing to a close and the men were due to return from the battlefields of Europe the following spring. There was a feeling of optimism in the land once again. The stage was now set for the coming halcyon days of the Dispro.

[15] The phenomenal success that the Model T was enjoying in those days was largely due to Ford's refinement of assembly-line mass-production techniques. Resultant cost savings permitted the price of the car to be constantly reduced until a Ford could be purchased far below the cost of any of its competitors and well within the range of the common man. By the early '20s over half of all cars in existence in North America were Model T's.

Cast bronze serial number plate from a 1916 model, the seventh Dippy ever produced. (Courtesy A.H. Duke)

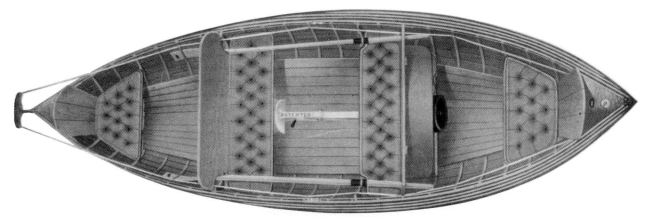

John Bull Model

Built-on Splash Boards.

Length, 16½ ft.

Beam, 4 ft. 11 in.

Depth, 1 ft. 8 in.

F.O.B. Port Carling, Ont., Standard Equipment, crated, $350.00.

Weight, 400 lbs.; crated, 500 lbs., complete.

Special Equipment 2-cylinder 6 H.P. Silent Dis-Pro, $500.00.

Speed, 9 miles per hour.
20 to 23 miles per gallon gasoline.
3 H.P. Silent Dis-Pro Engine.
Weight, 40 lbs.

Cushions as shown in this cut are supplied for all models, in plush, leatherette, etc., in a variety of patterns and colors. The filler is Kapoc, which is a life preserver. Also tarpaulins are supplied in khaki or white, in 12-oz. duck, being specially treated and guaranteed waterproof. One-man top, covers centre seats; complete with curtains and all fittings.

These are extras and prices will be quoted on request

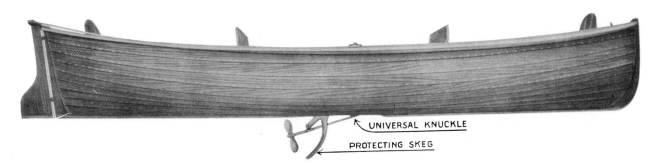

← UNIVERSAL KNUCKLE

PROTECTING SKEG ↙

Water-Ford Model

Built-on splash boards.

Length, 16½ ft.

Beam, 4 ft. 1 in.

Depth, 1 ft. 7½ in.

F.O.B. Port Carling, Ont., Muskoka Lakes, Standard Equipment, $300.00.

Weight, 350 lbs.; crated, 450 lbs.

Speed, 9½ miles per hour.
23 to 25 miles per gallon gasoline.
3 H.P. Silent Dis-Pro Engine.
Weight, 40 lbs.

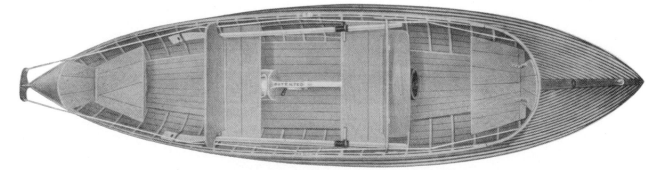

Uncle Sam Model

Length, 18½ ft.

Beam, 4 ft. 8 in.

Depth, 1 ft. 11 in.

Alternate strip-decking. Built-on splash boards.

F.O.B. Port Carling, Ont., Standard Equipment, crated, $400.00.

Weight, 425 lbs.; crated, 525 lbs., complete.

Special Equipment 2-cylinder 6 H.P. Silent Dis-Pro, $550.00.

Speed, 9 miles per hour
20 to 23 miles per gallon gasoline.
3 H.P. Silent Dis-Pro Engine.
Weight, 40 lbs.

The Good Years, 1919-1922

by Paul Dodington

THE PERIOD OF EXPANSION: 1919 — 1921

The 1919 catalogue announced the first attempt to improve the speed characteristics of the Dispro with the introduction of a new 2½ h.p. Kingfisher Model A-2 as standard equipment in all three models. This engine not only offered an increase of ½ horsepower but it exhibited a number of minor design improvements to make it more dependable. The purchasers of Uncle Sams or John Bulls were offered an optional power plant, a Waterman K-2, which was a beautifully-made 5 h.p. twin-cylinder version of the earlier Waterman K-1 engine. This option added $100 to the cost and a great deal of complication to the boat.

Although a number of these copper-jacketed twins were produced in the next few years, they never gained much popularity because their performance was somewhat disappointing. They consumed over twice as much fuel as the singles but offered a speed advantage of probably not more than 2 m.p.h. They were exceedingly cantankerous and required constant adjustment and fiddling to keep them running properly. The mediocre performance of the twins was due in good measure to their being coupled to the standard Dispro device housing, which offered insufficient clearance to swing an efficient propeller. Many frustrated owners later installed the more dependable single cylinder engines. Twins are consequently quite rare today.[1]

Like many other Canadian manufacturers of the time, the Disappearing Propeller Boat Company began to extol the virtues of its product as being exclusively Canadian made. In this fiercely patriotic period when returned men were experiencing the usual post-war difficulties in returning to the work force, "Made in Canada" products had a special impact on the buying public, a fact which did not escape the attention of the advertisers.

When the young men of Port Carling returned from Europe in the spring and summer of 1919, a large number of them were immediately given employment in the D.P. factory. Demand for the boats was steadily increasing now that the country was moving into a peacetime economy, and it soon became apparent that even the new factory facilities were much too small. An expansion programme was therefore begun and within the year the capacity of the factory was doubled.[2]

---

[1] The subsequent 6 h.p. Silent Dispro Model D-2 introduced in 1920, was similar in design, except for the timer, and was available as an option until at least 1928.

[2] According to the 1920 catalogue. The capitalization of the company was increased from $100,000 to $300,000 on Nov 11, 1919.

Twin-
Cylinder
Installation
(1924).

Model K-2—4-5 H.P.—60 Pounds.

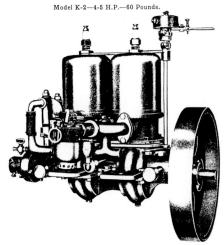

Model K-2 weighs less than the ordinary 1½ H.P. motor and you can therefore more than double your power without increasing the weight if you have a skiff, a small launch or yacht tender equipped with such an engine. Furthermore you can get rid of all the unpleasant vibration—vibration has always been one of the drawbacks against using an engine in a small, light boat. On this account you can use our model K motors in boats where the poorly designed and cheaply made engines would be out of the question—not simply by being uncomfortable to ride in but by being positively dangerous owing to the opening of the seams in the hull due to excessive vibration.

It is interesting to note—in these days of high priced gasoline—that the boat (shown on page 5) has a record of 45 miles in one run on less than two gallons of gasoline and at an average speed of 10½ miles per hour—23 miles to the gallon; What 6-passenger automobile can equal that record?

The model K-2 Waterman Twin
first introduced in D.P. boats in
1919. The model D-2 DIS-PRO,
introduced in 1920, was similar
except for the timer.

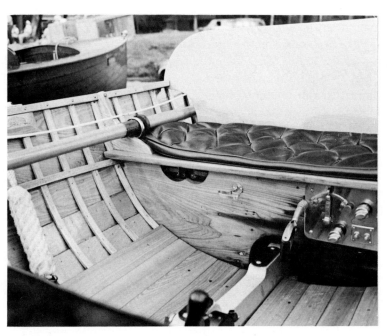

Dashboard arrangement of
a twin cylinder Model D-
2. Note the extra grease
cup to left of switches and
the two vibrator coils.

The Kingfisher A-1 engine 1918. The 1919 A-2 was externally similar, except for a water pump modification.

THE HIGHEST GRADE SMALL ENGINE IN THE WORLD

Reproduced from actual photograph. *Note the Timer.*

You can pour a stream of water over it without causing a misfire.

Due to its simplicity and ease of operation, the Disappearing Propeller Boat does not require an intimate knowledge of mechanical technicalities. It is a significant fact that approximately all Disappearing Propeller Boats are operated by laymen, who in the great majority of cases have had little or no experience with things mechanical.

The mastery of a thorough knowledge of the Dis-Pro motor construction is by no means a difficult or tedious task, and while it is not imperative for one to go into detail, yet it is desirable for the operator to acquaint himself with the essentials necessary for the proper functioning of the motor.

By following the rules set down in this Instruction book for the care and operation of the "Dis-Pro." motor, the operator will always be a master of the situation, secure more economy in its operation and maintenance, prolong its usefulness and derive untold pleasures from it.

The Motor

The motor used in the Disappearing Propeller Boat is of the two cycle type. This motor was adopted for its lightness and dependability, the lack of complicated parts in its construction, the simplicity of its operation and lubrication, etc.

Polished drawn copper water jacket, aluminum base, bearings, pump, connecting rod, timing lever and parts made of best phosphor bronze; carburetor connection and other parts of polished brass; nothing to bind, rust or give trouble. Built by expert mechanics, of the highest grade materials, duplicate parts interchangeable; in other words, no expense is spared to make The "KINGFISHER" Engine of the highest standard possible. AN ENGINE that will bring you home through rain or storm.

Hundreds of these engines are used in Disappearing Propeller Boats by men, women and children, giving the best of satisfaction.

This engine is manufactured by the A. D. Fisher Mfg. Co., Ltd., Toronto, Ont., and is guaranteed by them against defective workmanship and material.

"Kingfisher" Engine complete . . . Price $100.00

At the same time the plant was wired for electricity and the steam engine which had formerly powered all the machinery was soon replaced by a large electric motor. Five men were required to start the motor in cold weather — four men to yank on the 6 inch leather belt to rotate the armature and line shafting and one man to throw on the switch when sufficient speed had been built up! Power to operate all this electrical equipment came from a hydro-generating station on the falls at Bala, about 14 miles away. The transmission wires were nailed onto trees.[3]

Business was booming. The Water-Ford model was now selling f.o.b. Port Carling at $275, while the John Bull and Uncle Sam models were selling for $325 and $375 respectively. Kingfisher engines were sold separately, if desired, for $100, while the D.P. device could be purchased complete for installation in any suitable boat for $85.[4]

[3] Russell Cope of Bala recalled wiring the D.P. plant in Port Carling. (In a Feb. 3, 1980 interview with Paul Gockel.)
[4] 1919 Catalogue, Disappearing Propeller Boat Co., Toronto and Port Carling.

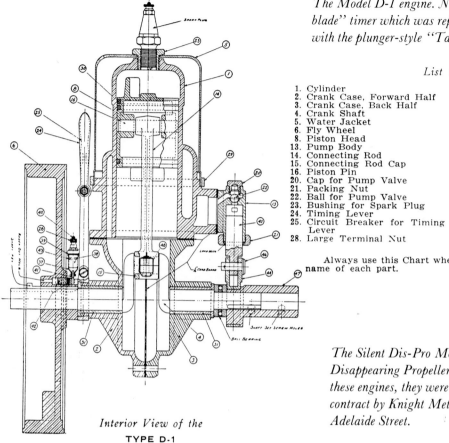

The Model D-1 engine. Note the early style "knife-blade" timer which was replaced in later production with the plunger-style "Tassie timer".

List of Parts:

1. Cylinder	29. Shrink Ring
2. Crank Case, Forward Half	30. Piston Ring
3. Crank Case, Back Half	31. Bearing for Crank Shaft
4. Crank Shaft	37. Finger for Timing Device
5. Water Jacket	38. Body for Timing Device
6. Fly Wheel	39. Fibre Washer for Timing Device
8. Piston Head	40. Stem for Timing Device
13. Pump Body	41. Contact Piece for Timing Device
14. Connecting Rod	42. Post and Binding Screw
15. Connecting Rod Cap	43. Finger Spring
16. Piston Pin	44. Eccentric Strap
20. Cap for Pump Valve	45. Pump Plunger
21. Packing Nut	46. Wrist Pin
22. Ball for Pump Valve	47. Pump Eccentric and Shaft Coupling
23. Bushing for Spark Plug	48. Connecting Rod Cap Screw Wire
24. Timing Lever	
25. Circuit Breaker for Timing Lever	
28. Large Terminal Nut	

Always use this Chart when referring to Engine. Give number and name of each part.

Interior View of the

TYPE D-1

The Silent Dis-Pro Model D-1 Engine. Although the Disappearing Propeller Co. claimed to be building these engines, they were in fact manufactured under contract by Knight Metal Products of Toronto, on Adelaide Street.

Weight
40 lbs.
3 H. P.

In a further attempt to increase the sales of the Dispro the company states in the 1920 catalogue:

"We are pleased to announce as standard equipment, the Silent DIS-PRO single cylinder, 3 HP High Speed marine motor...Also a Silent DIS-PRO two cylinder 6 HP high-speed marine motor which is special equipment for John Bull and Uncle Sam models. These engines are products of and guaranteed by the D.P. Boat Co. Ltd. In addition, we have adopted the well-known Maxim Silencer for use on all models of D.P. Boats, thus eliminating any possible noise."

The Maxim Silencers were vastly superior to the noisy little cast aluminum mufflers used previously and the increase in horsepower provided a moderate improvement in speed. While the new model D-1 engine contained a few minor design changes from the previous Kingfisher model A-2, it was really quite similar in most respects; many of the parts were still interchangeable with Kingfishers.[5] The really significant point here, however, is that the Disappearing Propeller Boat Co. now claimed to be manufacturing its own engines for the first time.

Over the past several years very close ties had developed between the Disappearing Propeller Boat Co. and Knight Metal Products of Toronto. Since 1916 this latter concern had manufactured all the devices plus most of the hardware and fittings used on Dispros so it was perhaps a matter of course that Knight's should now begin to build the engines as well. While the new engines were advertised as being "products of and guaranteed by the D.P. Boat Co.", both in catalogues and on the serial number plates of the engines themselves, they were in fact never manufactured directly by that concern but were built by Knight's on a contract basis. All single cylinder D-1 and E-1 models, plus the D-2 twins, were manufactured under this arrangement exclusively for the Disappearing Propeller Boat Co.[6]

This was certainly a cost-cutting move but it was also calculated to bring considerable prestige to the rapidly-growing enterprise. Henry Ford had previously established firm control over production costs of Model T engines, transmissions and axles by gradually incorporating the manufacture of these items into his own plant.[7] While the Disappearing Propeller Boat Co. was not yet in a financial position to undertake a similar venture, there were many advantages to be gained by at least appearing to follow in Ford's successful footsteps.

The Disappearing Propeller Boat Co. purchased the new engines from Knight's in job lots at a price of $36.50 apiece.[8] Allowing for inflation in the intervening years, this would still be considered remarkably inexpensive even by modern standards. While the basic design of the new engines had been tested and proven by previous experience with the similar Watermans and Kingfishers, it unfortunately soon turned out that not enough care was taken in the details of their manufacture.

"Sometimes over half of the motors in a shipment wouldn't run when we got them from Knight's," said one factory worker. "We'd have to dismantle them and install new piston rings and bearings in order to get enough compression."[9]

Individual parts were machined with such a broad range of tolerance, that the only really successful way to obtain an easy-starting, smooth-running engine was to use the

[5] Cylinder bore and crankpin dimensions were both increased 1/8 inch.

[6] Knight Metal Products of Toronto also supplied all engines, devices and hardware used in the American franchise plant in North Tonawanda, New York.

[7] For the first several years of Ford Model T production, many of the engine, transmission and axle parts had been manufactured by Dodge Brothers of Detroit under contract.

[8] Douglas Milner, in an interview with the author in 1974. W.J. Johnston maintained that they cost $39.00 apiece. (Interview with author, 1967.)

[9] Douglas Milner interview. Ibid. Former D.P. engineer William Croucher corroborated this statement in various discussions with the author between 1967 and 1983.

selective-fit system, a time-consuming method not compatible with low production cost.[10] The resulting lack of dependability of many of the model D Dis-Pro engines dogged the company for a long time and was a contributing factor to consumer resistance in subsequent years.

As a matter of fact, the instruction manual supplied with each new boat advised owners to "remove the spark plug and pour into the cylinder about ¼ cup of cylinder oil". This was a very effective technique for starting a balky Dippy, as the oil would temporarily seal the leaks around poorly-fitting rings and raise the compression sufficiently to bring the recalcitrant engine to life, albeit with accompanying clouds of blue smoke. Many Dispro owners relied exclusively on this treatment, urged on, no doubt, by a statement elsewhere in the manual that the "extra quantity of oil will harm no motor".

It was becoming apparent that the old 1916 design device housings, which were still being installed in boats as late as 1920, were not entirely satisfactory. Many developed a nasty tendency to leak profusely around the curved propeller inspection plate whenever the propeller was revolving in the raised position, sometimes rapidly filling the boat with water. A modification to the casting was made, early in 1920, to accommodate a flat cast iron cover plate which was much simpler to keep sealed. A year or two later an "aquascope" was offered as a $10.00 option to replace the cover plate. This was a popular item and became almost a trademark of the Dispro. The glass window allowed the operator to check at a glance whether his propeller had become fouled with weeds, without having to actually open the cover door.

The planking and ribs of all Dispros produced up to the late summer of 1920 had been fastened with iron clout nails which had been dipped in hot tin. Apparently, a number of prospective buyers at the annual boat show at the Canadian National Exhibition in Toronto that summer shied away, fearing that the tinned-iron nails would soon rust and rot away the surrounding wood.[11] As a result of these criticisms it was decided that an immediate change to copper nails, in spite of their considerable extra cost, would help to make the boats more attractive. Nevertheless, the occasional boat was built with tinned nails during the next year or two and others had combinations of copper and tin; these were likely sold as work boats at a reduced price.

Another serious drawback, as far as sales were concerned, was the lack of an efficient starting and control system for the engine. The method of operating the engine had remained unchanged from the earliest days and it was patently obvious by this time that many purchasers wanted something better. After all, even Henry's Model T could now be had with a self-starter and dashboard controls!

The 1921 catalogue announced the availability of several brand new options, most of which can probably be credited to the inventive genius of Harry W. Knight and his shop superintendents Bert Campton, and Henry R. Astridge, of Knight Metal Products. Of particular importance was a Dis-Pro Bow Light, an ingenious brass contraption which, "when not in use, folds down into the deck, leaving the deck flush".[12]

Also available, at long last, was a starter, a treadle affair which functioned much like the kick starter on a motorcycle.[13] In spite of catalogue reassurances that it was "a

[10] Henry Ford was able to achieve enormous production of Model T engines at very low cost by reducing human labour to a minimum. All engine parts were machined to such close tolerances that they were virtually interchangeable.

[11] Garth Tassie. Interview with author, 1977. It may be of interest to point out that a few of the "tinned-iron nailed" Dispros have survived to this day, and strangely enough, the passage of time has proven the criticism of these fastenings to be groundless, likely because of the high quality of tinning.

[12] So stated the 1921 catalogue. In actual fact, however, the light never did fold down flush, but rather folded into a cast bronze box above the deck surface.

[13] Ibid, p. 16.

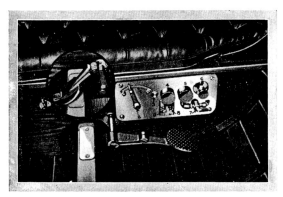

Showing Instrument Board with Starter Pedal.

1, 2. Spark Control.
3. Carburetor Adjustment.
4, 5. Main Bearing Grease Cups.
6. Primer.
7. Gasoline Shut-off Cock.

8, 9. Light and Ignition Switches.
10. Open and Close Priming Cup.
11. Starter Pedal in Use.
12. (Insert) Starter Pedal in Folded Position.

LITTLE THINGS THAT COUNT

The Dis-Pro Starter

The modern motor boat—like the modern motor car—should be equipped with a self-starting device. The self-starter of to-day is so efficient and so simple that little excuse, if any, can be offered against the use of one. There has been specially designed for the Disappearing Propeller Boat a wonderful little starter that costs nothing to operate, and that will start your engine with a slight pressure of the foot. It is so simple a child can operate it, and so designed that all danger from a possible back-fire is entirely eliminated.

This starter is not included in the regular equipment of the boat because some people may prefer to do without it. Nevertheless, we think it should be in every D.P. Boat, and we highly recommend it, not only for this year's model, but on all used D.P. Boats. It is comparatively simple to attach, and we feel sure that the initial cost will more than recompense every D.P.B. owner by the sturdy service it will give. The self-starter being in the centre of the boat, you simply stay in one place and, like the driver of a car, you have every appliance for the operation of your boat right at hand. This enables you to have your engine nicely encased, thereby adding to the appearance and the cleanliness of your boat.

Just for a moment let us imagine you are sitting on the seat, ready to start on that pleasant journey ahead of you. It's a fine summer day, the lake is like a vast sheet of glass,

a few pleasant companions are with you in the boat, all your troubles are forgotten, and you see only cloudless skies reflected in the depths of the blue waters. It is all yours, yours to enjoy, and you are about to glide into this fairyland of the earth.

So first you set the spark control and throttle. Then you open the gasoline adjustment needle. Next you prime the engine. Press your switch button. Then you press down on the starter with your foot, and immediately your engine starts. As soon as you take off your foot, the starter very conveniently folds out of the way.

Dis-Pro Bow Light

Should you have occasion to travel in the dark, get one of our Disappearing Special Bow Lamps. It is, we believe, the most compact two-way light you have seen. It sits on the foredeck firmly, and when not in use folds down into the boat, leaving the deck flush. This electric lamp is specially made for the D.P. Boat, and is a wise precaution against possible collision.

Disappearing Propeller Boat Cushions

Solid comfort cannot be obtained on solid seats, and we advise D.P.B. Cushions. These are exceptionally well made and being filled with Kapoc, make good life preservers. Covered with strong leatherette, they possess excellent wearing qualities. Colors are optional—brown, green and slate blue.

Disappearing Propeller Boat Tops

To provide protection from sun and rain, we have a really good D.P.B. Auto Top. It can be raised or lowered by one person, and when fitted with side and front curtains encloses the two centre seats. An additional bow and stern curtain encloses the boat completely. The celluloid windows at the sides, rear and front give an unobstructed view of your surroundings.

Disappearing Propeller Boat Tarpaulins

Where proper housing facilities are not available, we can supply a tarpaulin which entirely covers the boat. This tarpaulin is a specially treated waterproof duck, is simple to attach and detach, and affords ample protection against all weather. It is supplied for all three models, and will particularly appeal to those who desire to leave the boat moored or who want to leave it hauled up on shore for any length of time.

All the above mentioned accessories—the Starter, Dis-Pro Light, Cushions, Top and Tarpaulin—will add greatly to your boating pleasure. All of our accessories are made of the highest grade material.

We shall be pleased to quote prices upon request.

Two pages from the 1921 Disappearing Propeller Boat Co., catalogue showing the Instrument Board and the short-lived Treadle Starter.

wonderful little starter...that will start your engine with a slight pressure of the foot...so designed that all danger from a backfire is entirely eliminated", it proved to be entirely otherwise and was soon withdrawn.

Coupled with the starter, however, was a beautiful polished brass instrument board, which was located on the transverse bulkhead just ahead of the operator and within easy reach. This dashboard contained all the necessary engine controls: ignition and light switches, carburetor mixture adjustment, spark advance, main bearing grease cups, gasoline shut-off cock and priming controls. Now all necessity of leaping back and forth over the engine seatback was eliminated thereby vastly improving the operator's ability to control the boat, and incidentally making the craft more attractive to ladies. As instant access to the engine was no longer deemed necessary, all engines from this time on were enclosed in a box having two hinged covers, which was fitted on the forward side of the engine seatback. The new engine box afforded adequate protection from the weather and was a major improvement over the previous curved cover.

It appears that most of this optional equipment turned out to be unpopular in 1921, perhaps because of the $50 extra cost and the rather questionable performance of the treadle starter. The majority of 1921 models that have survived unmodified to the present have neither starter nor instrument board. The box-style engine covers, however, were retained as standard equipment on all boats from this time on.

Part way through the season, the ratchet-style device housing underwent its final modification. The embossed lettering "Disappearing Propeller Device" of former days was shortened to "Disappearing Propeller" because the raised lettering of the word "Device" had always run underneath the rock shaft inspection plate and had to be partially ground away to permit proper sealing of the gasket against water leaks. In addition, the two small inspection plates were made flat and horizontal, rather than curved and slanted as in previous models, and were fastened by round-head machine screws in order to permit ease of removal after they had rusted in place.

The factory facilities had been further expanded in the fall of 1920 with the addition of a large storage building, erected on cribs in the river, a few feet to the north of the factory itself. This warehouse had a capacity of about 400 boats.[14] Then, as now, boat sales were seasonal; boatbuilding took place mainly during the winter months, and the resulting pile-up of finished boats by early spring caused tremendous storage problems. The new warehouse, a three-storey frame affair, provided a welcome relief, and it helped set the stage for further increases in production.

SALES AND PROMOTIONAL TECHNIQUES

In just five years the Dispro had become one of the most popular production powerboats in the world. In fact, in the "Boatbuilders" section of the 1921 Toronto City Directory, the Disappearing Propeller Boat Co. was advertised for the first time as "the largest motorboat builders in Canada". Orders were coming in from all over the world. Garth Tassie, Office Manager at the Port Carling plant, remembered shipping carloads of Dispros in 1920 not only across Canada and the United States but to England, Ireland, China, France, and Brazil.

"We had to make a special model for Brazil," he recalled, "with the beam reduced by four inches so it would get through a rock cut which formerly had blocked all powerboats."

This marvellous boat did not, of course, sell itself but required a many-faceted approach to its successful promotion. The Head Office of the Disappearing Propeller Boat Co., now at a more prestigious location at 92 King Street West, Toronto, had a sign hanging out over the sidewalk in the form of a Dispro.[15] Just inside the window there was a

---

[14] Estimates of the capacity of the warehouse range from 150 to 400 boats. The latter figure, provided by varnisher Reg Stephen, seems the most realistic when compared to the estimated annual production figures.

[15] Previous Head Office addresses were: 33 Melinda Street, Toronto and 69 Bay Street, Toronto.

power-driven cutaway model of a Dis-Pro engine and device. Not only did the engine and shaft revolve, but the skeg and propeller moved constantly up and down. This proved to be a great attraction to passersby. In the showroom could be seen an example of each model, a "Waterford", a "John Bull" and an "Uncle Sam". A parts and service department was located at the back of the showroom.

Several distributors were appointed in addition to the Head Office sales agency. McMullen and Lee Ltd., 472-470 Yonge Street, Toronto were named Canadian Distributors in 1918, while Canadian Motor and Yacht Co. and Pike Yacht and Motor Co. of Montreal handled large numbers of Dispros in eastern Canada during the 1920s. There were doubtless many other agencies and distributors in addition to these.

Advertisements were taken out in various magazines as well. Examples have been seen in *Canadian Motor Boat* (1917), *Maclean's* (1918), *Popular Mechanics* (1923) and *Motor Boating* (1921 and 1925), among others. Apparently, catalogues and illustrative materials were available as early as 1916,[16] although the earliest brochure now known to exist dates from 1919. Each year from 1919 to 1921 a very handsome catalogue of up to 24 pages was produced. These had an embossed D.P. logo on the cover and numerous coloured plates inside. During the final two years of Port Carling production (1925 and 1926) the catalogue shrank to a single black and white printed sheet.

Around 1922 the Disappearing Propeller Boat Co. commissioned the writing of a song extolling the delights of a moonlight cruise by Dispro. Words and music were by Tom Vincent[17] and the song entitled, "Come Take a Trip in My Dippy-Dip-Dip". Whether the song ever reached the stage of being published and distributed in sheet music form is not known as only the cover art work and the words have survived.

Some of the more daring exploits attempted by Dippy owners were printed up and circulated as well. William G. Ogilvie[18], along with two other adventurers, made a 1,500 mile journey from Peace River Crossing in Alberta, down the Peace and Hay Rivers, across Great Slave Lake and down the mighty Mackenzie to Fort Norman in a brand new 1921 Waterford. His account of this incredible journey, originally published in the June 1922 issue of *Motor Boating* magazine, was subsequently printed up in a booklet form and distributed by the Disappearing Propeller Boat Corp. of New York under the title, "Fifteen Hundred Miles in the Canadian Wilds". (see page 142)

Another such expedition printed up in pamphlet form by the Disappearing Propeller Boat Co. was made about 1919 by Captain C.M. McCarthy of Elk Lake, Ontario along with a crew of 52 men. Two 38 foot pointers[19], each equipped with a Waterman K-2 engine and Disappearing Propeller Device, were launched at Pegway Bridge (300 miles west of Cochrane) on the Transcontinental Railway in Northern Ontario. The party travelled 300 miles down the Pagwachman and Albany Rivers to Port Albany (running the Limestone Rapids under power) and thence up James Bay another 100 miles to Attawapiskat. Wilderness expeditions such as these created considerable confidence in the viability of the Disappearing Propeller Device.

---

[16] In a letter to Johnston dated March 8, 1916, Hodgson states, "I hope to have literature soon, within a day or so". (Author's collection)

[17] Believed to be a pseudonym for Gordon V. Thompson, 1888-1965, a Toronto music publisher and popular song writer, who owned a cottage on Lake Muskoka, not far from Port Carling. See *Encyclopedia of Music in Canada*, (Kallman, Potvin & Winters) University of Toronto Press, 1981, Pages 913-14.

[18] William G. Ogilvie subsequently joined the sales staff of the Disappearing Propeller Boat Co., becoming its most successful salesman. By 1926 he had become General Manager of the Company.

[19] "Pointers" were very heavy, roughly-made flat-bottomed double-enders used extensively in early lumbering operations in Northern Ontario and Quebec. The stem and stern posts were set at a rakish angle to allow them to ride up over logs and onto beaches, hence the name.

Unique Power Boats Traverse the Waters of Hudson Bay

Captain C. M. McCarthy, of Elk Lake, Ont., relates some very interesting experiences with disappearing propeller boats in connection with an expedition to Port

Capt. C. M. McCarthy of Elk Lake, Ont., conveying Indians and Merchandise 300 miles North on James Bay, his 38-foot boat equipped with Disappearing Propeller Device.

Albany, Hudson Bay. Captain McCarthy and party started from Cochrane and travelled to Pegway Bridge, 300 miles west, via Transcontinental. The expedition was equipped with two 38-foot (7-ft. beam) Pointers, each one having installed specially for the trip north down strange and turbulent waters, a Disappearing Propeller Device and a Waterman K2 2-cylinder 5 h.p. engine.

Leaving Pegway Bridge, they ran down the Pagwachman River to Kenogami, thence down the Albany River to Port Albany, on the west coast of James Bay. During this run of 300 miles down river they ran under power the Limestone Rapids, making the 1½ miles of white water in an even five minutes. The Disappearing Propeller Device proved time and again to perform its automatic protection of the propeller when rocks or bars were hit. This is possibly the first instance of large boats heavily laden running rapids such as the Limestone under power in the North country.

Arriving at Port Albany, they then ran north a hundred miles in salt water to Attawpiskat, arriving in excellent shape after running 300 miles in 58 hours, cooking and sleeping aboard in the two Pointers. The actual time on this run was 58 hours, average speed 5.17 miles per hour, and average run per day, nine hours. Gasoline used was 36 gallons. For such large boats, heavily manned and laden, with only a 2-cylinder 5 h.p. Waterman engine and the Disappearing Propeller Device for power, this is really a wonderful performance.

The expedition, with 53 people all told, as shown in the picture, started back, running out of James Bay in heavy weather. There is a remarkable tide at the Princess Shoals, so much so that the two Pointers, when the tide went out as they were crossing the shoals, were left high and dry a full five miles from water. The tide coming in at 11.45 p.m., they got under weigh and ran till noon the following day, a steady twelve-hour run through, not only salt water, but muddy salt water, and in doing so conclusively proved the adaptability of the Disappearing Propeller outfit for salt water use. This run brought them to Kapisko River. A further run from 4.45 a.m. till 2 p.m. in salt water gave another excellent test, and engine and device stood up satisfactorily in every way. Two weeks later the party arrived back at Pegway Bridge and in Toronto in three days.

Soon the second expedition under Captain McCarthy started over the same route, and arrived at Port Albany

in a week, completing their mission, and arrived back in Toronto in a month, less three days.

The remarkable speed, allowing of two expeditions going from Toronto to Hudson Bay and return in practically three months and covering approximately 4,500 miles of primeval country and little known waters, opens up a wide field for the hunter or fisherman who wants to look over new spots, and get right back in the beyond, where it is still terra incognita.

The trip entailed a lot of hard work and some privations, but to hear the captain relate many incidents of the trip makes one envious. It is a trip anyone with a love of the wild naturally envies, and to think that one chap has done it twice in one summer makes it all the more remarkable.

At several points on the trip some curious customs were noticed. In three separate places there happens to be, at the juncture of a small stream entering the River Albany, a large rock in the main river and near by a small clump of poplar trees. Wherever this occurs, the rock is known as a Prayer Rock, and the Indians and natives invariably when passing place a small bit of tobacco on the stone to insure them of a safe trip down or up the river, and a successful hunt. Irrespective of wind, water or weather, they will place a small piece of their most valued treasure, tobacco, on the stone for the spirits.

Capt. McCarthy, when preparing for these expeditions, looked over the whole field of motors, and safety appliances for propeller protection, and selected the Disappearing Propeller Device for his two boats. On his return he stated they were wonderfully efficient in every way, and had helped most materially in the remarkable time made on these two trips. Th Captain disposed of one of the outfits on his return and it is now on its way back to Port Albany, Hudson Bay. The other is still giving splendid service and satisfaction at Elk Lake.

Capt. McCarthy was in Toronto recently and related his unique experiences to many friends who were keenly interested from a motor boating standpoint in the disappearing propeller device, which is conceded to be a great success.

At the sales offices of the Disappearing Propeller Boat Co., 69 Bay Street, Toronto, much satisfaction was expressed in the report of Capt. McCarthy on his remarkable trip, as it is justly regarded as being a supreme test of the utility of the disappearing propeller device. Boats

One of Capt. C. M. McCarthy's James Bay Craft heavily loaded at Fort Albany, James Bay, Ont.

thus equipped were first introduced on the famous Muskoka Lakes, where they are now as commonly used as some popular makes of cars in the large cities.

Each year, until at least 1926, Dispros were displayed under the old grandstand at the Canadian National Exhibition in Toronto. Here the boats received considerable exposure and a number of sales were made.

Much advertising was done directly from the Toronto office by mail and by direct telegraph and telephone communication with prospective purchasers and agencies. Perhaps the most fascinating efforts to sell Dispros, however, were put forward by the small entrepreneurs who operated one or two-man Dippy agencies.

Garth Tassie and R.B.Y. Scott, both bright young men recently returned from the war, obtained one of these agencies in the summer of 1919. Here is Mr. Tassie's story in his own words as related in an interview in December 1974 when he was 78 years of age:

> "The reason why I came to Port Carling is, perhaps, amusing. After returning to Canada after the war, a childhood friend and I were invited to board the first steel ship built in Toronto for her trial runs. The engines broke down in the middle of Lake Ontario; there was no food aboard and no drink except hard liquor and my friend and I did not use hard liquor. So we hunted around for a bucket and a rope; Lake Ontario was then clean and drinkable. In the search, we came upon an old magazine carrying an advertisement by the Disappearing Propeller Boat Company of Port Carling. We asked ourselves whether we were not entitled to a holiday after several years in the navy and army respectively and we decided that if we could obtain a Disappearing Propeller Boat agency, we might make our expenses for a good holiday. So we got our agency and purchased a John Bull model D.P. We fitted a weatherproof top, installed a wireless telegraphy set (we were both competent signallers) and finally took off down Lake Ontario. We stopped at about 4 or 5 o'clock each day and put up notices that the latest wireless news would be published by us at 6 p.m. Wireless was still a novelty and it was not surprising that quite a few people would gather. We sold a boat occasionally and gradually made our way down Lake Ontario and up the Trent Valley system to the Kawartha Lakes. We stopped at a cottage on Stoney Lake where a storm had been raging for several days. The cottagers were out of food, and especially milk for their children, so we borrowed a large, old-fashioned washtub, put a well-lidded pot inside it, well lashed down with canvas, and set out in our John Bull for Juniper Island store, two or three miles away. No boat had ventured out for several days. We returned with several milk bottles and bread and butter and bacon, without losing a drop of milk. This made our reputation locally, and we sold several boats. ...We continued about the Kawarthas until we had made enough commissions to pay for our holiday. We were really quite successful for an amateur sailor and an amateur soldier."[20]

William G. Ogilvie, who in later years founded the successful yacht brokerage firm, Ogilvie Bloss Ltd., developed his own special technique for selling boats during his years at the D.P.

"The personal touch was of utmost importance," he says. "You could mail out all the literature in the world but in the end it was your personal contact with a prospective customer that really brought results."[21]

[20] Excerpted from a tape-recorded interview, (1974) courtesy Aud. Duke, Port Carling.
[21] Interview with author, 1981.

R.B.Y. Scott and friend in AHMEEK, Stoney Lake, July 1919. This is the only D.P. known to have been equipped with a portable wireless receiver.

Garth Tassie & R.B.Y. Scott

Although 1921 had been a banner year for the Dispro many of the hundreds now in service were developing some rather disturbing problems.

The ratchet device, which had undergone only minor modification since 1916, was not functioning well. Unless the shaft and propeller were perfectly true, the skeg had a nasty inclination to creep either up or down, invariably in the wrong direction! True, frictional adjustment of the ratchet was provided for, however it was required so frequently that most owners simply gave up, and for the remainder of the life of their boats resigned themselves to holding the handle down with their foot. The ratchet devices seen today with flat spots worn on the top of the wooden handle bear mute testimony to this fault. And, if this problem weren't enough, the rather meagre packings on either side of the rock shaft often developed annoying leaks.

The early D-1 engines had shown a marked tendency to sudden failure, usually miles from home. It was found that as the engine crankshafts gradually developed slight end-play, the contacts of the "knife blade" style timer would be thrown out of alignment and the unit would be irreparably destroyed.

Garth Tassie, who by this time held the dual position of Office Manager and Assistant Factory Manager, developed a new timer in 1921 which consisted of a spring-loaded vertical plunger contacting a hardened steel shoe pinned to the rotating flywheel hub. This "Tassie timer", as it is affectionately known, was immune to the previous problems and, while it was only used as factory equipment on the later model D engines, it gained a reputation as the most dependable timer ever used on any of the D.P.'s. It had the distinct advantage of being easily interchanged with the two earlier styles. Consequently, most older engines were sooner or later improved by the installation of this unit.

In spite of the vast improvement in reliability offered by the Tassie timer, two other serious problems were becoming apparent with Model D-1 engines. The sleeve-type coupling between the engine and propeller shaft soon worked itself loose and wore so badly that serious misalignment of the shaft developed. This condition would gradually progress to the point that the resulting vibration would make the passenger's teeth chatter. And if this weren't enough, the flywheels, which were held in place only by means of a tapered key, had a nasty tendency to come off unexpectedly at high speed, roll up the side of the boat and, as often as not, end up overboard in the drink.

A far more insidious and serious problem began to manifest itself, however, late in 1921. The stress of the excessive vibration added to changes in moisture content in the wood itself were causing the copper clout nails, which had been in use for about a year, to loosen up, and the boats were literally falling apart! The old tinned-iron nails had been, naturally, much stronger than the new copper ones and structural problems had not been previously apparent.

But, not only was the strength of the nails found wanting, the quality of workmanship was suffering too. For some time all factory employees had been paid on a piecework basis, as an incentive to produce as many boats as possible. As time went on, the workmen naturally became much more efficient in the execution of their various tasks, but they also began to take short cuts, some of which affected the quality of the finished product. While every boat was carefully inspected and visible defects corrected before varnishing, there were sometimes hidden flaws which would not be caught by the inspector and which would not become apparent until a boat had been in service for a time. The nailers had found, for example, that by drilling the nail holes in the planking extra large, one operation in the nailing procedure could be entirely eliminated, thus significantly increasing their productivity.[22] The soft copper nails combined with the oversize holes soon gained the boats a reputation as "leakers" during the summer of 1921. Swift corrective action was necessary to salvage the reputation of the Dispro.

---

[22] Bert Riddiford, Port Carling, in an interview with the author, 1981.

A MOTORBOAT THAT WILL GO ANY PLACE YOU
=CAN ROW=

RELIABILITY
SIMPLICITY
ECONOMY
DURABILITY

A
REALLY
SILENT
MOTOR

A
STRONG
SEAWORTHY
HULL

BACKED BY GUARANTEE AND VOUCHED FOR BY THOUSANDS OF ENTHUSIASTIC OWNERS

ONE-MAN TOP .:. DIS-PRO STARTER
SUPPLIED AS EXTRAS

SEND FOR FULLY DESCRIPTIVE LITERATURE. PLEASE ADDRESS ALL COMMUNICATIONS TO HEAD OFFICE

DISAPPEARING PROPELLER BOAT CO.
HEAD OFFICE & SHOW ROOMS   LIMITED
92 KING STREET WEST,
TORONTO, CANADA   FACTORY, PORT CARLING, ONT.

THE DISAPPEARING PROPELLER DOES IT =

ROCKS, LOGS, SHOALS, DRIFTWOOD, ETC.,
HOLD NO FEAR FOR THE OWNER OF A

DISAPPEARING PROPELLER BOAT

THE PROTECTING SKEG IMMEDIATELY
RAISES THE PROPELLER INTO ITS HOUSING, OUT
OF ALL DANGER, AUTOMATICALLY

A FEW POINTS

1. Lifting of lever automatically controls speed of engine and boat.
2. Any speed from slightest forward movement to 9½ miles per hour.
3. Increase of from 2 to 2½ miles per hour over rear-driven propeller.
4. One pull of control lever gives as clean a keelson as skiff.
5. Automatic propeller protection.
6. Propeller mid-ship stablizes as centre board to sailboat.
7. Can remove propeller while sitting in boat.
8. Vibration eliminated.
9. Steers from all parts of boat.
10. Boat always on even keel.
11. Propeller at all times thoroughly submerged.
12. Engine and device so placed no available room lost.
13. Lever up, boat stands still, automatically throttling engine, making one way clutch.
14. Can be pulled out on beach or dock same as a rowboat.
15. So simple of operation a child can run it.

UNCLE SAM	JOHN BULL	WATER-FORD
MODEL	MODEL	MODEL

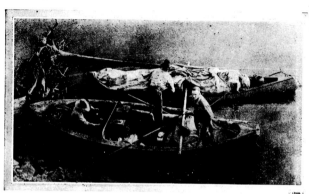

ASSOCIATED UNDERWRITERS, LIMITED
FINANCIAL AGENTS

263 ST. JAMES STREET

Montreal, Dec. 18th, 1920.

Pyke Motor & Yacht Co., Ltd.,
374 Notre Dame St. W.,
Montreal.

Att. Mr. Pyke.

Gentlemen:—

I am enclosing herewith a photograph of the "Uncle Sam" Model Disappearing Propeller Boat you sold us, and shipped to Edmonton last spring.

This photograph will give you a pretty good idea of what this small boat had to carry, as well as the big freight canoe, heavily loaded, which she towed throughout the entire journey.

We left Peace River Crossing on July 10th, for Mackenzie River, more than 2,500 miles down the Peace River, across the entire length of Great Slave Lake and again down the Mackenzie River.

I cannot speak too highly of this boat and its engine as it is absolutely the first motor boat to have made this trip of more than 3,500 miles practically without repairs, which, as you know, are impossible in this country.

Unfortunately we only used one pint of cylinder oil to five gallons of gasoline, which I found out later, was not sufficient, and this cut the connecting rod bearings very rapidly, so that before the end of the return journey one connecting rod and piston had to be removed, the cylinder plugged up and the engine was run back the balance of the trip on one cylinder, a feat which would have been absolutely impossible with most makes of engines.

I will send you in my order at an early date for two more boats for spring delivery, and I want the same model and just a few minor changes regarding the steering arrangements and exhaust connections, which are not exactly suitable for the heavy work we have to carry on. The model of the boat, however, is the best I have ever seen, as while out on the Great Slave Lake we went through a blow when every other boat on the Lake stayed in, and even the big ferry boats were afraid to go out.

I refused time and time again to sell my boat at double what I paid for it, and at the end of the season after running more than 3,500 miles, I sold it for practically what it cost, and I believe there will be hundreds of these boats sold in this district this season as it is unquestionably the only perfect boat for these waters, and your engine is so easily operated anyone can run them successfully. My boat was named "Just Right." Its proper name.

Yours very truly,

R. A. BROOKS.

THE GREATEST LITTLE MOTOR BOAT AFLOAT

This letter will be of interest to those contemplating journeys in unknown waters.

D.P. advertising during this period focussed on "reliability, simplicity, economy and durability," as well as the boat's ability to "go any place you can row".

Early in 1922 all three models were redesigned with oak ribs on 4 inch centres instead of the previous 8 inch centres. Not only were the ribs doubled in number but the plank nailing was increased as well. The net result was that each plank was fastened every 2 inches along its length instead of 2 5/8 inches. These improvements of course added extra weight to the hull but the increase in stiffness and strength turned out to be well worth the extra pounds, and the extra cost.

The quality of workmanship of the nailing was brought back up to an acceptable standard by the institution of an hourly wage for nailers, and this policy shortly was applied to all workers throughout the plant.

By March of 1922 a redesigned device was ready for installation in the new boats.[23] The novel feature of this new unit was the elimination of the old ratchet and the substitution of an adjustable friction brake to lock the propeller in any desired position. The rock shaft upon which the skeg pivoted up and down was also redesigned to provide proper bearings with adjustable watertight packings.

These device improvements were invented by Henry Astridge, Plant Superintendent of Knight Metal Products in Toronto. He applied for a patent in April 1922 and assigned it to the Disappearing Propeller Boat Company. The modification proved so successful that the design was carried basically unchanged, right through to final production in 1958.[24] (See patent drawing)

Even the Silent Dis-Pro engine was redesigned. The new model, known as the E-1, sported many improvements over the old D models. The new-style Maxim Silencer, from Wilcox Crittendon, was much simpler to disassemble and decarbonize and being of totally cast iron construction, it usually didn't leak when re-assembled.[25] The flywheel was now mounted on a tapered crankshaft and securely fastened by an acorn nut.

While vibrator coil and battery ignition was retained, the Tassie timer which had been in use for only a brief period, was replaced with an entirely new unit. This new timer consisted of a spring-loaded button running against a fibre disc on the rear face of the flywheel. This arrangement provided greater economy of battery current, but it nevertheless required the use of a larger, more expensive 7½ volt dry battery. In spite of the extra voltage, it eventually developed a tendency to misfire at high speed.

Why the proven Tassie timer was superceded by this less satisfactory unit is not known, but a possible explanation is that the Model D flywheel hubs were seriously weakened due to the hole drilled to attach the timer shoe and many of the hubs had subsequently developed cracks. This had been a major cause of flywheels coming off at high speed. Unfortunately, the Tassie timer was not readily adaptable to the new Model E engines and consequently most surviving Model E's are now found with a plethora of "backyard" ignition timing devices, demonstrating the wide range of inventiveness of their respective owners.

[23] In a letter dated March 2, 1922, J.R.C. Hodgson writes to Johnston, "New devices put them in all boats from now on. How do they look to you?"

[24] These new devices were officially known as the "D2-22" model. It is believed that they were initially designed and intended for use with the Model D-2 twin cylinder engines because of the latter's tendency at full power to overcome the ratchet restraint on the old "No. 16" devices. In actual practice, however, all boats, regardless of engine, were equipped with the new-style unit after this time. The few old "No. 16" ratchet devices still in stock were used up subsequently in the occasional economy model.

[25] Some early E-1's may have been fitted with the earlier Maxim Silencer as found on D-1 engines until stocks were used up.

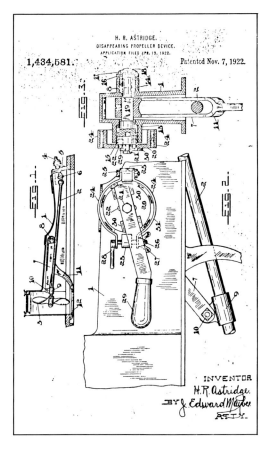

The aquascope, introduced about 1922, was such a popular option that it soon became almost a trademark of the Dispro.

U.S. Patent drawing of Astridge's brake restraint device 1922 (Canadian Patent No. 225,945). This is the last improvement patented on the D.P. device.

Various styles of Astridge's brake restraint device in use from 1922 to 1958. Left: 1922 to 1926; Centre: late 1926 to 1950 (no u-joint plate); Right: late Greavette, 1951 to 1958.

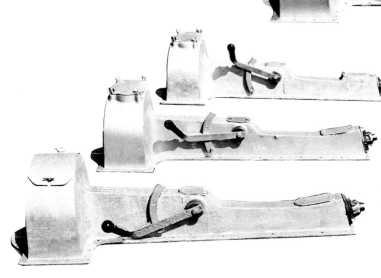

The three styles of ratchet device. L. to R.: curved top 1916-20; early flat top 1920-21; late flat top 1921, early 1922.

The new model E-1 engine serial number plates (right) de-emphasized the previous "Made in Canada" aspect, and were now more international.

At first, Model D-1 engines were shipped from Knight's in Toronto to the Port Carling factory in crates...

...soon they were arriving by the bargeload!

The E-1 engines were provided with a special two-piece propeller shaft coupling in order to accommodate the new cable rewind starter. These couplings improved the alignment of shaft and engine, thus helping materially to reduce vibration. The new so-called "pull-starter" consisted of a pull handle and cable arrangement protruding through the bulkhead just to the left of the brass dashboard. Operating through a series of pulleys, it engaged a ratchet wheel on the forward propeller shaft. These recoil starters proved to be very successful, so much so that most models sold after this time were factory-equipped with them. Owners of earlier Dispros in many cases had the new starting equipment and instrument boards installed in their older boats.

The new engines were thankfully easier to start than most of the older D models. This was due in part to the addition of a third piston ring which helped improve compression. No longer was it necessary to endure the choking clouds of blue smoke when starting up.[26] An examination of surviving E-1 engines reveals that there was considerable improvement in production standards and quality control, so a much more dependable power plant was the result.

In line with the new international status of the Dispro, the serial number plates on these new engines dropped the former "Made in Canada" wording and now read "Disappearing Propeller Boat Co., Toronto and Buffalo". Ironically, the failure of the recently-established manufacturing plant in North Tonawanda, New York, occurred only about a year after the introduction of these new plates.

All boats continued to be equipped with one pair of beautifully-made sitka spruce spoon oars, either 7 feet 8 inches long for Uncle Sams, or 7 feet 4 inches long for John Bulls and Waterfords. Most of the oars up to this time had been handmade by W.J. Johnston Sr., who had otherwise retired from the boatbuilding operation in 1916. The leathers were made up and installed by C.J. Amey in his local Port Carling harness shop.

While all three models continued to be built as before, their names in advertising brochures and literature were changed.[27] *All* boats were now known as Water-Fords, and the three different styles were officially known from this time on as "Water-Ford Scout" (formerly the Water-Ford), "Water-Ford Utility" (formerly John Bull) and "Water-Ford Deluxe" (formerly Uncle Sam). However, the old names by this time had become well established, and they were perhaps more evocative as well, so that this new nomenclature really didn't catch on to any degree, at least in Canada. Even today, the three models are usually referred to by their original names.

With the introduction of the new 1922 models, the Dispro was now close to its highest state of development.[28] Clair Hodgson shared his enthusiasm over the new boats with Billy Johnston in a letter dated March 2:

"New starter looks and acts like a real job. New timer according to your reports does also and also reports from shop here. I will say we are going to have some boat this year what say you?"[29]

---

[26] A few of the late production D-1 engines were fitted with this third piston ring as well.

[27] First appearance of these new names is in a 1922 Tonawanda catalogue. Like "Dis-Pro", the name "Water-Ford" gradually lost its hyphen in subsequent spelling.

[28] The "Sport Special" model produced in small numbers in later years at Lindsay was admittedly more complex in that it had 10 rounds of planking and more elaborate decks. Also, a square-stern model was produced around 1930 but it was a failure. Both of these models were equipped with an engine much inferior to the earlier E-1's which proved to be very troublesome and prone to vibration. Except for the introduction of electric starting in 1941 there were really very few significant improvements indeed after 1922. After 1942 in particular, most changes were made with a view toward reducing production cost and complexity rather than maintaining or improving the quality of the boat.

[29] Excerpted from a copy of a letter in the author's collection.

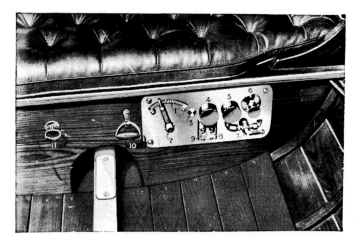

The new pull starter for 1922. Compare with the previous treadle unit shown on page 53.

Showing Instrument Board with Pull Starter.

1, 2.—Spark Control.
3.—Carburetor Adjustment.
4, 5.—Main Bearing Grease Cups
6.—Primer Bearing
7.—Gasoline Shut-off-Cork.
8, 9.—Light and Ignition Switches.
10.—Starter Handle.
11. Open and Close Priming Cup

Instructions for operating DIS-PRO. Starter

See that grease cups are well-filled—use lubrication freely for new motor.

Fill Gasoline tank : proper proportion One Quart Medium Grade Gasoline Engine Oil to five Gallons of Gasoline. Strain through chamois.
Extra quantity of oil will harm no motor.

Inspect wire and gas connection before attempting to start Motor, thus avoiding difficulty in starting.

To Start :

First—Be sure D.P. Device Lever is fully up.

Second—Move spark control No. 1 to extreme left or retarded position. Do not push to right or advance position until after Motor is started.

Third—Pull out No. 3 to give engine more gas from carburetor for starting only. Do not push in until motor has run for a few minutes, then push in close against dash plate.

Fourth—Push No. 11 to extreme end to open petcock and allow gas from primer to enter cylinder of engine. Do not close until after engine has been primed, then pull out ½ way until you hear click of notch, which is closed or running position.

Fifth—Turn on gasoline No. 7.

Sixth—Unscrew primer head No. 6 and draw out to load—pushing two or three times to prime motor, then close and screw tight—after this operation close petcock as described under fourth operation.

Seventh—Pull out ignition switch No. 8.

Eighth—To start engine pull handle No. 10 to extreme length of rope, then release. After motor starts advance to the right spark control Lever No. 1 and then lower device lever for boat movement and grade of speed.

In case motor does not start after three or four attempts, open priming cup No. 11 by pulling out rod, then pull starter handle a few times until an explosion occurs ; close priming cup by pushing in rod No. 11 and again pull handle to start motor.

21

W.J. Johnston Sr. (left) and W.J. Johnston Jr. at factory dock, summer of 1920. The boat is a Water-Ford model with accessory top.

The Disappearing Propeller Device had proven itself to be a gadget of obvious merit but this fact alone does not account for its phenomenal rise to preeminence in the small motorboating field in the early 1920s. The real success of the venture was essentially due to Johnston's and Hodgson's unique personal qualities plus their ability to gather about them a group of outstanding individuals whose various talents and skills combined to function as a very effective unit.

The fantastic output of the Port Carling factory of the Disappearing Propeller Boat Co. was due mainly to the untiring efforts of Johnston and some of his close associates. Young Billy was not only a very skilled boatbuilder, but was a man of tremendous drive as well. Many of the factory employees recalled that he would often be on the job at 5 o'clock in the morning, well before any of the other workmen, and that he himself cut out many thousands of planks, stems and sternposts in addition to his duties as Factory Manager. He was well-liked by his employees and apparently treated them fairly. He had gathered about him a nucleus of loyal, young energetic workmen who became the backbone of the boatbuilding operation.

It is said that Douglas Milner became so efficient that, to settle a bet, he once planked a complete boat (less ribs) in only 2½ hours. This was a job that would normally take 8 to 12 hours for a skilled boatbuilder. His brother, Cameron Milner, who in later years became the owner and manager of the Honey Harbour Boat Works on Georgian Bay, could "finish" an Uncle Sam in one day — that is, he could make up and install the decks, splashboards, gunwales, coaming, seats, knees, seat backs, and trim.[30]

There was Reg Stephen in the varnish room, of whom it is said that he varnished just about every Dippy built between the time he returned from overseas in 1919, and the time when the Disappearing Propeller Boat Co. ceased operations in the early 1930s. (Legend has it that Reggie would sing from morning till night as he and his helpers would go through 25 to 30 gallons of varnish per day.)

There were many others as well, every one hand-picked by Johnston to perform a particular task according to his individual skills.

Of course, credit for the initial establishment of the company and for its tremendous growth, during the first few years at least, must go to its President, J.R.C. Hodgson. Believing firmly in the viability of the Dispro right from the beginning, he turned all his considerable entrepreneurial talents to its promotion. Like Johnston, he gathered about him men of proven ability and used their talents well. In the Toronto office at 92 King Street West was his cousin, Judd Wight, who acted as company secretary and salesman, while Frank Erickson-Brown acted as solicitor. On the sales staff as well were Neil Wilson, (later Managing Director of the ill-fated Tonawanda plant,) and the aggressive young salesman, William G. Ogilvie.

As we have seen, Hodgson had formed an early association with the firm, Knight Metal Products of Toronto, and its President, Harry W. Knight.[31] This company (which was also known variously over the years as Automotive Products Ltd., Clear Vision Pump Co. Ltd. and Service Station Equipment Ltd.) had two very capable shop superintendents: Bert Campton, reknowned as a skilled welder and metalworker, and Henry R. Astridge, a superb mechanical draftsman and designer who had patented the brake restraint device. The development and and production of the Model D and the improved Model E engines, the Dis-Pro Light, aquascope, instrument panel and recoil starter were largely due to their efforts.

---

[30] Several surviving employees of the Port Carling plant have mentioned these speed records.
[31] Knight was also a member of the Board of Directors of the Disappearing Propeller Boat Co. of Delaware (the U.S. patent-holding company) and Managing Director for one year at the North Tonawanda plant.

With such a formidable array of energetic and skilled people behind the many aspects of the boat's production and promotion, success seemed assured. By 1922 this group had managed to solve most of the serious technical problems affecting both the machinery and hulls of the Dispro and a highly efficient factory operation was now coupled with an effective sales and promotional organization. The factory in Port Carling was now employing upwards of 40 men during peak periods, and while the boatbuilding operation remained essentially labour-intensive, there was a serious attempt at specialization of operations within the factory.[32] As in the Ford Motor Co., each man performed his own specific operation, be it planking, nailing, finishing, installing engines and devices, varnishing, or whatever, according to his ability. But while the key to Ford's phenomenal success with the Model T had been due to mechanization of production, coupled with the specialization of human labour, it was not possible to apply mechanization to the production of Dispro boats. This is where the analogy between the Model T and the Dispro ultimately broke down. The boatbuilding operation, in spite of various attempts made to mechanize it, continued because of its very nature to be based largely on the labour and skills of the factory personnel.

It had taken several years to build up this corporate edifice. When it was shattered a short two years later, and the various talents and skills scattered to the winds, the halcyon days of the Dispro were at an end.

[32] Estimates of the number of factory employees vary considerably. The figure quoted above represents not only the boatbuilders but also factory office staff, repairmen, engine installers and machinists, plus personnel involved in shipping completed craft by barge to the railway station at Bala. The number involved in actual boatbuilding operations is believed to have been about 20.

To demonstrate the durability of the Model T Ford, dealers often heavily overloaded it with passengers. Photographs such as these undoubtedly prompted Tassie to try the same stunt with a Dispro. [From "Tin Lizzie" (Stern) 1955, Simon & Schuster]

Eighteen people crowded into a De Luxe Model. Approx. weight 3126 lbs. Still 9 inches freeboard and boat making headway.

Left to Right:

1. Bert Hurst, Nailer
2. Reg Stephen, Varnisher
3. Cameron Milner, Finisher
4. Harold Cooper, Engineer
5. Harold Clark, Engineer
6. Doug Milner, Planker
7. Alf Croucher (partly hidden), Planker
8. Unknown
9. W.J. Johnston Jr., Factory Manager
10. C.J. McCulley (behind Johnston), Assistant Office Manager

11. Tom Croucher, Planker
12. Dunc Batten, Mechanic, Blacksmith
13. Tip Massey, Helper
14. Bill Croucher, Misc. Woodwork & Engineer
15. Bill Sweet, Woodworker
16. Garth Tassie, Office Manager, Assistant Factory Manager
17. Leslie Brown, Woodworking, Machinery
18. Johnny Johnston, Misc. Woodwork

Garth Tassie (third from stern) apparently was the instigator of this famous photograph, which eventually enjoyed widespread publication. It is said that at the last moment Garth passed his camera to a friend who happened to be visiting the Port Carling D.P. plant at the time, and jumped into the stern of the Uncle Sam just in time to become immortalized with his fellow workers.

List of personnel in modern "18 in a Dispro" photo taken in Sept. 1982. Bow to Stern: Bert Hurst, Roger Dyment, Alex Posiliko, Bill Fraser, John Cooper, Paul Dodington, Bill Otton, Joe Fossey, Jim Domm, Ron Hill, Paul Gockel, Tom Myatt, Jeff Hill, Jim Smith, Rob Haggar, Linda Jackson, Kimberley Clarke, Bruce Clarke.

A barge-load of boats being prepared for shipment, summer of 1920.

Life in the D.P. Factory

by Paul W. Gockel III

"The hum of industry can be heard throughout the year for Port Carling is the home of the Disappearing Propeller[1]...." Over the years, this fact has been substantiated by many who lived and worked in Port Carling at the time of the D.P. In the early '20s, the large, three-storey factory is alleged to have employed as many as 40 men at one time.[2] From raw lumber to finished product, an enormous amount of skilled and unskilled labour was concentrated in the plant on the Indian River in order to have built some 2,000 boats.

The first floor of the D.P. factory consisted mostly of dock space. Here the engines were stored and installed along with their necessary accessories. There was a limited amount of machine tools such as a lathe, a drill press and a worn out keyway cutter, to do the almost limitless repair work required on D.P.'s. The shafts were made up with the universal joints and the devices were then assembled. There has also been reference made to a concrete test tank on the first floor, the purpose of which was to test all D.P. devices for leaks[3] as this was a common problem, especially in the early years. Because of the hill behind the plant, the first floor was smaller than the other two floors so little more than testing, machining and installing engines could be undertaken here.

Although the steam engine and boiler were in a stone shed at the dock level also, the machinery they powered was on the second floor of the plant. All these machines were run from a ceiling line shaft which had a series of pulleys. Great wooden levers hung down from the shaft which enabled the operator to engage or disengage each machine.[4] From laying the keel to installing the seats, all the boatbuilding was done on the second floor. During the boatbuilding season, the second floor of the D.P. was probably the busiest place in Port Carling.

The third floor, which had about one-half the area of the second, was where all the varnishing was done and it was here also that the devices were installed.

[1] "History of Port Carling", *Port Carling Ripple*, ed. S.M. Beach (Port Carling: 1921), p. 10.
[2] The number 40 is more than likely exaggerated. 20 to 30 at one time seems more realistic.
[3] Garth Tassie, former office manager, D.P. Co., Port Carling, taped interview with Aud Duke at Port Carling, 1974.
[4] Charles F. Amey, former planker at D.P. Co., Pt. Carling, personal interview with the author, Port Carling, October 15, 1981.

Work generally started at 7:30 a.m. and finished at 5:30 p.m., the ring of a gong marking the times.[5] First thing in the morning, a workman would stoke the boiler to get up steam to heat the building,[6] to fill the steam box and to run the enormous steam engine that ran the band saw, planer, jointer, table saw, sander and chip blower. Billy and Johnny Johnston, who were usually there long before anyone else,[7] were the men who used the large machinery most. They roughed-out stems, stern posts, ribs, planks and anything else that would be needed for the day's building. Johnny could often be seen walking around the shop with an enormous pile of wood under his arm.[8]

Lumber arrived on the railway at Bala then went via barge or sleigh, depending on the season, to the D.P. factory. In the winter it would come by road to the plant down the steep cliff behind the factory on the factory's skid[9] and be stored next to the plant. A certain amount would be brought inside the plant immediately and sorted.[10]

The lumber that was brought in was dressed on both sides so all pieces could be carefully examined. It was dressed from 1¼-inch rough lumber to a finished 1-inch. This gave the sawyer an opportunity to examine the material for knots, splits, shakes, sapwood or any other adversity that would make an inferior keel, plank or rib. If the stock were considered good, the piece would be cut from patterns. Keels, requiring no less than three patterns to shape them correctly, were made up full-length on a long bench.[11] Accurate bevelling of these was accomplished by extensive use of a drawknife and thumbplane. The previously hewn stem and stern post were fastened to the keel, stopwaters were installed in the joints, the assembly plumbed right-side-up on the stocks and the moulds fastened to them. This spinal assembly was now ready to receive the planking.

In the D.P., as in most production boat shops, plank shapes were derived from plank patterns — one pattern for each round of planking, thus each model of D.P. boat had at least nine plank patterns.[12] When the sawyer had determined that he had found a good piece of lumber from which a plank could be made, he would cut out the plank shape on the band saw and then hand-plane the edges to obtain a fair and accurate curve. Then the plank was re-sawn into two halves, dressed to 3/8-inch and run through the sanding machine to remove all machine marks. Finally, completed planks would be stored in labeled bins until the planker was ready for them.

The planker's job was to take care of bevels, plank rabbets, hood ends, scarphs and steaming if necessary. He would usually use the matched re-sawn pairs in planking up the boat so a symmetrical appearance resulted; one plank on the port side, its mate on the starboard. Once the plank was in place on the boat, the job of the nailer began. The nailers had to be fast to keep up with the top-quality plankers who worked there. If the nailers were slow, the plankers complained and the foreman gave the planker a new nailer and

[5] From an untitled poem by W.G. Ogilvie, former general manager at Port Carling. Copy in author's collection.

[6] Ibid.

[7] Bert Riddiford, former D.P. employee, personal interview with the author, December 21, 1981, Port Carling.

[8] W.G. Ogilvie, interview with the author, April 9, 1980.

[9] The lumber slide was used to remove boats from the plant in the winter so they could be shipped to Bala. Russell Cope, the electrician who undertook wiring of D.P. factory, personal interview with the author, February 3, 1980, Bala, Ontario.

[10] Charles Amey, October 15, 1981.

[11] Ibid.

[12] It is believed that more than nine patterns may have been needed per boat. Because the D.P. is a powered craft, the stern tends to "squat" while underway. To compensate for this undesirable effect, the top three rounds of planking aft were made slightly taller, thereby increasing the height of the stern. This added height aft is especially noticeable in Water-Fords. In these last three rounds of planking therefore, it is believed that bow *and* stern patterns were required, bringing the total number of patterns per boat to 12.

*Resawing
a plank*

vice-versa, depending on who was interviewed. There was usually one nailer and one planker per boat.[13]

So adept were the plankers at the D.P. that all the planks with their scarphs and even their bevels could be prepared well ahead of actually installing them on the boat. The planks were delivered to the planker's bench in reverse order. They were piled up on the back of his bench with the sheer plank at the bottom, the garboard at the top. While the nailer was busy setting up the stem, stern post, and keel assembly on the stocks and then putting the moulds in place, the planker was bevelling as many rounds as could be done before the nailer was ready to begin. Perhaps five rounds could be bevelled before they started planking. If the nailer fell behind the planker anywhere along the planking process, the planker could continue to bevel the remaining rounds.[14]

Although they were exceedingly fast, accuracy was not sacrificed. The only problem was overcoming boredom. This was usually eliminated by holding races between the various planking/nailing parties. With up to three boats being planked at once, races were commonplace.[15]

Parallels can be drawn between the techniques used in the D.P. factory with those used by Ford in his manufacture of automobiles. At the Ford plant for example, one man would put a bolt in place but would not tighten it; tightening was the job of another man. Likewise in the D.P., one man would cut a plank, a second would fit it to the boat and a third one would fasten that plank securely. While the nailer was nailing, the planker could be getting out another plank, and so went the process until the boat was finished.

The first three rounds of planking off the keel were steamed in order to soften them so the severe twisting of these bottom planks could be successfully accomplished. The last six rounds, those at the top, went on cold[16] so speed was somewhat increased as the workers did not have to wait for the planks to conform to their new shape.

After the boat was planked, props were shoved under the bottom edge of the sheer plank to keep the hull from spreading and the boat was then ribbed. It took about three

[13] C. Amey, March 14, 1981.
[14] Charles Amey, February 18, 1983.
[15] Ibid.
[16] Ibid.

Douglas Milner (R.) and Cameron Milner (L.) installing ribs in a newly-planked hull in the D.P. factory, Port Carling about 1922. Moulds, seen hanging near the window at left, were attached to the swinging brackets overhead, and dropped in place over the keel which had previously been placed up on the stocks. Stem and sternposts were plumbed by means of triangular braces as shown above Cam Milner's head. After the planking and ribbing operations, the hulls were moved down to the end of the room, where two boats can be seen, to have the finishing work completed. A supply of extra stems and sternposts is hanging between the windows.

men to rib a boat: one man to run between steam box and boat while carrying as many as three hot ribs at once, and two men at the boat hammering the ribs into position and then nailing them during the minute or so while they remained soft. It was a hot and tiresome job.[17]

When the ribbing was completed, the boat was removed from the stocks so another boat could be set up. The completed hull was then taken over to the finishers where seats, bulkheads, knees, decks, splashboards and similar items were installed. This was the part of construction that required the most careful craftsmanship for it was in the decks and seats that the quality manifested itself to the public. A bad job here and the entire boat would have had a poor appearance.

Once the boat reached this stage everything was ready to be numbered. The hull was given a serial number, probably by a finisher, and every seat that went with the boat was given the same number so that the pieces could be identified properly after the boat was varnished. When all this had been accomplished the boats went up to the third floor via an outside crane mechanism[18] to the varnish room where they would receive three to four coats of either Nor-Var or Scarfe's varnish.[19] Also up here in the varnish room, the hole for the device would be cut and two men would spend their time installing the devices. Probably the messiest job in the plant, varnishing consumed about 25 to 30 gallons per day as about 15 boats could be done at a time.[20] Once the boats received their varnish, they were considered finished and went, without engines, over to the storage shed. Engines were not installed until the boats were ready for shipment.

The most difficult boats to build were the John Bulls. So unpopular were they in the D.P. factory that if a planker knew he was to plank a John Bull the following day, he and most of his associates would call in sick. They were more awkward boats to work around than the Uncle Sams or Water-Fords and more difficult to plank and rib. Garboard planks on the John Bulls gave the most trouble in that they were too wide and had too much twist in them, considering the ratio of their length and width. When the time came to rib one of them, again difficulty was encountered in clenching the nails at the bottom due to the excessive width of the boat. Bulls were only built when the pressure to build Uncle Sams and Water-Fords was low. Needless to say, in the D.P. factory they were not popular boats[21] and as a result, there are few of them today.

Working conditions in the D.P. factory were probably the best in Port Carling during the early 1920s. The plant was centrally heated and the pay was excellent. Although there were a fair number of accidents, they did not seem to deter the men from wanting to produce. A planker could eventually receive as much as 80¢ per hour and could plank two boats per day as an absolute maximum.[22] The men in the varnish room received 30¢ per hour[23] but a finisher could get $12.00 per boat or about $1.20 per hour.[24] One finisher was known to have finished two Uncle Sams in one day but could only do so if he were mad enough. Also, legend has it that not one of his screws in those boats ever saw a screwdriver, but rather the face of a hammer![25] It should be remembered when such high production figures are seen that all materials were prepared ahead of time so no time was lost in starting from rough lumber.

[17] Ibid.

[18] Riddiford, op. cit.

[19] Reginald Stephen, former head of varnish department, Port Carling D.P., personal interview with the author, Port Carling, April 12, 1980.

[20] Ibid. It seems a bit high but may have been a peak production figure.

[21] Amey, op. cit.

[22] Ibid.

[23] Stephen, op. cit.

[24] Amey, December 16, 1981.

[25] Ibid. November 10, 1982.

View of the Port Carling factory from the south, winter 1921. The boiler house at the base of the chimney supplied steam for space heating, steaming ribs and planking and running the steam engine which drove all the machinery. (The steam engine had been replaced with an electric motor about 1920.) The hoisting arrangement visible above the varnish room door on the third floor was used to raise the boats from the woodworking department on the second level. The lower storey was used for engine installation and testing of completed boats.

Working in the D.P. factory sounds as though it may have been appealing but it was a driving operation. The men worked nine to ten hours per day with no breaks except for lunch. Work consumed about one-half of their Saturdays also. Couple all this with the fact that most of the boatbuilders went off to other jobs during the summer as little boatbuilding was done during the summer,[26] and a potentially tedious winter is portrayed.

The plant was by no means a static place. Over the years, the facilities changed from a small shop with skylights in the roof for lighting, to a large, modern, electrically-operated plant. Innovations came and went, as did employees and building techniques.

In 1916 the plant had been a small operation, employing perhaps only five or six men. Later it grew to meet an expanding market of D.P.'s. In 1919 the factory size was doubled and it was electrified.[27] In the fall of the following year the storage shed was built north of the factory and could store 250 to 400 boats.[28]

The story of electricity coming to the plant is significant of rural electrification techniques at the time. The generating plant of the Bala Electric Light and Power Co. was completed in 1917.[29] By 1919 Port Carling and other communities were connected as well.[30] The transmission lines were wrapped around green bottles which had been fastened to trees along the route of the Bala-Port Carling road.[31] After the First World War, Russell Cope, a young electrician from Bala wired the D.P. factory.[32] Electric lights enabled boatbuilding to be carried on into the dark, early winter evenings. Sometime shortly thereafter the steam engine which had powered all the machinery was replaced by a large electric motor.[33] Starting the motor on a cold morning was an ordeal, usually requiring as many as five men. Four would start pulling on the belt in unison to get the armature rotating. When the RPM's were thought to be sufficient, the fifth man would throw the knife switch on the wall and if all went well, within the 30-second time allotment, the machinery would start to move. On a cold morning however, difficulties were usually encountered and the proceedure had to be done many times.[34]

For years the plant had operated on a piece-work basis. The more each man produced, the more money he received. This seemed a good method in the early days but as time went on the workers tried to produce boats faster by taking shortcuts and even eliminating some necessary operations. One example of cutting corners which resulted in an inferior product was in the nailing process. All nail holes in the planking were pre-drilled to a certain size permitting the nail to be pushed in only about half-way with the thumb. This was a good sign, showing that the hole was the correct size and that the boat would probably not leak around the nail. It meant however, that the nail had to be hammered into position, clenched and then re-hammered. To eliminate one step of the process, the workers began to drill the holes too large, allowing the nails to be pushed in with ease. When it was later discovered that most of these boats developed problems in service, the piecework method was discontinued and the hourly wage plan was adopted.[35]

The boatbuilding process at the D.P. factory had varying degrees of dependency on labour and on machinery. As time passed, the dependency on the machinery increased slightly over previous years as an attempt was made to increase production. Although most

[26] Riddiford, op. cit.

[27] D.P. Catalogue, *Disappearing Propeller Boats*, ca. 1921, p. 1.

[28] *Port Carling Ripple*, op. cit. frontispiece, 1921. There are conflicting reports as to the number of boats that could be stored in the warehouse.

[29] Plaque in Bala at site of ruins of old hydro station.

[30] Ibid.

[31] C.F. Amey, December 10, 1981.

[32] Russell Cope, op. cit.

[33] C.F. Amey, op. cit.

[34] Ibid.

[35] Riddiford, op. cit.

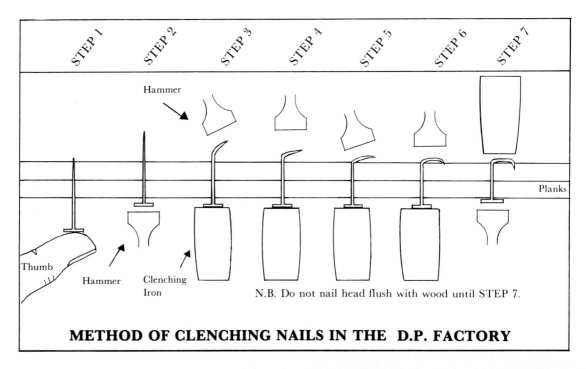

STEP 1   STEP 2   STEP 3   STEP 4   STEP 5   STEP 6   STEP 7

Hammer

Planks

Thumb

Hammer

Clenching
Iron

N.B. Do not nail head flush with wood until STEP 7.

METHOD OF CLENCHING NAILS IN THE D.P. FACTORY

The dock space between the factory and warehouse was used as a repair area. In this photo, W.J. Johnston Jr. (L.), Reg Stephen (C.), and an unidentified factory employee are launching a 1921 Water-Ford. The garage in the background was used as a storage area for oil and gasoline. The two large vertical posts supported an overhead rail, by which completed hulls were moved from the third floor varnish room to the warehouse. Timber piled on the dock was used to crate boats.

93 engines.

of the work required to fabricate stems, stern posts and keels involved hand labour, especially in the early years, the preparation of the planking, ribs and trim involved the machinery. Finishing again relied on craftsmanship.

During the early years the posts were carved out by hand by one man who stood at his bench and attempted to make both rabbets symmetrical. Later, the table saw was rigged to speed the process by cutting some of the rabbet.[36] However, by 1925, Mr. Astridge devised a method involving a milling cutter in a drill press chuck which made the previous methods obsolete. So thorough was this final method that almost no hand work was necessary and the time requirement was greatly reduced.[37]

Although most of the actual boatbuilding mentioned in the factory was done in pairs (two men to plank, two men to rib, and two men to finish) there were some one-man jobs too. Most of the machinery was operated by either Billy or Johnny Johnston, with several assistants. Bench work, or that work which did not apply directly to the hull of the boat, was also necessary and required most exacting craftsmanship. A few good men were needed to make rudders, seat backs and seats, motor covers, oars, bulkheads, engine beds and floorboards. All these things were made up in bulk and then fitted to the individual boats by the finishers. Such work usually rotated among the men to help eliminate boredom.[38]

Such was life in the D.P. factory during the winter months in the early 1920s. During the summer however, the pace of life changed, and from a boatbuilding operation dealing mostly with woodworkers, efforts shifted to the mechanical end of production of D.P. boats.

In the spring and summer when the ice had gone, engine-less boats were removed from the storage shed where they had rested all winter and were brought into the first or dock-level floor of the factory. A shipment of engines from Toronto would usually arrive at the plant in the spring. Numerous men would be busy installing engines, gas tanks, propeller shafts, starters, dashboards and making up the numerous copper gas and grease lines and fitting them to the individual boats. Probably small things like steering rope eyes, pulleys, oarlock plates and oar retention leathers were also installed.

After the boats had been thoroughly outfitted, each was run up and down the river to ascertain whether all systems were functioning correctly. Many boats were run over the rapids at Port Carling to see if the devices were doing what they were supposed to be. It is not known how many boats came back for new propellers! If systems on the boat were all right, a chart was made and sent with its respective boat,[39] claiming that previous motor experience was unnecessary. All one had to do was follow the chart.[40]

When all installations, testing and chartmaking had been accomplished, the boats which were intended to leave Muskoka were shipped to Bala. Some were first crated and put on a barge while others were towed nose-to-tail behind a larger boat. From Bala, the boats were shipped throughout Canada and around the world.

[36] Ibid.
[37] Ibid.
[38] Ibid.
[39] D.P. Catalogue, *Disappearing Propeller Boats*, ca. 1920, p.2.
[40] Ibid.

EVERY BOAT IS TESTED

Every boat is tested in the water under its own power. From this test a chart is made, which is sent to each purchaser. Previous motor experience is unnecessary— simply follow the chart.

Quality control testing of an early Water-Ford: running the Port Carling rapids in both directions.

Due to the lack of rail connections at Port Carling, boats shipped to points beyond the Muskoka Lakes had to be transported by water to the railway station at Bala, 14 miles distant. Sometimes the launch PRISCILLA would move the boats by scow as in the above photo, but often they would simply be towed stern first as shown below.

Dispros being crated in preparation for rail shipment, summer of 1920.

Dispros were often used as work boats around the factory. Here, Harold Clark, engineer, tows a scow and two crated Dippies. Riding the scow are C. J. McCulley (in white shirt) and Garth Tassie (centre). The new warehouse can be seen in the background. (Photo, 1921)

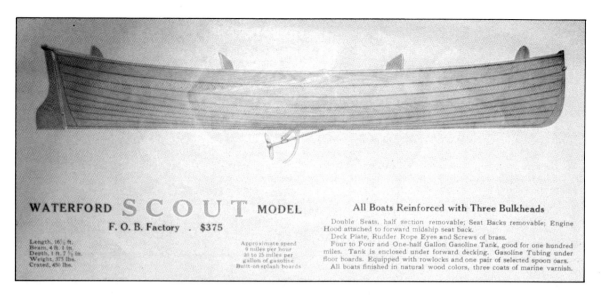

WATERFORD **SCOUT** MODEL

F. O. B. Factory . $375

Length, 16½ ft.
Beam, 4 ft. 1 in.
Depth, 1 ft. 7½ in.
Weight, 375 lbs.
Crated, 450 lbs.

Approximate speed
9 miles per hour
20 to 25 miles per
gallon of gasoline
Built-on splash boards

All Boats Reinforced with Three Bulkheads

Double Seats, half section removable; Seat Backs removable; Engine Hood attached to forward midship seat back.

Deck Plate, Rudder Rope Eyes and Screws of brass.

Four to Four and One-half Gallon Gasoline Tank, good for one hundred miles. Tank is enclosed under forward decking. Gasoline Tubing under floor boards. Equipped with rowlocks and one pair of selected spoon oars.

All boats finished in natural wood colors, three coats of marine varnish.

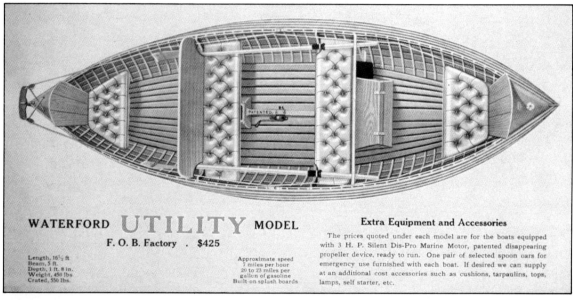

WATERFORD **UTILITY** MODEL

F. O. B. Factory . $425

Length, 16½ ft.
Beam, 5 ft.
Depth, 1 ft. 8 in.
Weight, 450 lbs.
Crated, 550 lbs.

Approximate speed
7 miles per hour
20 to 25 miles per
gallon of gasoline
Built-on splash boards

Extra Equipment and Accessories

The prices quoted under each model are for the boats equipped with 3 H. P. Silent Dis-Pro Marine Motor, patented disappearing propeller device, ready to run. One pair of selected spoon oars for emergency use furnished with each boat. If desired we can supply at an additional cost accessories such as cushions, tarpaulins, tops, lamps, self starter, etc.

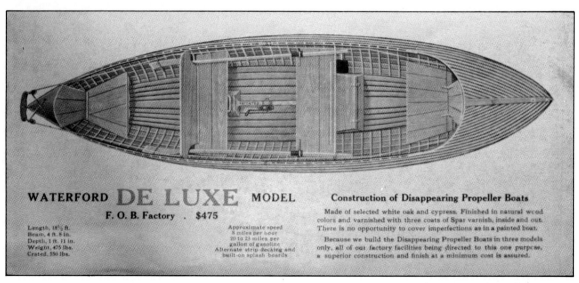

WATERFORD **DE LUXE** MODEL

F. O. B. Factory . $475

Length, 18½ ft.
Beam, 4 ft. 8 in.
Depth, 1 ft. 11 in.
Weight, 475 lbs.
Crated, 550 lbs.

Approximate speed
8 miles per hour
20 to 25 miles per
gallon of gasoline
Alternate strip-decking and
built-on splash boards

Construction of Disappearing Propeller Boats

Made of selected white oak and cypress. Finished in natural wood colors and varnished with three coats of Spar varnish, inside and out. There is no opportunity to cover imperfections as in a painted boat.

Because we build the Disappearing Propeller Boats in three models only, all of our factory facilities being directed to this one purpose, a superior construction and finish at a minimum cost is assured.

North Tonawanda Catalogue, 1922.

The United States Venture, 1920-1923

by Paul W. Gockel III

Popularity and sales of the Dis-Pro boat in Canada increased steadily from 1916, and by 1920 the influence of the boat had been felt in the States to such an extent that American production facilities were considered viable. The unprecedented success of the Canadian operation up to this time turned the eyes of J.R.C. Hodgson toward what he thought would be the still greener pastures in the south.

In his excess enthusiasm, however he failed to conduct adequate market studies in the United States. Particularly suited to areas with smaller, uncharted waters where travelling distances were not great, the D.P. was to find a limited market in the U.S. Certainly there were suitable places, such as the exposed shield of northern Michigan, the Finger Lakes, New England and the Florida Everglades, and here the Dippy did well. However, it was not much of a success elsewhere in the States.

However, J.R.C. Hodgson's zeal to exploit the Dis-Pro boat, with Harry W. Knight's cooperation, led them both to meet on March 6, 1920 at which time they made an agreement.[1] Later that same month, the Disappearing Propeller Boat Co. of Delaware was incorporated and "subsequently acquired the patent rights to Disappearing Propeller Boats and Trade Names used in connection therewith, for the United States from the Canadian Company."[2] The American company in Delaware paid $50,000 cash, 600 shares preferred stock and 8,000 shares common stock to purchase these U.S. patents from the Canadian Company on August 21, 1920.[3] Hodgson, Knight and Brouse became the directors of the American company.

The purpose of the Delaware company was to license district companies throughout the United States for the purposes of manufacturing and marketing Dis-Pro boats on a royalty basis.[4] The Delaware company was to sell the motors and propeller devices to the proposed various district companies and be the holding company for the patents and the trade names in the U.S.

---

[1] Disappearing Propeller Boat Co. v. Hodgson, #2914-24, Affadavit article 6. York. (F.C. Clarkson) February 12, 1925.

[2] Office of the Provincial Secretary, Prospectus: *Disappearing Propeller Boat Co.*, February 25, 1922; p. 2.

[3] Ibid. p. 5.

[4] Ibid. p. 3.

Numerous district companies across the States were started, including ones in Wisconsin, Seattle and North Tonawanda, New York.[5] It was hoped that each district company would out-produce the one Canadian company. Only one of these district companies ever made it to the production stages however, and even that was short-lived. This was the Disappearing Propeller Boat Corporation of New York, in North Tonawanda.

The directors of this first district company assembled on September 9, 1920 in Buffalo, New York and organized the first stock corporation in America to manufacture D.P. boats. The document of incorporation was notarized September 17 and filed in the Erie County Clerk's Office at 3:04 p.m. on September 27, 1920.[6] Early in 1920 an unidentified man, perhaps a naval architect,[7] visited the Port Carling factory. He toured the plant and measured every part of each boat. Keel angles, seat patterns, engine locations, trim details — nothing escaped his eyes.[8] From these measurements he was able to draw the plans necessary to produce boats in North Tonawanda. Everything needed to manufacture and finish a boat was copied from the Canadian operation.

Office space was rented at 725 Main Street Buffalo[9] and the plant was located at 332 Robinson Street in North Tonawanda.[10] The plant had formerly been that of the Niagara Paper Company and the machinery came from the Curtiss Aircraft factory. The employees, all of limited or no skill, were mostly of Polish and Ukranian descent.[11]

If any one person played a major role in the success of forming the North Tonawanda plant, it would have to be E. Douglas Milner of Port Carling.[12] Not only did he see to the establishment of the shop and its operation, he, as an excellent planker, made an attempt at training immigrant labour to build boats, which would have been a formidable task even without the language barrier.

The association of Doug Milner with W.J. Johnston was based on mutual trust. Milner had had the job of running Johnston's Port Sandfield boat livery for many years before the D.P.[13] He also was associated with Johnston for some time after the liquidation of the Port Carling factory.[14]

Exactly when production started, ceased and how many boats were produced in North Tonawanda is unknown. All records have been lost. However, Doug Milner is reputed to have said that one boat could be produced there per day, at best.[15] The fact that boats were produced there is evident. Boats identical to those known to have been produced in Port Carling exist but with unusual serial numbers. Instead of the four numerical digit scheme used at Port Carling, the New York boats appear with such numbers as "A 255". These numbers refer only to the hulls and not to the engines. Engine numbers, it is believed, correlate exactly with the Canadian engines since all the

[5] Ibid.

[6] Erie County Clerk's Office, State of New York, Treasurer's Office. *Certificate of Incorporation of Disappearing Propeller Boat Corporation of New York*, pp. 4-6.

[7] W.G. Ogilvie, former office manager, Disappearing Propeller Boat Co. Ltd. Toronto, Ontario, personal interview with the author at Lakefield, Ont. March, 1982. He thought it was a man named Mr. Harley but knew no more.

[8] Charles Amey, former planker with the Disappearing Propeller Boat Co., Port Carling, personal interview with the author at Port Carling, December 2, 1981.

[9] D.P. Catalogue, *Disappearing Propeller Boats*, ca. 1921, p. 3.

[10] Small, square advertisement, source unknown, ca. 1922, author's collection.

[11] Doug Milner, former planker with the D.P. Co. Ltd., interview with co-author, Port Carling, ca. 1970.

[12] Ibid., also C. Amey, op. cit., March 5, 1981.

[13] C. Amey, Ibid.

[14] Leila Cope, *A History of the Village of Port Carling* (Bracebridge: Herald-Gazette Press, 1956), p. 65.

[15] Doug Milner, op. cit.

Rocks and Snags Can't Injure the Propeller—

It automatically disappears inside the housing (see above diagram) the instant the protecting skeg strikes an obstruction.

UNIVERSAL KNUCKLE
PROTECTING SKEG

Skating the rapids in a Waterford.

A picnic party in a Waterford.

Graham Bell in his faithful Waterford.

Tilting stern out of water—propeller still submerged.

Navigating a Waterford safely through the tropical wilderness of the Everglades.

MOTOR B

The Waters Call To Summer Joys

The cool blue lake, the breezy bay, the hidden inlet, the swiftly gliding river, the creek gurgling amid its leafy banks invite you to share Mother Nature's summer delights — the fish — the "old fellows" that have been playing with you for summers past dare you to catch them.

Go Anywhere in a Disappearing Propeller Boat in perfect safety from submerged logs, rocks and sand bars.

Propeller Disappears

The instant the protecting skeg —the exclusive feature of this motor boat—touches any submerged obstacle it raises the propeller and propeller shaft into its housing, at the same time throttling the engine. The boat glides over as easily as the lightest skiff. The propeller and skeg act as a centerboard keeping boat on even keel making it possible to stand up to fish or shoot or to dive with absolute safety.

DISAPPEARING PROPELLER BOATS

Driven by 3 H.P. single cylinder engine equipped with Maxim Silencer and copper water jacket. 20-25 miles per gal. of gasoline. 9 to 9½ m.p.h. Simple one lever speed control —a child can operate it with ease. Built in 3 models, Waterford $375; John Bull $425; Uncle Sam $475. Specifications: 16½ to 18½ ft. and 4½ ft. beam.

Before planning your summer outing read "Vacation Days", a beautifully illustrated story of the out-of-door season sent free together with a list of Disappearing Propeller Motor Boat owners. See a Disappearing Propeller Motor Boat demonstrated. A limited number of agencies open.

DISAPPEARING MOTOR BOAT COMPANIES
97 King St., W., Toronto, Can.   731 Main St., Buffalo, N. Y.

Disappearing Propeller Boat Corporation
OF NEW YORK

NORTH TONAWANDA, NEW YORK

Dad! I can run her—

YOUR boy will be proud when he meets "Dad" for the first time with the new *WATERFORD*. Mother and the children will enjoy their summer this year if you provide them with this sturdy, reliable motor boat that they can run in absolute safety—over rocks, snags or in shallow water. Your week-end at the cottage will be a delight—you can reach the spot where they're biting without tiresome oar work.

Write today for the story of this wonderful boat "1500 Miles in Canadian Wilds."

DISAPPEARING PROPELLER BOAT CORPORATION
331 Robinson St.   North Tonawanda, N. Y.

WATERFORD
The Disappearing Propeller Boat

* * *

Neil Wilson, managing director of the Disappearing Propeller Boat Corporation of North Tonawanda announces orders have been received for the construction of more than 500 boats, sufficient to keep the plant busy for some time to come. Lionel Barrymore, the movie actor, is a purchaser of a boat. Many boats have been shipped to Florida for winter tourists.

* * *

Various ads, 1921.

machinery came from Canada. Surprisingly enough, in a listing of surviving E-1 Dis-Pro engines in Canada, there is a conspicuous void of numbers from 3000 to 3350. All these engines may have been sent to the North Tonawanda plant. If they were, it gives a clue as to the American production. Another clue is that in February 1921, orders for 500 boats had been received.[16] However, if Doug Milner's statement of one boat per day is accurate, it seems probable that as many as 500 were produced in North Tonawanda.

The existence of the North Tonawanda company is manifested in the business directories of that city for only two years, namely 1921 and 1922.[17] During both of these years George Gooderham was president. Neil Wilson was mentioned as managing director and secretary-treasurer for both years also.[18] Wilson had held this same position with the Canadian firm from 1916 to 1919, inclusive.[19] His name disappears from the Toronto annual returns in December 1920 and after this date he apparently went to New York. The third person prominent in both companies is Harry W. Knight, managing director of North Tonawanda.[20] His name appears only in the 1922 directory. Harry Knight owned and operated the Knight Metal Products Co. in Toronto and it is believed this firm manufactured all the machinery for the boats including the engines, devices, dashboards and lights.

Power Boating magazine for 1921 mentions the North Tonawanda company as having orders for over 500 boats and that some were being shipped to Florida.[22] Even Lionel Barrymore, the famous movie actor, had purchased one.[23] Later, in June, 1921, small boats with low powered engines were entering races sponsored by the Buffalo Launch Club. These races were being conducted up the Niagara River with a trophy being offered to the winner by the Disappearing Propeller Boat Company.[24]

According to the colour advertisements put out by the North Tonawanda firm for 1922,[25] the boats produced in the States were identical to the boats of Port Carling including the three horsepower Dis-Pro engine, device, cypress-over-oak construction, dimensions, models and even price, allowing for the exchange rate on the dollar. (All boats were $15.00 cheaper in the U.S.) The North Tonawanda ad is the earliest known to show engine box covers rather than the curved hood, four-inch rib centers rather than the eight-inch and the use of the brake restraint device rather than the old ratchet type.[26] This final feature unquestionably dates the catalogue to 1922. Unfortunately, only one, poor ad from Port Carling has been found after 1921 displaying all of these features.

The fact that no ads appear in the North Tonawanda city directories for the Disappearing Propeller Boat Corp. after 1922 gives good reason to believe that the North Tonawanda company had ceased to exist by this date. There is some evidence to back up

[16] "Along the Niagara Peninsula", *Power Boating*, (February, 1921) p. 36.

[17] North Tonawanda City Directories: 1921, pp. 79, 186; 1922, pp. 65.

[18] Ibid.

[19] Toronto Corporate Records, File on Disappearing Propeller Boat Co. Ltd., Notes from that file, p. 1, Author's collection.

[20] N. Ton'a. City Dir's., op. cit.

[21] Port Carling Factory Photograph #154, taken by Garth Tassie, former plant manager, D.P. Co. Ltd., Pt. Carling Author's collection.

[22] "Along...Peninsula", op. cit., p. 36.

[23] Ibid.

[24] Ibid., June, p. 44.

[25] Advertisement from Disappearing Propeller Boat Corp. of New York, ca. 1922. From the collection of the Museum of the Tonawandas.

[26] It is important however, not to contribute these advances to any sort of progress on the part of the North Tonawanda firm. It is believed that they had enough difficulty just trying to build good boats without being innovative. As employed here in the text, these details serve only as a medium for more accurately dating the catalogue rather than as a source of falsely inflating the quality of the North Tonawanda boats.

this theory. Penn Yan Boats of Penn Yan, New York bought the assets of the New York D.P. firm which included 350 hulls, devices, motors and equipment.[27] That number, 350, is surprisingly close to the number of E-1 engines not previously accounted for. Hodgson later bought all these boats back from Penn Yan, through one Mr. Herman[28] for $150,000.00 with the conditions that Penn Yan would complete and crate the hulls for Hodgson.[29] This comes to $428.57 per boat. It seems highly unprofitable for the D.P. company to have done this when one considers that they sold boats for $425.00!

In the summer of 1923 William G. Ogilvie of Toronto was sent to Penn Yan to sell boats. He sent out about 50 wires at the advice of Hodgson to various dealers in the States and sold most of the boats, the balance being sold by J.R.C. Hodgson's nephew.[30] Ogilvie liked selling the boats in the States, claiming it was "like taking candy from a kid."[31]

There could be numerous reasons for the demise of the North Tonawanda operation. One is the outboard motor. Although this will be dealt with in more detail in a later chapter, suffice it to say that it is doubtful whether the outboard can be held entirely responsible. Although with its speed and convenience, it certainly made the D.P. look antique, there were other contributing factors.

One of those was the royalty arrangement between the district companies and the Delaware company. The Buffalo company was required to pay to the Delaware company royalties of $75,000[32] — a figure established when production and sales hopes were high. If sales and/or production were grossly lower than planned, as was more than likely the case, royalty payments could not be met, rendering an unprofitable operation. A third theory is to consider advertising costs. In 1922 between 40,000 and 60,000 pamphlets on the McKenzie River trip were printed, all of which went to Penn Yan. The bulk of these were thrown away.[33]

A fourth consideration is the general economy of the U.S. during this time. In 1919 the postwar U.S. markets were booming, even with the modicum of inflation which was present.[34] From July 1920 to March 1922 however, the U.S. experienced a major economic decline when prices plummeted and unemployment soared. Farm prices, auto prices and even the consumer/price index all dropped sharply in 1920 and were not to recover, or at least improve, until 1922.[35] By mid-1921 unemployment was 5.75 million.[36]

This period of economic hardship came at precisely the time when the American Disappearing Propeller Boat Company was in its formative stages. The North Tonawanda company was incorporated in September 1920, only two months after the economic disaster had struck. Although the Delaware company had been formed when conditions were favourable, the district company perhaps could not see its way clear of royalty payments in the midst of the poor economic conditions.

Although the economy was improving by 1922, the D.P. had already sown its unfruitful seed in the United States. Last-ditch attempts at saving the company, like the prospectus of 1922, failed. Furthermore, the parent company was beginning to experience hardship at home in Canada. Perhaps the economic recovery can be credited to the ease

[27] W.G. Ogilvie interview, op. cit., 1981.

[28] Mr. Herman of Penn Yan tried to devise some hydraulic reverse mechanism for Dis-Pro's but it was not successful. (From a phone interview with Ogilvie, September 21, 1979).

[29] Ogilvie, op. cit. 1980.

[30] Ibid.

[31] Ibid.

[32] Ogilvie phone interview, December 12, 1981.

[33] Ibid.

[34] Garrity, John A. *The American Nation. A History of the U.S. Since 1865* (New York: Harper and Row, 1975) Vol. II, p. 681.

[35] Ibid. p. 705.

[36] Ibid.

which Ogilvie had in selling the boats, but for all purposes, American production was finished.

If all of these reasons are coupled with the earlier stated belief of the poor marketable potential of the D.P. in the U.S., then a good view can be had of the failure of the company. Whatever the reasons, the North Tonawanda-based Disappearing Propeller Boat Corp. of New York ceased to exist either at the end of 1922 or early in 1923, and the corporation was officially "dissolved by proclamation of the Secretary of State" on December 12, 1929.[37] The Delaware company was definitely dead by December 28, 1929,[38] but how many years previous to that is unknown.

[37] State of New York, Dept. of State, Corporations Bureau. Letter to the author, April 24, 1978.
[38] Toronto Corporate Records. Author's notes. p. 8.

C.J. McCulley at his desk in the D.P. factory office, August 1921.

The Decline and Fall of the Disappearing Propeller Boat Company

by Paul Dodington

SHOALS APPEAR ON THE HORIZON

The failure of the North Tonawanda plant came as a serious psychological and financial blow to the D.P. interests in Canada, and although production figures for 1922 in Port Carling were almost as high as they had been in 1921, by 1923, the Canadian operation was beginning to experience serious difficulties as well. The new models, with their 4-inch rib spacing, their dashboard controls and recoil starting systems, involved the use of considerably more materials and labour than earlier designs, and were therefore more costly to produce. Nor could they be built as quickly as before, so production began to drop somewhat while costs rose.

Close examination of the serial numbers and features of surviving Dispros from this period reveals that boat production during 1922 and 1923 was gradually slowing down, and that the factory had already reached a maximum annual production of about 350 boats in 1921.[1] As workers were now being paid wages instead of the former piecework system of remuneration, the incentive to keep up the breakneck pace was now lost. Nor was there adequate supervision of the employees with regard to punctuality and diligence. Declining production figures after 1921 reflected this increasingly lackadaisical state of affairs.[2]

The institution of a wage system throughout the plant was met by considerable resistance by the workers, especially those who had been particularly productive under the old system. Although provision for bonuses was added to the basic wage offered, the men were still apparently dissatisfied.

In a letter from Hodgson to Johnston, dated March 2, 1922, he alludes to some employee unrest in the Port Carling factory and suggests that Johnston as Factory Manager should take immediate steps to get the situation under control. He says,"...if there is anyone who is not most satisfactory to the business and yourself fire them at once please". He also asks Johnston to discourage any more worker requests for bonuses. He

---

[1] None of the original company records are known to have survived. Therefore, production figures given in this book have been extrapolated from many varying sources, mainly a listing of serial numbers and features of about 150 existing boats, which has been compiled by the author over the past 20 years. Exaggerated tales of production reaching over 1,000 boats per year in the early '20s are not substantiated by a close examination of this listing. Former Port Carling finisher, Cameron Milner, once stated that 355 boats were built there in the most productive year.

[2] Several factory workers recalled this state of affairs in various discussions with the author.

says, "It certainly is too bad the boys do not appreciate what we are trying to do for them, however I understand things are getting better and will hope for a good run on boats this month."[3]

Hodgson's occasional appearance at the Port Carling factory at the wheel of a brand new Packard convertible did little to improve the morale of the factory staff, particularly when the men were being told by management that generous increases were not in the offing.

A demand from the Toronto office that henceforth all books and records were to be kept only at the Head Office simply created more mistrust in the minds of the factory personnel. In fact, C.J. McCulley, who had succeeded Garth Tassie as Factory Office Manager on the latter's resignation in July of 1922, began to keep a secret duplicate set of books, unknown to the management of the Toronto office and in direct contravention of orders from Hodgson.[4]

Tassie maintained years afterward that he had begun to suspect the Head Office management in Toronto as early as 1922. In a letter dated 5th June 1925, he mentions that he had felt obliged to resign his position at the D.P. because he foresaw, "the impending wreck of the company through its city branch."[5]

To top it all off, there were rumours that shipments of boats had disappeared into thin air and charges that company property was being misappropriated by the Toronto office.[6] Garth Tassie even claimed to have thwarted a serious attempt at arson. Tassie, at 78 years of age, recounted the story in his own words:

> "I remember one occasion when our regular night watchman, Bob Ennis, was ill with pleurisy and I had been tipped off that there was likely to be some trouble. So I got an old .38 calibre revolver and some blank cartridges and on my rounds I carted this with me. One night, about the third of my job as night watchman, I heard two people climb up on the boiler house roof and force open the varnish room door upstairs, and I waited till they got in and I turned on the lights and fired a couple of blank shots. They leaped out of the varnish room door, wide open and landed in the river. I don't know where they went then, but there was considerable splashing."[7]

While employee unrest in the Port Carling plant certainly existed, the situation never really came to a head because of the lack of any alternative opportunities in the area. Indeed, the boat factory provided the only winter employment in the vicinity in those days, other than cutting cordwood in the bush at $1.50 per day. By comparison, factory wages at $85 a month were generous indeed!

The Port Carling factory was now building a better quality boat than ever before at a fairly reasonable production level but it was becoming increasingly difficult to sell the product. The lion's share of the boats had been previously absorbed in the Muskoka Lakes area alone, but this lucrative market was becoming glutted by 1923. More and more effort

---

[3] Excerpt from a letter in the author's collection.

[4] The confidential set of books is mentioned in a copy of a letter from Johnston to his solicitor, R.H. Parmenter, K.C., (of Tilley, Johnston, Thompson and Parmenter, Toronto) dated September 8, 1924. (Author's collection)

[5] Excerpt from a letter from J.S.G. Tassie to Furniture Manufacturers' Assoc., Toronto. (Author's collection)

[6] In a letter from Johnston to Parmenter, dated September 2, 1924, he asks the latter to investigate some of these alleged misappropriations. (Copy in author's collection)

[7] J.S.G. Tassie, taped interview, op. cit. (1974).

had to be expended in promoting the virtues of this little craft, farther and farther afield, sometimes in waters less suited to its unique capabilities.

Judd Wight was sent to Montreal during the winter of 1922 to promote sales of Dispros and returned with immediate orders for a carload to be shipped around March 15th. Hodgson wrote, "We will hope for good business from Montreal this year."[8]

Even university students were hired during the summers to travel about selling Dippies.

As has been previously noted, the construction of the new Dispros with their 4-inch rib spacing and increased mechanical complication was much more labour-intensive than earlier models. While Ford's mass-production techniques involved constant simplification of parts and mechanization of factory operations, the D.P. boat was heading in the opposite direction and becoming increasingly complex to build, involving more man-hours, and, of course, more expense.

Although this increased complexity was reflected to some extent in slightly higher selling prices, the profit margin must have become very narrow indeed. There was a reluctance to raise the price of the new boat substantially for fear of losing the already weakening market. The boating fraternity, which had been carefully conditioned to view the Dispro as the "Water-Ford" might not take kindly to a stiff price increase.

The most sinister threat to the continuing success of the Dispro, the outboard motor, was rapidly becoming a major competitor. The introduction of vastly improved and more dependable outboards by 1922, such as the Johnston and Elto, dealt a crippling blow to the vulnerable Dispro. These new outboards were designed, as the Dispro, to afford protection from underwater hazards by tilting up automatically, but they were much simpler to portage, transport, service and store for the winter. They were also becoming cheaper, and thus appealed directly to the same class of consumer who previously might have purchased a Water-Ford.

Outboard motors were also generally faster than Dispros and could be used on any suitable hull. They were much more maneuverable and the Dispro, with its fine lines and simple, yet eloquent craftsmanship, could not hope to compete with such noisy contraptions in the Roaring '20s.

As outboard speeds increased, the Dippy gradually gained a reputation as a slow boat. On Georgian Bay, for example, Dispros were derisively nicknamed "Disappointing Propeller Boats", because of their maddening inability to get to safe shelter quickly when a storm threatened. Due to the displacement hull design of the Dispro, and the lack of a suitable engine of higher horsepower, it was not possible to improve the speed performance of the boat significantly in order to make it more competitive with the outboard. Nor was research and development capital available to the Disappearing Propeller Boat Co. on nearly the scale that it was to the various American manufacturers of outboard motors.

By the summer of 1923, the financial picture of the company was beginning to worsen. In July of that year, a one year loan was taken with the Bank of Nova Scotia in Port Carling for $55,000. This loan was increased in November to $75,000, with J.R.C. Hodgson and A.H. Britton, directors of the company giving personal securities as collateral in excess of $75,000.[9]

[8] Copy of letter, Hodgson to Johnston, March 2, 1922, (Author's collection)

[9] D.P. vs. Bank of Nova Scotia, 1924, op. cit. (Statement of Claim) There is substantial evidence that Hodgson's cottage and property on Lake Joseph were put up as collateral. If this is true, his willingness to sacrifice his personal property in an attempt to save the foundering Disappearing Propeller Boat Co. is evidence that he still believed the Dispro to be a viable proposition and that the economic woes were temporary.

*During its early years, the Dispro
had offered many advantages over
the slower, noisy, cantankerous
outboard motor. (1915 Evinrude
advertisement, Muskoka Lakes
Blue Book Directory — courtesy
Port Carling Pioneer Museum)*

*The Johnson outboard
motor (1922) enjoyed
immediate and lasting
success. By the early 20s
the outboard motor had
become much more versatile
than the D.P., and was
luring many potential
customers away.*

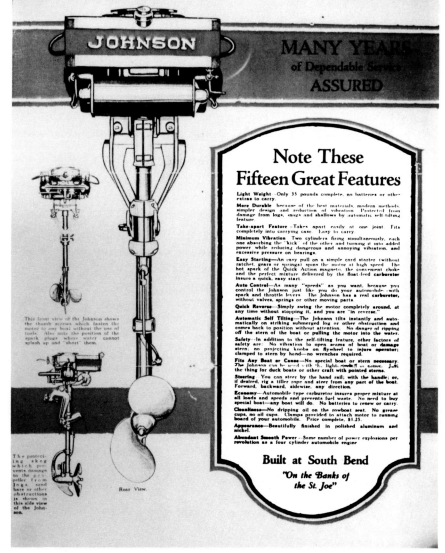

In an attempt to broaden potential markets for the Dispro across Canada, increase the capital of the company and thereby reduce its debts, J.R.C. Hodgson with the company secretary, A.H. Britton, decided in 1923 that the Disappearing Propeller Boat Co. should apply for a Dominion Charter to replace the old Ontario Charter under which it had operated since 1916. This move was expected to produce several beneficial effects and it was hoped that it would provide the means whereby the company might ultimately proceed to even greater heights.

The proposed Dominion Charter would permit the new company to do business directly in all provinces in Canada. The new Dominion Company would simply be a reorganization of the old Ontario Company at increased capitalization and would take over the assets of the business. It was hoped "that by such sale of stocks in the new company and profits, [the Disappearing Propeller Boat Co.] might pay off its obligation by the end of the 1924 season."[10]

According to a newspaper account of evidence given in a subsequent trial, Hodgson was alleged to have approached several of the senior employees in the factory, about August of 1923, and to have put pressure on them to subscribe to stock in the new company. Evidence given by W.J. Johnston, witness for the Crown against J.R.C. Hodgson, in a trial held in York County Judge's Criminal Court in March 1925, was summarized as follows:

> "...The business appeared to flourish for several years, and [Johnston] was led to believe difficulty had been encountered in 1923. About August, he said, [Hodgson] wrote to him requesting that employees be approached and asked to invest or to purchase shares in the proposed new company. [Johnston] said [Hodgson] visited him, mentioned losses of about $75,000 and stated his desire to sell about $50,000 worth of stock... [Johnston] said [Hodgson] asked that employees be brought into the office one by one, then asked them to acquire $2,000 worth of stock in the new company."[11]

When the workers were individually apprised of the financial state of affairs of the company, and of the very real prospect that it might soon have to suspend operations, many of them made a serious personal commitment to keeping the plant functioning. Johnston and six other senior factory employees invested many thousands of dollars in the form of cash, bonds and promissory notes in the new enterprise.

Hodgson undoubtedly hoped that this move would have a double-barrelled positive effect. Not only would some essential investment capital be obtained, but by involving key factory personnel in this way Hodgson may also have been hoping to provide some much-needed incentive to get production figures climbing once again.

By the spring of 1924 the financial picture was not improving as expected. The establishment of the proposed Dominion Company had been repeatedly postponed, possibly due to the lack of interest shown by potential investors and also to Hodgson's involvement during this period in the winding up of the defunct Tonawanda operation. At last, on April 10, 1924, formal application was made for Dominion Letters Patent

---

[10] Ibid.

[11] From a undated newspaper account of the proceedings (circa March 1925) in the author's collection. Johnston himself is known to have subscribed to stock as early as July 3, 1923, according to his Statement of Defence, Johnston vs. Hodgson, op. cit.

incorporating the new Disappearing Propeller Boat Co. Ltd., which was to take over the assets of the old Ontario Company. The Dominion charter was finally granted on July 30.[12]

Boat production had continued unabated during the winter of 1923-24. For the first time there were no changes in either hull or mechanical design except for a handful of special models built in the late spring of 1924.

With the increasing affluence of Muskoka cottagers during the 1920s, more elegant boats built of mahogany were now becoming *de rigueur* among the most up to date. In much the same way that Henry Ford sought vainly to bolster sagging interest in his obsolete Model T during its last years of production by making a series of superficial changes in body styling, the Disappearing Propeller Boat Co. attempted to create renewed interest in the Dispro. About a half-dozen special deluxe models were built, which were planked in mahogany instead of cypress.[13] These sported a small afterdeck in a laminated design like the foredeck and splashboards, in place of the standard "skyboard", plus two lockers under the second midship seat. One of these boats was displayed at the Canadian National Exhibition in the summer of 1924 and attracted considerable attention; but other events were taking place swiftly and it was already too late to save the company.

THE D.P. BOAT COMPANY ON THE ROCKS

The very next day after the company had received its new Dominion Charter, the Bank of Nova Scotia "reduced into possession the assets of the Ontario D.P. Boat Co., and for three days put into the Toronto office of the company its representatives, claiming to be taking possession. This entry extended to all the books and records of the company, and on August 30, 1924, the Bank caused a petition of bankruptcy to be filed against the D.P. Boat Co. Ltd., and obtained an interim injunction restraining the company from carrying on business without the Bank's written consent."[14]

A week or so later, on September 9, 1924, the bank obtained an order declaring the Disappearing Propeller Boat Company bankrupt and appointing E. Jas. Bennett custodian of assets.

The disaster had finally occurred. All the factory employees were laid off and most of the families of Port Carling now faced a very uncertain winter. The complete story of the collapse of the largest enterprise in the village's entire history is still only vaguely understood nearly 60 years later. The demise of the D.P. spawned a series of hearings and court cases, some of which took years to resolve. Unfortunately, the records of some of these cases and the accompanying documentation have since been destroyed, while others lie forgotten in musty archives in various states of completeness.

While it may no longer be possible to tell the story in its entirety, a probable scenario can be pieced together from the scattered bits of evidence which have survived.

As has been previously stated, the Bank of Nova Scotia precipitated the collapse of the company by its action of July 31, 1924. In the subsequent hearing, lawyers for the bank alleged that for "many months prior to the filing of the bankruptcy petition...the company was in a hopelessly insolvent condition..."[15]

---

[12] File #23792, Dept of Provincial Secretary, Toronto. The officers of the new company were:
   1. Arthur Beresford Mortimer (Barrister)
   2. Alfred Bunting (Real Estate Agent)
   3. Ernest Middleton Lee (Student-at-Law)
   4. Ida May Beament (Stenographer)
   5. Sallie Gillies MacKellar (Stenographer)
[13] According to W.J. Johnston in an interview with the author, 1967. One local resident recalls that Hodgson had one of these mahogany boats at his cottage.
[14] Statement of Claim, D.P. vs. Bank of Nova Scotia, 1924, op. cit.

Solicitors for the company, on the other hand, maintained that the actions of the bank prevented the company from re-organizing, selling stock or carrying on business. Therefore, they argued, the bank ruined the company's credit and its power to repay the loan and attempted to force the company into bankruptcy.

On November 13, 1924, the Disappearing Propeller Boat Co. was declared to be insolvent and liable to be wound up. G.T. Clarkson became the liquidator for the company.

Some months previously, J.R.C. Hodgson, along with the company Secretary, A.H. Britton, had forseen the impending collapse of the enterprise. In what appeared to be an attempt to salvage the patent rights and trademarks, Hodgson was alleged to have executed an agreement with Britton on March 14, 1924 which stated, "In certain events, the various patents and patent rights should become the property of J.R.C. Hodgson". This agreement was also said to include the trademarks "Disappearing Propeller Boat" and "Dis-Pro".[16]

So, when the liquidator took over the assets of the company the following November, the various letters patent and trademarks had disappeared. This precipitated another court battle between the Disappearing Propeller Boat Co. in liquidation and J.R.C. Hodgson, as the liquidator could not proceed to sell the company until the ownership of the patents and trademarks was properly established.

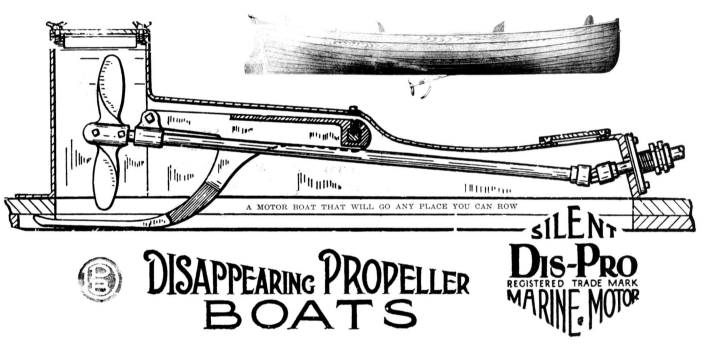

A MOTOR BOAT THAT WILL GO ANY PLACE YOU CAN ROW

DISAPPEARING PROPELLER BOATS

SILENT DIS-PRO REGISTERED TRADE MARK MARINE MOTOR

In this case, the company claimed that it had purchased the various patents and trademarks from Hodgson at sundry times and that they were therefore the legal property of the company. In addition, the company claimed that the agreement of March 14 between Hodgson and Britton was null and void as it had been signed when the company was insolvent and unable to pay off its debts in full — and when both the company and Hodgson knew it.

Hodgson's defense was essentially that he had never agreed to transfer ownership of the patents to the company until they were paid for in full, and until the Disappearing Propeller Boat Company was able to give him and other shareholders a good return.[17]

[15] Ibid.
[16] See Statement of Claim and Statement of Defense, D.P. vs. Hodgson December 18, 1924, #2914-24, Ontario Archives.
[17] Ibid.

Mr. Justice Kelly, however, saw otherwise. He found the agreement of March 14 to be null and void and that the patents and trade names were rightfully the property of the company. He ordered Hodgson to transfer all patents and trademarks to the Disappearing Propeller Boat Co., but added that the company still owed Hodgson any unpaid balance due him. Hodgson appealed the decision but again the judge found for the company. Mr. Justice Orde, of the Appellate Court, said in summarizing his decision:

"This hazy, nebulous idea of retaining the title seemed to exist only in the mind of Mr. Hodgson."[18]

Thus, J.R.C. Hodgson finally lost all control over the patents and the company and he and his associates were forever restrained from selling the patents and trade names. He ended up with only a couple of minor claims and expenses and his rights against the company in liquidation for the unpaid balances of what he was to receive for the patents.

Meanwhile, the liquidator had ordered W.J. Johnston to re-open the factory late in the fall of 1924 and to rehire a small select group of men for the purpose of converting the large inventory of materials and lumber into finished boats and thereby improve the financial picture of the company.[19]

Johnston, therefore, rehired six of his best men: Johnny Johnston, (his brother), on band saw; Bert Riddiford, nailer; Doug Milner, planker; Cam Milner, finisher; C.J. McCulley, office; and Reg Stephen, varnisher. It must have been difficult indeed for Johnston to decide which men to rehire and which men would have to work in the bush that winter.

This small group of men worked diligently during the winter of 1924-25 and it is estimated that they turned out three or four boats per week. Late that winter Johnston was called to Toronto for a day or so and C.J. McCulley as Office Manager laid off all the men. Upon Johnston's return, he rehired the men and kept them all on staff for one more month.

"During that month," says Riddiford, "Not one boat was built. Some of the men sat around the shop, while others built furniture out of the mahogany that was lying around."

By this action, Johnston was viewed locally as a benefactor who, when he finally realized that the company was not going to survive, did what he could to see that the workmen benefitted as much as possible from the liquidation. It is possible, as well, that his own solicitor may have pointed out to him that by continuing to build boats, he was increasing the value of the assets of the defunct company, thereby reducing his own ability to later purchase the assets from the liquidator. Johnston, in his disillusionment over the recent course of events, now began to lash out against Hodgson as though the latter were personally responsible for the debacle. About March 7, 1925 Johnston entered an action in the Supreme Court of Ontario against Hodgson, suing the latter for $10,000 damages.[20]

Johnston's Statement of Claim was delivered on March 21, by his solicitors, Tilley, Johnston, Thompson and Parmenter. In this document he indicated that as he was a man of little education who had little or no experience with business and finance, he had trusted in Hodgson and had relied on his integrity to protect his interest in the patents and financial affairs of the Disappearing Propeller Boat Comapany. He claimed that Hodgson had misconducted himself in his dealings with Johnston's shares, finances and affairs and had acted adversely to his interests, by which he had suffered substantial damages. There followed a long list of specific claims in addition to the $10,000 asked for damages, most of which involved accountings on stock dividends, purchase money in respect of Johnston's interest in the patents and monies received by Hodgson for subscription to stock in the new Dominion Company.

On April 2, Hodgson's solicitors, Bone, Jenner & Teskey, delivered a very elaborate

[18] Quoted from an undated contemporary newspaper account of the proceedings entitled, "Company Owns Patents", (Author's collection).

[19] According to Bert Riddiford, one of the small group of former employees rehired.

[20] Supreme Court of Ontario, Johnston vs. Hodgson, #578-25.

Statement of Defense complete with two schedules of affidavits. The latter consisted of several signed agreements and letters dating back to 1916 with respect to Johnston's sale of the patents, Hodgson's Power of Attorney and the Johnstons' exchange of the original buildings and plant in Port Carling and Port Sandfield for stock in the company. A very complete but complex accounting was given with regard to Hodgson's dealings with Johnston's affairs under the Power of Attorney. The statement concluded with a claim that Johnston's action should be dismissed with costs and, that according to Hodgson's accounting, Johnston had already been overpaid.

Whether the case ever came to trial is not known. Nevertheless, much can be gleaned from the scraps of evidence which have survived. The Johnstons, Sr. and Jr., had transferred most of the assets of their previous business in Port Carling and Port Sandfield to the newly-established Disappearing Propeller Boat Co. in exchange for capital stock. Young Billy's patent interests were at various times obtained by Hodgson largely in exchange for company stock, and in most cases any stock dividends payable to Johnston were reinvested in the business too. The Johnstons therefore had built up a sizeable stock investment in the company.

Hodgson, through his Power of Attorney, had probably arranged Johnston's affairs in this manner in order to encourage the latter's continued exclusive commitment to the enterprise. Johnston had concurred with these arrangements in the belief that the business was a sure thing and that his investment in the company would eventually bring him untold riches.

Now that the Johnstons were faced with the immediate prospect of losing practically all of the equity that had been built up since the days of the first Johnston rowing skiffs, over 50 years earlier, it is perhaps understandable that Hodgson would be viewed as the scapegoat. In an interview with the author, some 42 years later, Johnston was still very much adamant in his assessment of Hodgson:

"That business was a gold mine," he said emphatically. "I was done out of it by a sharp promoter."[21]

While Johnston vs. Hodgson may in fact have been settled out of court, Hodgson was at the same time under attack from another more formidable group of investors seeking legal redress. As a result of his actions with regard to the disposition of funds and promissory notes he had obtained from company employees back in 1923, which were intended to be applied to stock in the new Dominion Company, Hodgson was now faced with 27 counts of theft. He was tried before Judge O'Connell in York County Judge's Criminal Court at a series of hearings during the winter of 1925.[22]

The Crown alleged that Hodgson, as former President of the Disappearing Propeller Boat Co. of Ontario, had procured cash and securities totalling $13,375 from various individuals[23] for the purpose of allotting shares in a proposed new Dominion Company of the same name, but that he had appropriated these for his own use. A newspaper account of the proceedings quotes as follows:

"Crown Attorney McFadden sought to show that the employees were induced to invest, and that the money, rather than going to the new company, had been used otherwise."

Judge O'Connell: "Stop there. That's not the issue. The case is, having got the money, how did he apply it?"

[21] W.J. Johnston Jr., interview with author, July 1967.
[22] Papers in the author's collection, courtesy Mrs. W.J. Johnston Jr.
[23] Most were employees in the Port Carling factory. Hodgson was alleged to have stolen from Edgar H. Clark, $2,500; C.J. McCulley, $2,400; A.R. Duke, $1,000; J.C. Milner, $2,449.50; and T.H. English, $1,000.

STARTED IN 1916.

Evidence given by W. J. Johnston, inventor of the disappearing propellor contrivance, was that Hodgson had arranged with him in 1916 to promote the business on a fifty-fifty basis, witness conducting a factory in Port Carling. The business appeared to flourish for several years, and witness was led to believe difficulty had been encountered in 1923. About August, he said, accused wrote to him requesting that employes be approached and asked to invest or to purchase shares in the proposed new company. Witness said Hodgson visited him, mentioned losses of about $75,000, and stated his desire to sell about $50,000 worth of stock.

The Court—"That would not cover the losses."

Witness said accused asked that employes be brought to the office "one by one," then asked them to acquire $2,000 worth of stock in the new company. An action entered by witness against Hodgson relevant to the old company is still in abeyance, witness saying the present case had no bearing upon same.

Crown Attorney McFadden sought to show that the employes were induced to invest, and that the money, rather than going to the new company, had been used otherwise.

Judge O'Connell: "Stop there. That's not the issue. The case is, having got the money, how did he apply it?"

Mr. McFadden: "He got it to hold and not to apply to the old company in any fashion."

Arthur D. Mortimer, barrister, testified that he had been instrumental in promoting the new company in April, 1924, upon receiving instructions from Hodgson.

BANK MANAGER TESTIFIES

Recalls Dealings of J. R. C. Hodgson Charged with Theft

Evidence for the Crown was given by George G. Glennie, manager of the main branch of the Bank of Nova Scotia, at the resumed trial in County Judges' Criminal Court of J. R. C. Hodgson, charged with theft of moneys and securities totalling $13,274.

Witness said bank officials had approached accused in 1923 in reference to the latter's liability to repay a loan, and the bank had been asked to carry the account for another year. The bank offered to advance another $10,000 on receipt of securities, and Hodgson and another official of the Disappearing Propeller Company stated their intention to sell stock and tender notes to the bank representing such sales. Witness said discount notes were brought to the bank later, some of them from persons from whom Hodgson was alleged to have stolen. The defence previously set up was that the bank had withheld securi—

Various newspaper accounts.

100

BOAT COMPANY IN TANGLE

J. R. C. HODGSON ON TRIAL

Charged With Theft of the Funds— Defence Claims Assets Withheld.

Facing 27 counts of theft, including moneys totalling $4,000, and promissory notes representing $9,944.60, as well as Dominion of Canada bonds and savings certificates, J. R. C. Hodgson was placed on trial today before Judge O'Connell, in the County Judges' Criminal Court. Previously arraigned, accused had pleaded not guilty.

The Crown alleged that Hodgson, as former president of the Disappearing Propellor Boat Company of Ontario, procured these sums and securities for the purpose of allotting shares in a proposed new company designated as the Disappearing Propellor Boat Co., of Canada; but that accused appropriated same for his own use. Most of the securities were said to have been obtained from six employes of William J. Johnston, boat-builder, of Port Carling, inventor of the propellor, the sums and securities totalling: From Edgar H. Clerk, $2,500; C. J. McCulley, $2,400; A. R. Duke, $1,000; J. C. Milner, $2,449.50; H. G. Cooper, $1,200; E. D. Milver, $2,825, and T. H. English, $1,000.

ASSETS HELD BY ASSIGNEE.

In defence, T. H. Lennox, K.C., and C. A. Thompson said they aimed to establish that assets of the company has been held by the assignee which prevented the new corporation from functioning. Hodgson was always prepared to carry out the arrangements, providing the assets could be procured from the assignee. The contract with complainants would be lived up to if Hodgson could be enabled to deal with the shares. The liquidator was said to have paid $39,000 for the assets of the original company, while a bank was declared to be holding $80,000 securities belonging to Hodgson. In the latter case, Mr. Lennox advised that a suit was pending.

President of Boat Company Liable for Commissions

April 24/25

J. R. C. Hodgson, director and president of the Disappearing Propeller Boat Company, is held liable to the liquidator for $5,120 received by him as commissions on the sale of stock of the company, and $1,431 for commissions paid to others, according to a decision of Charles Garrow, K.C., Master of the Supreme Court, who declares that the letters patent of the company show no authority for payment of commissions. With reference to a credit balance of $3,734 on the books of the company, Mr. Hodgson is allowed to rank as an ordinary creditor. A further claim for salary and expenses is yet to be dealt with.

Mr. McFadden: "He got it to hold, and not to apply to the old (sic) company in any fashion."[24]

Hodgson's lawyers claimed in defense that the assets of the company had been held by the assignee, which prevented the new corporation from functioning. Hodgson was always prepared, they claimed, to carry out the arrangements, providing the assets could be procured from the assignee. The contract with complainants would be lived up to if Hodgson could be enabled to deal with the shares.

George G. Glennie, the Manager for the main branch of the Bank of Nova Scotia, testified on behalf of the Crown that when the bank had asked for security on an additional $10,000 bank loan taken out back in 1923, Hodgson had presented discount notes to the bank, some of them from persons from whom Hodgson was alleged to have stolen.

On March 10, 1925, J.R.C. Hodgson was convicted by Judge O'Connell on 26 counts of theft of securities and monies. His Honour, in summing up the case, stated that the evidence showed that those who had subscribed for stock in the new company had done so on the understanding that their money was not to be used to reduce the liabilities of the original Ontario company. Judge O'Connell indicated that anything done by the accused by way of restitution during the interim would be considered and would carry a great deal of weight at the time of sentencing, which was to take place on March 20th.[25]

THE SALE OF THE DISAPPEARING PROPELLER BOAT CO. BY THE LIQUIDATOR — THE END OF THE JOHNSTON ERA

On April 17, 1925 the assets of the now defunct company were put up for sale by the liquidators by order of the Supreme Court of Ontario. The assets were divided into three separate parcels and sealed tenders were invited for any or all of the parcels.[26]

The first parcel included the property and factory, warehouse and wharves in Port Carling; the boathouse, oilhouse, machine shop and docks at Port Sandfield; the tools and machinery; stock-in-trade; engines; office furniture, and Canadian Patents Nos. 161292, (the R.A. Shields Patent), and 225945, (the Astridge brake device patent) and trade-marks.

The second parcel included the foreign patents and manufacturing rights in the U.K. and Isle of Man, France, India, Italy, Newfoundland, Australia and Holland.

The third parcel included the three U.S. patents.

W.J. Johnston Jr. immediately set out to purchase the assets from the liquidator. Understandably, he was most anxious at this time to get the business back so he proceeded to round up the necessary investors.

In a letter to Dr. R.J. Hutchinson[27] of Grand Rapids, Michigan, dated April 27th, 1925, Johnston stated that he was trying to make a bid on Parcel One. He indicated that he already had a promise of $5,000 from Mr. Shields[28], that he could raise another $5,000 locally, and then asked Dr. Hutchinson to invest $5,000.

[24] Quoted from an undated newspaper clipping in author's collection. The final statement contains an obvious misprint. It ought to read, "And not to apply to the *new* company in any fashion."

[25] It is not known whether Hodgson later appealed this decision, nor is it known what sentence was handed down by Judge O'Connell, on March 20th. Again, the pertinent records have been destroyed. According to Garth Tassie, Hodgson did, in fact, make restitution. Some sources interviewed insist that Hodgson went to jail for his various offences; others are just as adamant that he did not.

[26] Notice of Judicial Sale of Assets — undated Toronto newspaper clipping in the author's collection.

[27] Copy of this letter in author's collection.

[28] This is the same R.A. Shields who sponsored the original patent application back in 1914.

It is believed that this consortium did in fact put in a tender to the liquidator on Parcel One for about $15,000; however, a small notice in Toronto papers on May 14, 1925 indicated that the liquidator had rejected all bids for the company and that negotiations were being conducted by the liquidator for private sale. So it appears that for reasons of insufficient capital, Johnston and the other members of his consortium were sent away licking their wounds.

The small nucleus of key workmen who had been chiefly responsible for building Dispros at such high production levels was now gone forever. Never again would Dispros be built in such volume nor with such consistently high quality.

Understandably, from this time on, there was a determined effort by Johnston and his associates to defeat any resurrection of the Disappearing Propeller Boat Co. by going into direct competition.

With his Sunday dinner finished, his belly bulging coat,
Mr. Astridge goes on drawing line of the Dis Pro Boat.
With sketching board before him and the T square in his hand,
He draws in ribs and keelson of the boat that "Billy" planned.
To scale he marks them off so the men they can't go wrong,
He wants them to start off right with the first ring of the gong.

So with compass and divider, he plots each rib with care,
Even using drafting ink so the lines will never wear.
Overtime he works upon it breaking all the Sabbath rules,
Eager to get it finished and to put away his tools.

Finished he hangs it where each workman's eye can see,
Ther'll be no excuse for placing ribs where the gas tank ought to be.
And no excuse for building one boat longer than the other,
Or for fashioning a stern post that looks like a rudder.
Ther'll be no basket building from the day the sketch is done,
The Dis Pros will be straighter than the conscience of a nun.
The keelson will be truer than the tree that gave it birth,
Ther'll be no better boat in Carling, nor in all this blessed earth.

And when the lumber heaves in sight and the saws begin to rend,
The steam box will grow red hot and the oak ribs start to bend.
Ther'll be Johnny cramming Cyprus into the saw's malicious maw,
And Duncan cursing softly when a drill runs through his paw.
While aloft our little Reggie will be sluicing on the spar,
Till the blooming o'ergrown rowboat is shining like a star.
It will keep George busy shovelling to dry the tacky dope,
But he'd rather stoke the boiler than drink with a pious Pope.

Bill Ogilvie
circa 1925

The D.P.'s Last Brief Appearance in Port Carling

by Paul Dodington

THE DISAPPEARING PROPELLER BOAT COMPANY RESURFACES UNDER THE DOMINION CHARTER AND NEW OWNERSHIP

About the end of May, 1925, the assets of the defunct Disappearing Propeller Boat Co. were purchased by Thomas Hodgson of Lindsay, Ontario, a cousin of J.R.C. Hodgson and a director of the Hodgson Bros. Chemical Co. Ltd. of Lindsay. According to a letter he sent to Johnston, dated May 26, 1926, he had paid the liquidator a total of $30,400 for parcels 1, 2 and 3, (including legal costs and fees).[1]

Henry Astridge, who had recently retired as Superintendent of Knight Metal Products and who had redesigned the device in 1922, was hired as factory manager and a number of former workmen were rehired. Several carloads of cypress were ordered and production began once again in the Port Carling plant.

Things apparently got off to a very slow start. Most of the patterns and moulds had mysteriously disappeared during the two months or so that the factory had been closed and it became necessary to start all over again from scratch.

Measurements were therefore taken from existing boats and new patterns and moulds made up. Astridge, with his background in drafting and mechanical design was horrified at the rule-of-thumb techniques used by the woodworkers and set out to standardize the construction of the boats.

The old John Bull model (more recently known as the "Utility") was dropped from production and all energies were devoted to the Waterford (Scout) and Uncle Sam (Deluxe). Apparently Astridge, for the first time in the history of the Canadian Operation, made up complete detailed sets of blueprints and posted copies on the walls of the plant. It is doubtful that the workmen paid any attention to them, particularly in view of the fact that many of them couldn't read anyway.[2]

Serious problems were encountered with the shipment of cypress that year. A large proportion of it was sapwood, which has a tendency to turn blue and then quickly rot away. This may explain why relatively few of the boats built during that summer seem to have survived. Some of those which still do exist have planking of heartwood, while seatbacks and floorboards have a decidedly bluish cast! In order to compensate for the shortage of good cypress, a few boats that summer apparently were planked in British Columbia cedar instead. None of these are known to have survived to the present.

---

[1] Copy of letter, T. Hodgson to Johnston, May 26, 1926, (Author's collection)
[2] W.G. Ogilvie mentions this in a taped interview of his reminiscences, 1982.

Prior to this time, most of the boatbuilding had been done in the winter, mainly to take advantage of the fact that many men who normally had good-paying jobs at summer hotels and cottages during the season from May to October would be available for hire in the off-season.[3] During the summer months the remaining staff had been concerned mainly with the delivery of new boats, maintenance of older models, engine installation and testing and the transportation and preparation of materials for the boatbuilding operations to take place the following winter.

Now, for the first time Dispros were being built only in the summer months and the handling characteristics of the planking were considerably different, particularly the cedar. Apparently, it was found to be necessary to hose the hulls down before ribbing them to prevent planks from splitting.[4]

Astridge also developed a method of routing out the major part of the rabbet in the white oak stems and sternposts using a milling cutter mounted in the chuck of a drillpress. Formerly the manufacture of these posts had been almost entirely a hand operation, involving many hours of careful chiselling. Astridge's method saved considerable time on this very labour-intensive part of the hull.

In a cost-cutting move by management, however, Henry Astridge was replaced partway through the summer by William G. Ogilvie, as plant manager. Boatbuilding continued until well into the fall and then the plant was shut down for the winter.

COMPETITION FOR THE D.P.: THE FOUNDING OF THE PORT CARLING BOAT WORKS

When their tender for the purchase of the old Disappearing Propeller Boat Co. was rejected by the liquidator in May of 1925, Johnston and several of his key employees found themselves literally out on the streets of Port Carling. Undaunted, they soon decided that amongst themselves they possessed more than sufficient skills to set up a successful independent boatbuilding operation. So, with the additional financial support of R.A. Shields and Dr. R.J. Hutchinon, they busied themselves with plans to set up a brand new boat manufacturing concern, to be known as "The Port Carling Boat Works Ltd."

Harold Cooper and Harold Clark, former D.P. engineers, and C.J. McCulley, former Office Manager, rented the old H.L. Bastien Boat Livery above the locks, which had in recent years been used by the Ditchburn Boat Co. Here they set up a D.P. repair agency and they soon took the lion's share of the maintenance and repair business away from the new owners of the Disappearing Propeller Boat Co.

Former head finisher Cameron Milner left to work temporarily at Ditchburn's in Orillia, while his brother Douglas, planker, spent the summer making arrangements for the construction of a large new boat works above the Port Carling locks.

W.J. Johnston, Jr. locked himself in a loft above the Port Carling Garage, which belonged to Uncle Billy's son-in-law, Bill Massey, and here he secretly set about designing a brand new craft which was to totally revolutionize the small motor boat industry, and thereby supercede the Dispro. It must be remembered that "Young Billy" over a 25-year period had developed a very loyal following among Muskoka boaters, so it was felt that the success of the new venture was therefore assured.

That autumn the new factory was erected as planned and the following winter construction of the first production boats began. The new craft, known as "The Johnston Special", was Billy Johnston's answer to the Dispro. As a matter of fact, although slightly larger, it looked very much like a super-deluxe Dippy, with a laminated deck at each end. Like its predecessor it had an engine which was designed especially for the boat. Known as

[3] Bert Riddiford interview, December 1981.
[4] Ibid.

Johnston Special

Length 19′ 1″—Beam 4′ 11″—Depth 22″.

DESIGNED to fill the need for a motor boat easily operated by any member of the family.

A splendid sea boat, perfectly balanced and easy to handle as a rowboat, even for those unaccustomed to a motor boat.

It comfortably seats eight to ten people. The floors are raised and level. You may steer from any place, and the boat being decked at both ends, with spray boards all round ensures a dry trip even in choppy water.

This hull is so designed that there is practically no chance of the protected propeller coming in contact with a log, rock, or other obstruction while running.

Planked with clear British Columbia edge-grain cedar, copper fastened, with oak ribs close spaced and further reinforced by oak bulk heads, the Hull is the strongest and lightest of its class in Canada. It is light enough to be easily hauled out on shore or onto the dock without injury.

All seat backs are removable for ease in stowing baggage or other extras. A pair of oars are furnished as regular equipment, and the hull is finished in natural wood clear varnished.

Powered with a Firefly engine specially built for and installed in the centre of the boat, ensuring fine riding qualities and maximum safety, you may travel at any speed up to ten miles per hour. All controls are centrally located alongside the engine hood, and the Bull dog reverse gear, a most essential equipment when manoeuvring a boat in traffic or about docks, is standard equipment, a feature left out in most boats of this size.

Advertisement for the Johnston Special

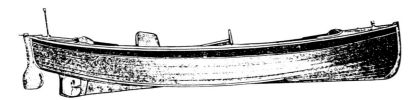

the "Firefly", this new single-cylinder 4-stroke power plant was built by Buchanan Engines in Orillia, Ontario. While the boat was not, of course, equipped with the Disappearing Propeller feature, the hull was so designed that there was little chance of damage to the protected propeller. The really unique feature, however, was that it was the first craft of this general style to be equipped with a reverse gear and as such it was expected that it would soon render the Dispro obsolete.

The Johnston Special, while it cut considerably into Dispro sales, was not nearly as successful as anticipated. It proved to be somewhat unsatisfactory in service. Due to its lack of buoyancy at the stern, it tended to ride very high at the bow when under way. One disgruntled owner complained that the only way he could ever hope to keep up with a Dispro was to move up front where his weight would help to keep the boat on an even keel!

Nevertheless, the Johnston Special continued in production for at least three years, but as the interest of the boat-buying public was now swinging away from old-fashioned "double-enders" toward transom-style launches, Johnston and his associates gradually abandoned the Johnston Special and concentrated on the design and construction of larger square stern motor launches.

The enterprise grew rapidly over the next few years, despite a disastrous fire in the fall of 1931, when the entire factory was lost. It was immediately rebuilt and during the season 1933-34 the Port Carling Boat Works built and sold more inboard motor launches than any other company in Canada.[5]

[5] J.S.G. Tassie, "A Sketch of the Boatbuilding Industry in Port Carling", op. cit.

The D.P. factory remained closed during the winter and early spring of 1926. Bill Ogilvie, who was understandably getting sick of selling Dippies by this time, agreed to return for one more season only if the directors would raise his former 10% commission per boat to 20%. Their agreement to this proposition is evidence of the fine reputation Mr. Ogilvie had developed as a Dispro salesman. By early March he was hard at work, getting orders for the upcoming season's production.

By mid-May he had secured orders for about 60 boats, while Neil Wilson, former managing director of the Tonawanda operation, who had been selling from the Toronto office, managed to get only 10 to 15. Wilson was accordingly relieved of his duties about this time and Ogilvie was made General Manager of the company.[6]

Meanwhile, Bert Riddiford, a nailer, had received a letter from the company asking him to come back to work on March 15th. He had given up a winter job in Toronto at Massey-Harris to return to his beloved Port Carling but the factory did not open as anticipated and he was forced to take a job cutting cordwood all spring.

Tom Hodgson was clearly disenchanted with his new operation and concerned about the stiff competition. In May of 1926 he made a serious attempt to sell the Disappearing Propeller Boat Co. back to Johnston and his associates at the Port Carling Boat Works. He offered them the whole company for the sum of $40,000 or a half-interest at $15,200. He states:

"the reason for this offer is that I want to get away from the manufacturing end of the business... .

"The profits must go to all the shareholders and everyone given a square deal " he said. "There would be a full and proper set of books kept and audited by a competent auditor. I believe we could jointly make a big success out of the business."[7]

Johnston and his associates did not take him up on the offer. Perhaps they were caught up in the flush of enthusiasm generated by their new business and the introduction of the Johnston Special; perhaps they did not trust anyone named Hodgson; or perhaps they were beginning to realize that the D.P. had had its day. It is believed that Tom Hodgson subsequently formed a syndicate of Lindsay investors in order to finance the operation for one more summer.[8]

After he was made General Manager, Bill Ogilvie was sent off to Detroit, where he hand-picked 20,000 board feet of cypress to be sent to Port Carling. This was done to avoid a repetition of the previous summer's disaster when 40% of the cypress had been found unsuitable. The fact that a substantial number of 1926 boats have survived to the present day, is, perhaps, a testament to his success.

The factory eventually opened its doors toward the end of May to a group of about 20 workmen. Bert Riddiford, who worked as a nailer that summer, recalls that Eric Stephen and Johnny Johnston prepared planking, stems and miscellaneous woodwork, Tom Croucher was the planker, and Charlie Amey assisted Vern Harris with the finishing (seats, decks, splashboards, etc.)

Up on the third floor Reg Stephen could be found, as always, singing to his heart's content as he slapped the traditional three coats of spar varnish on each boat. Bill Ogilvie's duties carried him back and forth between the factory and Head Office at 92 King Street West, Toronto, so there were often times when there was no adequate supervision of the workers. Consequently, production was rather slow that summer.

[6] W.G. Ogilvie, interview with author, 1981.
[7] Letter, T. Hodgson to Johnston, May 26, 1926, op. cit.
[8] Bill Ogilvie recalled dealing with the "Lindsay Syndicate" that summer.

Late in the summer, all the Model E-1 Dis-Pro engines which had been left over from the liquidation of the original Disappearing Propeller Boat Co. had been used up and a new engine was installed for the first time.[9] This was the 3 h.p. Caron, produced in Montreal by Caron Bros. This peculiar engine was used along with its larger 6 h.p. version in almost all Dispro production from this time up to the Depression. (An occasional twin cylinder, copper jacket Dis-Pro engine was still making an appearance up into early Lindsay production.)

A minor change to the device housing took place very late in 1926, when the inspection cover over the universal joint (which could not easily be removed in situ anyway) was discontinued and the device casting made without the hole.

After the last of the folding Dis-Pro lights had been used up, late 1926 models were equipped with the larger bronze navigation light shown lower right.

The last of the old folding Dis-Pro lights were used up that summer, as some late 1926 boats have been seen with a larger bronze navigation light on the foredeck. The bottom edge of the rudder was now angled downwards towards its trailing end to improve the steering characteristics, and, for the first time, the rudder sported a polished aluminum tiller bar, having a flagpole socket cast in. This style of tiller continued in use with a series of minor modifications right through until Dispro production ended in 1958.

Some boats appeared with an angled extension on the lower cover door of the engine hatch. These "modesty panels" were designed to protect the feet of passengers riding in the forward seat from the rotating flywheel. Later Lindsay-built models continued to have these same extensions.

---

[9] Why Caron engines were installed when the Clear Vision Pump Co. of Toronto, (formerly Knight Metal Products) still had a stock of copper jacket Dis-Pro engines is not clear. Perhaps Knight's were reluctant to extend credit to the re-organized Disappearing Propeller Boat Co.

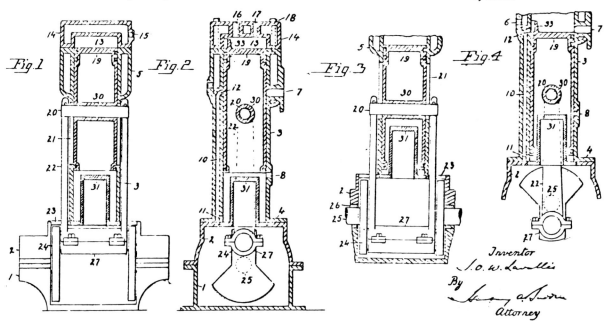

J. O. W. LAVALLEE.
INTERNAL COMBUSTION ENGINE.
APPLICATION FILED APR. 14, 1920.

1,437,428.   Patented Dec. 5, 1922.

Caron engine patent, 1922.

*Earliest known 3 h.p.
Caron installation.*

Disappearing Propeller Boat Co. Limited

ADDRESS ALL CORRESPONDENCE
TO
HEAD OFFICE & SHOW ROOMS
92 KING STREET WEST
TORONTO - CANADA

CABLE ADDRESS
"DIS-PRO"

FACTORY
PORT CARLING, ONT.
MUSKOKA LAKES

INSTRUCTIONS FOR THE OPERATION OF THE CARON MOTOR

Before Starting to get the Motor Read the Following:

1.   See that all electrical connections are secure.

2.   Examine the oil gauge on the side of the motor, if the indicator rod is up this means there is sufficient oil in the base to start and run for hours. NOTE one quart of oil (reputed) is sufficient oil to fill the base and make the needle show full. If you put more oil in than is required, it will splash out at the flywheel. This motor should need only about 1 pint of oil every 25 running hours. We recommend, as the best oil for these motors, something similar to MOBILE MEDIUM OIL.

3.   Before starting motor remove the spark plug and pour in about ¼ cup of oil, turn motor over by hand a few times, and replace spark plug.

4.   To Start Motor - See that shut-off cock at the FILTRAP strainer on the tank is open, gas can be seen in the glass bowl, then open small gas cock at the carburettor, priming can be done either by the special spark plug for cold weather or by choke attached to carburettor control rod - the other rod is for opening the needle also which makes easy starting, see that spark is retarded to the left position, push needle rod in full and pull choke full out. Then give the motor about 3 good turns by the starter, then put on and start and crank again until motor starts. After it starts advance spark, before motor has run a few minutes examine the water drain cock to see if the pump is working, then feel the aluminum jacket so that the jacket shows signs of being just warm to the touch - the water cock on the pump connection regulates this and same is set at the factory - this should not be wide open, as the motor will get cold and not function properly.

5.   The timer is well packed in grease and is oiled inside by the splash system and it will only be necessary to put a few drops into the small hole on the top weekly, also the small grease cup needs a turn down now and again, - the eccentric has a special oiler on filled with wick and this needs oiling about a few drops a day.

      TO DRAIN OUT WATER IN FALL shut off sea cock and open petcock. Start motor, run for a few minutes, then stop your entire cylinder and pump is now drained out.

      Examine the FILTRAP under the tank weekly. This is where the dirt collects. To remove the bowl unscrew the knurled nut down, then push the strap to one side, and the bowl will come out. Before doing this shut the gas off at tee handled shut-off.

One prototype boat was made up having a laminated bridge deck with hatch doors over the engine and a forward-facing "Mother-in-law" seat in the bow. This was Bill Ogilvie's own design, and although it was displayed in the annual Dispro exhibit under the grandstand at the Canadian National Exhibition, for the first time not one boat was sold there.[10] It must have been a very discouraging time for employees and management alike.

Due to the lack of interest shown by the boat-buying public at the CNE, and the unwillingness of the syndicate to invest any more capital in the enterprise, the Port Carling manufacturing plant closed its doors in late September of 1926 for the last time and the company was put up for sale. While the lower part of the plant was re-opened during the next summer or two by the subsequent owners as a repair shop serving the hundreds of Dispros still in service on the Muskoka Lakes, no more boats were ever built there.

As Bill Ogilvie put it so aptly, "The Dispro had had its day. We were flogging a dead horse."

Three years later, on May 1st, 1929, W.J. Johnston Jr. severed his connection with the Port Carling Boat Works. He then purchased the old D.P. factory back from the Disappearing Propeller Boat Co. and tore off the upper two storeys. Thereafter, he used the lower storey as "W.J. Johnston's Boat Works" until his retirement in 1956 at age 75. Late in 1930 the former D.P. warehouse, which was by that time rented to Duke Motor Service as a winter storage facility, burned to the water. Hundreds of fine Muskoka launches were lost, and arson was strongly suspected, but never proved.

But while the palmy days of the Dispro were now long gone, the skills acquired within the walls of the old D.P. factory were long-lived. When the company was sold to C.J. Barr in the fall of 1926, all the machinery and equipment was moved to the premises of Sam Botting's Lindsay Boat Company, in Lindsay, Ontario. Many of the former Port Carling employees who now found themselves with few prospects for employment packed up their families and moved to Lindsay, where they were put to work in November, building a large two-storey addition to Botting's shop.

These men taught Botting, who was more familiar with the Peterborough cedar strip tradition of boatbuilding, the techniques of building the lapstrake Dispros. Until the Depression, most of Botting's staff was composed of these former Port Carling employees. Because of this continuity of personnel, coupled with the continuity of serial numbering, it is virtually impossible, when examining existing boats, to identify any sudden changes of workmanship or design which pinpoint the change of location from Port Carling to Lindsay.

Many of the former D.P. men later became involved in other boatbuilding operations in the Muskoka area. Some, like Bert Hurst and Charlie Amey, were employed in the Ditchburn factory at Gravenhurst. Some worked later at Greavette Boats, as well as at Duke Motor Service and the Port Carling Boat Works. Others were involved in the construction of the famous "Fairmiles" during the Second War. Billy Johnston himself, in addition to the many fine launches he designed and built for such personalities as band leader Howard Cable, also built 58 whalers for the Government during the war; and Charlie Amey, who started with the Disappearing Propeller Boat Co. as a 16-year-old boy in 1919, is still building the occasional lapstrake rowing skiff today, using the original patterns of Old Uncle Billy's.

While most of these men are only fading memories now, many fine examples of their craftsmanship have survived, and the tiny handful of those hardy souls who remain with us yet are living reminders of those far-off golden days when Billy Johnston's Dispro was truly "The Greatest Little Motor Boat Afloat".

[10] This "bridge deck" prototype served as the inspiration for the later "Sport Special" model produced at Lindsay and subsequent Greavette deck treatment as well.

One of the last views of the defunct Port Carling D.P. factory and warehouse, Winter 1928. Some of the hockey players are former employees.

DISAPPEARING PROPELLER BOAT CO. LIMITED,

ADDRESS ALL CORRESPONDENCE
TO
HEAD OFFICE & SHOW ROOMS
82 KING STREET WEST
TORONTO - CANADA

CABLE ADDRESS
"DIS-PRO"

FACTORY
PORT CARLING, ONT.
MUSKOKA LAKES

Port Carling, Ont.
September 20th/26

      To whom ever it may concern.

         We have found Chas. Amey, boat finisher
and planker, who has been in our employ for
the past four months, to be a quick and
effecient workman.

         Being about to curtail our building for
winter months , we recommend him to any boat
building concern.

                    The Disappearing Propeller Boat Co. Ltd.
                    per;

                                    W.G. Ogilvie
                                        Manager.

The Port Carling plant closed its doors for good at the end of the summer of 1926. In this letter of reference, young Charlie Amey was recommended as a boat finisher as well as a planker, although he had never "finished" a D.P. boat. Undoubtedly, Mr. Ogilvie felt that the extra prestige would be to Charlie's advantage. (Courtesy Charles Amey)

Lindsay Boat Company Brochure, 1926.

PROVINCE OF ONTARIO.) WE, Jesse T. Perrin, Samuel Botting and

COUNTY OF VICTORIA.) Ernest W. Gardiner, all of the Town of

) Lindsay, in the County of Victoria, Boat

) Manufacturers, hereby certify :-

1. THAT We have carried on and intend to carry on trade and business as boat manufacturers at the Town of Lindsay, in the County of Victoria, in partnership under the name and Firm of "Lindsay Boat Company.

2. THAT the said Partnership has subsisted since the Second day of May, A.D.1921.

3. THAT we are and have been since the said day the only members of the said Partnership.

WITNESS our hands this Twenty-Third - - day of May, A.D.1921.

WITNESS :-

Jesse T Perrin

Samuel Botting

Ernest Gardiner

Partnership agreement, 1921. (Courtesy Archives of Ontario)

Sam Botting

112

LINDSAY
1927–1936

The Lindsay Boat Company

by Dr. James L. Smith

A BRIEF HISTORY OF THE LINDSAY BOAT COMPANY

The misfortunes of the Disappearing Propeller Boat Company at Port Carling during 1926 could easily have spelled the end of the boat's production. However, the decree of fate was otherwise and promise of a new life for the craft evolved from the association of two men, Charles J. Barr, businessman and Samuel Botting, boatbuilder, an association which later was to end in litigation.[1]

In Lindsay, the Perrin Boat Company had been active well before 1921. Ontario Archives record a partnership declaration dated 23rd May, 1921 between Jesse T. Perrin, Samuel Botting and Ernest W. Gardiner for the purpose of carrying on trade and business as boat manufacturers at the town of Lindsay, the firm to be known as the Lindsay Boat Company. The Lindsay Registry Office discloses that a mortgage was granted on July 15, 1922 covering the property comprising numbers 64-66 Ridout Street, Lindsay, on the banks of the Scugog River. An amount of $5,500 is mentioned with George and Samuel Botting as guarantors. This would suggest that Samuel's father, George, assisted him in establishing himself in the boatbuilding venture on these premises. The brick residence at No. 66, formerly occupied by Jesse Perrin, served as home for the Bottings and at No. 64 the wooden buildings served for business operations. The larger two-storey building nearest the road was used for making, assembling and finishing the boats. A second building nearer the river housed the engine and machine shop. Docks and a three-slip boathouse were located to the rear of the residence at No. 66. The canoes, called Big Chief canoes, were of cedar or basswood, copper-fastened and trimmed in butternut. They ranged in price from $45.00 to $75.00. Rowing skiffs 16 feet long, made of cedar, copper-fastened and trimmed with mahogany were also made and sold at prices ranging from $75.00 to $100.00. They were available in either smooth-skin or lapstrake style. An 18½ foot motorboat in lapstrake construction and powered with the St. Lawrence engine was offered for $385.00.

The partnership with Messrs. Perrin and Gardiner was relatively short-lived. Although the time and circumstances of the change are obscure, it is known that Perrin retired before 1926 and Gardiner did not care for boatbuilding so he returned to Orillia, Ontario to work in a furniture store. Botting became the sole proprietor.

---

[1] Sam Botting 1891-1954. Born Medonte, Ontario. Obtained early boatbuilding experience at J.H. Ross Boat Company, Orillia, Ontario. Moved to Lindsay 1921.

Premises of Lindsay Boat Company: circa 1926

    The picture was taken from a position near the Scugog River. To the left can be seen the brick residence at 66 Ridout Street with the boat slips behind it at the water's edge. The boat building and assembly was done in the lower part of the wooden structure to the right of the residence. This section contained the saws, boiling tank etc. A Lister gas engine was located outside the building and used for running the band saw and ripsaw by means of overhead shafts and belts. The upper part of the building was used for painting, varnishing and storage. In the picture a truck is being loaded with a craft and Sam Botting is holding the prow with Pat Saunders at the stern. At a later date an addition was placed on the side of this building nearest the residence giving considerable improvement in housing the saws and machinery. The extra woodworking machinery installed in the improved plant was obtained when the Port Carling operation closed.

    The second wooden building towards the water was a engine shop where engines were stored or prepared for installation. Engine repairs were also carried out there. This building had an attic where moulds and patterns were stored.

    The Lindsay shop was small compared with the Port Carling operation. Lindsay's plant in 1929 was only 2,000 square feet and was heated with two box stoves, one at each end of the building. Each was fired with wood or coal. All bending operations were done with hot water, boiling rather than steam.

    All frame buildings have now been removed from the property. The brick building is still standing.

Photo by Fulton Stewart

THE DISAPPEARING PROPELLER BOAT COMPANY LIMITED
UNDER CHARLES J. BARR, 1927-1931

In the fall of 1926 a business transaction took place which was to have a profound effect on the Lindsay Boat Company. Charles J. Barr, a resident of both Toronto and Lindsay, bought all the assets, patents and name of the Disappearing Propeller Boat Company from Tom Hodgson. Among the assets was a large inventory of parts for Silent Dis-pro engines and possibly some new Caron engines. Now owning the rights, Barr brought a proposal to Sam Botting to build the Dispro at the Lindsay facility. Undoubtedly he pointed out to Botting the past wide success of the boat at the time of the Port Carling operation and the pair envisioned a suitable degree of success again for it. The exact terms of the contract in the matter of finances, cost and profit between them are open to conjecture but the appeal must have been sufficiently attractive for Botting to direct a portion of the company's facilities for Dispro construction while still continuing his regular line of canoes and skiffs. Arrangements were made to bring all materials, engines and frames pertinent to Dispros and possibly some completed boats from Port Carling to Lindsay during the fall and winter of 1926-27. Many extra pieces of woodworking machinery, such as planers and sanders, arrived from Port Carling and took up a lot of space at the small Lindsay plant; necessitating an addition to the building nearest the road. Workers, including Eric Stephen, came down from Port Carling to assist in building the addition which was completed in November, 1926. The exact date when construction of boats started is not known but Pat Saunders suggested that it is unlikely that the first Lindsay-built Dispro appeared before May, 1927. According to Mrs. Botting the first order presented by Barr to Botting was for not more than 20 boats. The first one produced was of Waterford style and continued to be named Scout. Production was not constant. It occurred in batches seasonally or as materials, demand and finances were available and the necessary workers hired. During the Barr period experienced former workers from the defunct Port Carling plant were hired from time to time. These included Charles Amey, Johnny Johnston, Eric and Reg Stephen. In view of this it was not surprising that the early craft built at Lindsay resembled and appeared to be a direct continuation of those built at Port Carling. This is particularly true of the Scout and DeLuxe models where very few changes in construction can be discerned. Longer seat risers were used in the Lindsay boats extending from bow to stern seats. In general the Lindsay boats of this period did not seem to be as well finished in detail with tool and saw marks apparent and quality varying from boat to boat, particularly in the cheaper models. In some, efforts were made to repair cracks rather than replace planks. In others, engine hatches were installed out of line. Evidently the matter of economics entered in and attempts were being made to save on time, materials and maintenance of tools and machinery. Apparently Johnny Johnston was sent to purchase the first load of cypress. He got 'tank grade cypress' but it was found to be too thin to re-saw into two planks and consequently many early Lindsay Dippies did not have matching planks on both sides. There was much waste of wood that year!

A summary of Dispro models built at Lindsay under Barr would include five styles, as follows: (1) Waterford (Scout): length 16 feet 5 inches; width 4 feet 1 inch. (2) John Bull (Utility): length 16 feet 6 inches; width 4 feet 11 inches. (3) Uncle Sam (Deluxe): length 18 feet 6 inches; width 4 feet 8 inches. (4) Sport Special: length 18 feet 9 inches; width 5 feet. (5) DeLuxe square stern.

An advertisement in the June issue of *Rod and Gun* magazine for 1928 described the merits of the Sports Special model available in the spring of that year. This craft had some similarity to a Dispro which appeared at Port Carling during the last months of the company's operation there. Bill Ogilvie had redesigned the top decks and trim of the Uncle Sam model and put in a bridge deck in an obvious effort to endow the craft with greater

6 h.p. Caron engine.   *A restored Sport Special.*

June 1928.

T. Eaton Catalogue, Spring 1927.

luxury and appeal. Only one of this style was built at Port Carling and it was displayed at the C.N.E. in the summer of 1926.

The Sport Special model built at Lindsay in 1928 used Ogilvie's top styling, having elaborate spruce and mahogany laminations on both fore and aft decks, on motor hatches and completely around the gunwales. There were distinctive oak coamings both fore and aft and on either side of the centre deck. The forward-facing front seat, sometimes spoken of as the "Mother-in-law" seat, was somewhat cramped and would only accommodate an adult of moderate size or possibly two children. The rear seat was comfortable and of ample size for one person and was provided with a back rest. This model, however, differed from Ogilvie's "Special" Uncle Sam in some important respects. It was fitted with the 6 h.p. Caron Engine and it had ten rounds of planking instead of nine. It was longer and wider and would have required completely new sets of plank patterns and its own special moulds. Someone at Lindsay obviously spent a lot of time designing it!

Barr made an arrangement with the T. Eaton Company of Toronto for retail sales of the boats and an Eaton's ad for the spring of 1927 offered the DeLuxe model "complete with starter" for $525. The starter mentioned would, of course, be the hand-pulled spring-return starter. Interested buyers were asked to write for the illustrated folder describing the other models, Utility and Scout. Although the Utility or so-called John Bull model was mentioned in the ad, it is thought that Barr had only a total of six of these built and these only on special order for the Duquesne Hunting and Fishing Club of Georgian Bay. They were made about 1927 or 1928. All boats built during the Barr regime made exclusive use of the Caron engine except for an ocasional D2 Dispro twin which was probably old stock from Port Carling. Engines were brought in as complete units from Caron Bros. Inc., Montreal.

The association continued, with Botting making the boats and Barr taking care of sales and publicity. For this purpose Barr retained the premises at 92 King Street West, Toronto as head office of the Disappearing Propeller Boat Company for sales and parts. A business report dated December 31, 1928, submitted as a government requirement, listed as Company Personnel the following: President C.J. Barr; Secretary C.J. Barr Jr.; Treasurer H.R. Barr; Director Esther R. Barr; Director Margaret Barr; all of 77 Douglas Drive, Toronto. Assets mentioned included land at Port Carling $1,000 with associated factory and boat storage $19,500.

Dispro production in Lindsay occurred at a time of great progress in outboard motors and boats. For example, by 1928 the Johnson Outboard Motor Company had devised an engine of 25 h.p. and the very next year a four-cylinder engine of 26 h.p., and had embarked on production of racing motors. Other manufacturers, such as Evinrude, Elto and Caille, also offered large and speedy motors, and boats were being made to accommodate them. The outboard engines were becoming more dependable than their earlier counterparts. The popular appeal and convenience of this equipment had the effect of lessening interest in the relatively low-powered Dippy and contributed to its reduced sales. Dispro production at Lindsay also coincided roughly with the Depression era and this, together with legal problems encountered in 1931 and 1932 must have gravely affected sales and therefore the number of boats built. The actual beginning and ending serial numbers are not known but it is thought that Barr continued the numbering from Port Carling, possibly leaving a void and starting at 3800. The earliest Lindsay serial registered with the Dispro Owners Association is 3802. Little is known of boats of the 3900 series. No. 3928, a square-stern cypress boat, is thought to have been built in 1930 during the Barr era, possibly on special order. Barr may have had this craft designed as an experiment to test the market with a more modern style or as a craft which would accept an outboard motor as alternative power. Eighteen feet in length, it had the 6 h.p. Caron motor installed, a forward-facing front seat, and was trimmed like the DeLuxe model. Only one other of this type has been known to exist. The March 1931 issue of *Canadian*

Power Boating contained an advertisement by the Disappearing Propeller Boat Company under Barr which described "a Modern Runabout with the Protected Propeller Feature with Design and Construction Supervised by Bert Hawker." This runabout had an enormous cast aluminum Disappearing Propeller Device and it is probable that only one prototype of the craft was made. The only conclusion that can be drawn from the experimentation with the square-stern Dispro and the runabout is that Barr was aware of the inroads being made by outboards and launches but regrettably his effort was tantamount to clutching at straws. This occurred in the waning period of Barr's association with the Lindsay Boat Company when he was already encountering financial difficulties and facing a more severe onset of the depression with consequent reduced sales.

The Barr Runabout.

"Giant" housing (almost 6' long) compared with regular housing. It was intended for use in the Runabout but the project was never completed.

The following serial numbers are offered as an approximate guide, open to updating on receipt of further evidence. 1927: Numbers 3800 to 3830 — 1928: 3831 to 3865 — 1929: 3866 to 3895 — 1930: 3896 to 3930.

Barr is said to have lost money in the stock market crash in late 1929 and in the difficult economic period which followed he apparently fell behind in his financial commitments to Botting. Leslie M. Frost, a Lindsay lawyer and later Premier of Ontario, advised Botting to sue Barr. Legal proceedings were entered into in 1931 and as a result of the court decision on April 30th, 1932, Botting was awarded ownership of a majority of the assets of the Disappearing Propeller Boat Company because of the debts owing to him. He and George Thompson, who was employed in the engine and machine shop section of the firm, purchased the remaining assets for $1200 cash and received a further judgment of $2,400 under the Landlord's Provisions. As creditor he was to get this through the receivers. Because of these legal and financial problems it is probable that few if any Dispros were produced in 1931 or early 1932 and there is no evidence that the King Street showroom at Toronto was retained after this time.

THE LINDSAY DISAPPEARING PROPELLER BOAT COMPANY UNDER SAM BOTTING, 1932-1936

Having secured the patent rights and assets, Sam Botting now continued the manufacture of Dispros. Acting on the advice of his lawyer he changed the name of the company and called it the Lindsay Disappearing Propeller Boat Company, thus avoiding responsibility for any outstanding legal claims against the former company. The Lindsay Disappearing Propeller Boat Company is believed to have begun building Dispros sometime after April, 1932, starting the serial numbers at 4000. However, the number of Dispros made was relatively few compared to the golden years of 1927 to 1929. Sales were conducted only from Lindsay and general economic recovery through the Depression was sluggish. During this period some of the advertising was incredibly distorted and it was apparent that Botting was attempting to make the boats appear far more popular than they actually were. His 1933 catalogue claimed "over 5000 in use" and the 1936 catalogue "over 6000 in use". This is open to question as total production of Dispros up to this time, including those from Port Carling, fell rather short of this figure and it is thought that production during the Botting regime averaged only ten Dispros a year. The latest Lindsay serial registered with the Dispro Owners Association is 4031. Since 4031 is presumed to be in the last year's production (1936) it is unlikely that more than 40 boats were built by the Lindsay Disappearing Propeller Boat Company. During an interview in August 1980, Mrs. Botting was definite in the opinion that the serial numbers were stamped on by Sam Botting himself. Regrettably, it appears that no written record was kept of production numbers or, if it was, it has long since been discarded.

George Thompson sold out his share of the company to Botting in July, 1933. He thought there might be more profit in running a boat storage place so he opened one at Long Beach on Lake Erie near Port Colborne. In the late 60s Thompson was employed as a tool and die maker for General Motors in Oshawa.

At Lindsay under Botting only three sizes of Dispros were made. They varied little in appearance from those made under Barr. The smallest, the Scout, was considered an economy model. It had no elaborate trim and was powered with either the Silent Dis-Pro or the St. Lawrence engine. It served as an excellent boat for fishermen or as a general utility craft. The largest size, the Sport Special, was continued with little change except that it was powered with the 3 to 4 h.p. St. Lawrence engine as regular equipment. The DeLuxe model was offered as an in-between choice with somewhat less trim than the Sport Special, no centre deck, and no laminations on the rear deck. It was three inches shorter than the Sport Special and four inches narrower, and was powered with either the Silent

DISAPPEARING PROPELLER BOATS

FOR YOUR FAMILY

At the summer cottage DISAPPEARING PROPELLER BOATS solve the motor boat problem. They are safe—fool-proof—easily operated—sturdily built—beautifully finished in natural woods, and sold at a price that enables every family to possess one.

A dependable seaworthy craft that will take you anywhere a boat can go and bring you safely home again. Although not sold as speed boats, the speed of all three models is remarkable for boats of this size. They will travel faster than any boat of similar size and weight equipped with a three horse power motor and fixed propeller. Women and children soon become accustomed to operating these safe family boats and derive great pleasure from this new sport.

Purely a Canadian product designed by Canadians to meet conditions met with on our many thousands of Inland Lakes and Waterways. The best sea-going boat built today for its size. Can weather any storms. 6,000 now in use.

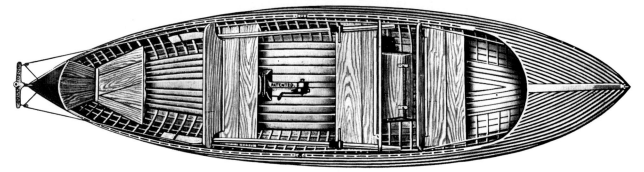

Length—18 ft. 6 in.
Beam—4 ft. 8 in.
Depth—1 ft. 11 in.
Weight—500 lbs.

Standard Boat Equipment consists of one paddle and one pike pole, or 1 Pair Oars.

Model De Luxe

Complete with 3 H.P. St. Lawrence Motor—$550.00
Complete with 3 H.P. Dis-Pro Motor $500.00
Tax Extra.   F.O.B. Factory

Speed—9-10 M.P.H.
Fuel used—24 M.P. Gal.

Life Preserver Kapok Cushions extra equipment at $36.00 per set.

CHOSEN FOR THEIR SEAWORTHINESS AND ADAPTABILITY

In greater demand than ever. New improvement with standard equipment. All boats ready to run, complete with one paddle, one pike pole or 1 pair of oars. Other equipment extra — Cutten & Foster Guaranteed Life-Saving Cushions; Water-proof tarpaulin; Regulation running lights; Flag-pole with sockets; Oars, are all extra.

The St. Lawrence Marine Motor is standard equipment in all models.

Length—16 ft. 5 ins.
Beam—4 ft. 1 in.
Depth—1 ft. 7 ins.
Weight—425 lbs.

Life Preserver Kapok Cushions extra equipment at $36.00 per set.

SCOUT MODEL

Complete with 3-H.P. Dis-Pro Motor — $475.00
Tax Extra.   F.O.B. Factory.

Speed—9-10 M.P.H.
Fuel used—24 M.P. Gal.

Standard Boat Equipment consists of one paddle and one pike pole, or 1 Pair Oars. Oars are extra equipment at $8.00 per pair.

OVER 6,000 ARE IN USE

From 1936 catalogue.

IT'S THE IDEAL BOAT FOR YOU

FOR THE SPORTSMAN

As a fishing boat they are not surpassed. In trolling any speed desired can be obtained by merely raising or lowering the propeller operated by the spade handle near the centre seat. When casting you will note the steadiness of these sturdy boats, and to reach the favorite spots of the fighting bass, you can run in close to the rocky shores—along the weed beds and lily pads. For shooting, the boats are roomy enough to carry dogs, decoys and other equipment. These boats are practically noiseless, being fitted with a New Style Silencer.

THE GREATEST LITTLE MOTOR BOAT AFLOAT

Length—18 ft. 9 ins.
Beam—5 ft.
Depth—1 ft. 10 ins.
Weight—650 lbs.

Fuel used—16 M.P. Gal.
Speed—9-10 M.P.H.
Oil Used—59 M.P. Qt.

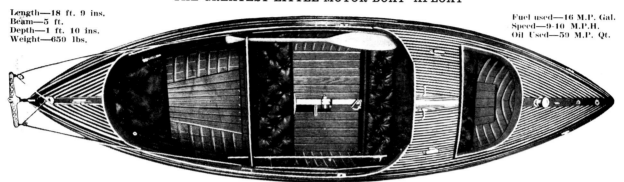

This Sport Model has the 3 H.P. St. Lawrence Motor fitted as standard equipment and gives you a boat with extra reserve power for off shore fishing and cruising on larger lakes.

The Sport Special

Complete with One Paddle, Pike Pole or One Pair Oars
$600.00

6% Tax Extra.   F.O.B. Factory

Life Saving Kapok Cushions
extra equipment.
$36.00 per set.

The St. Lawrence Engine

EQUIPMENT

Carburetor

Spark Plug

Dry Battery

Switch

Battery Wire

Jump Spark Wire

Spark Coil

Shaft

Shaft Coupling

Stuffing Box

Propellor

Seacock

Muffler

Grease Cups

Wrench

Price $115.00
6% Sales Tax Extra

3 Horse Power

Bore 3¼", Stroke 3½"

The 1936 Motors are fitted with Aluminum pistons and light steel connecting rods, and are free from vibration at all speeds.

This engine is suitable for replacement in Disappearing Propellor boats, with most satisfactory results. A large number are now in use for this purpose.

THIS ENGINE IS STANDARD EQUIPMENT FOR DIS-PRO BOATS.

Silent Smooth Running Disappearing Propeller Boat, Free from Vibration.

Dis-Pro or St. Lawrence engine. The use of Caron engines was discontinued by Botting and a catalogue of 1933 vintage lists only St. Lawrence engines supplied with all models. Subsequently the St. Lawrence engine was used in the Sport Special and optionally with the Silent Dis-Pro in the DeLuxe. The Silent Dis-Pro was then used routinely in the Scout with St. Lawrence optional. Botting secured the Silent Dis-Pro engines from Service Station Equipment Company Ltd. of Toronto. The firm had a stock of engines left, possibly as many as 200, when the Port Carling operation ceased. Botting received the St. Lawrence engines from the St. Lawrence Engine Company of Brockville, Ontario. The Lindsay Disappearing Propeller Boat Company had its own engine section with Fred Tillcock in charge. He succeeded Bert Campton, Bill Griffiths and George Thompson who managed the section in earlier years. Only single-cylinder engines were installed as standard equipment. Boats with large Caron or St. Lawrence engines were fitted with three-blade propellers and those with Silent Dis-Pros, two-blade.

The 1936 brochure described the Sport Special model as giving 16 miles per gallon of fuel at a speed of 9 to 10 m.p.h. and available with one paddle, pike pole or one pair of oars for $600. Life-saving kapok cushions were an extra at $36.00 a set. The DeLuxe model had the laminations only on the forward deck and to a point about three-quarters of the distance to the stern where they tapered. It had a smaller after deck or skyboard and a motor box similar to Port Carling's Uncle Sam. The picture shows no deck hardware although a later page in the catalogue specified that bow and stern decks were complete with chocks and cleats as standard equipment. Extra equipment consisted of bow and stern lights with flagpole wired for $15.00, and bow flagpole for $1.00, aquascope for $10.00 and oars for $8.00. The rowlocks were also extra for $2.50. The Scout model had very short skyboards and single seats fore and aft with the forward passengers riding backwards. Two other seats amidships accommodated two people each. It had a pull-start Dis-Pro engine or optional St. Lawrence and sold for $475. All boats were of lapstrake construction, planked in either cypress or cedar with preference for cedar in later years. They were varnished inside and out, receiving one coat of boiled oil and three coats of spar varnish. Some were painted red under the floorboards. Botting went down to the Robert Bury Lumber Company in Toronto to inspect and order the wood to be used in the boats and then had it shipped by rail to Lindsay. Saunders earned $10.00 a week in earlier years and then arranged for an improvement in his earnings to 50 cents an hour. Mrs. Botting assisted in administrative and paperwork for the company. In addition, she made seat cushions for the craft if they were specially ordered. These were probably of standard type as the kapok-filled variety mentioned in the catalogue were made by Cutten and Foster of Toronto.

Some later boats in the 4000 series have a hexagonal brass plaque on the coaming or on the foredeck with the inscription "Lindsay Disappearing Propeller Boat Company". This type of plate appears on boat No. 4028. A diamond-shaped plate has been observed ón boat No. 4031 built subsequently. Boat No. 4028, previously mentioned, had several special features in its construction, such as a locker under the foredeck. These were obviously factory-installed and would indicate that Botting was willing to provide custom work on his craft as an enticement for the customer to order. Botting did not change the boats significantly except for such special features. He had to produce and sell boats to ensure continuation of rights and patents. Botting did not rely entirely on the Dispro but carried on manufacture of a variety of other boats such as canoes, rowing skiffs and inboard launches. The 1936 catalogue drawn up in the final year of the company's Dispro production was elaborate and would suggest that Botting was putting his company in the best possible light for a potential buyer.

On December 12th, 1936, Botting sold the rights for the Dispro to Thomas Greavette of Gravenhurst, Ontario. The name of Botting's firm then reverted to the Lindsay Boat Company but parts and service for Dispro boats were still available. Under Botting's

Boat No. 4028, with hexagonal plaque and locker.

ownership the firm carried on manufacture of other types of boats until November, 1939 when the facilities were sold. The buildings were later used as a depot for a milk transport company. Only the brick residence at No. 66 remains standing today.[2]

While the Lindsay phase of Dispro manufacture may be considered minor by many observers, it was a significant link in the chain of the Dispro history in that it preserved continuity over a very difficult economic period. Admittedly, the boats there were not numerous but they were of fine quality, particularly the DeLuxe and Sport Special models. The Scout model made available the utilitarian benefits of the Dippy to many who could not afford the more expensive ones. As business conditions improved by the late thirties, and with the cessation of the war in 1945, an opportunity was presented for expansion in recreational enterprises. Greavette was in a position to capitalize on a demand which was not available to either Charles J. Barr or Sam Botting at Lindsay during the early and mid-thirties. Let us hope that those who possess the relatively few examples of the Lindsay craft which remain will be avid in their care and take pride in their ownership.

[2] Sam Botting later become associated with Shepherd Boat Company at Niagara-on-the-Lake, Gordon Boat Company of Bobcaygeon, Ontario and with Henry Boats of Lindsay before his death in March, 1954 at age 63. His wife survived him until February, 1981, age 90.

Aerial view, Greavette Boats, Gravenhurst, Ontario. (Courtesy Bruce Wilson)

GRAVENHURST

1936–1958

The Dispro Returns to Muskoka

by Joe Fossey

A BRIEF HISTORY OF THE GREAVETTE BOAT COMPANY

The Dispro moved back to Muskoka, its birthplace, in December, 1936, when Greavette Boats of Gravenhurst, Ontario acquired the patent rights and assets of the Lindsay Disappearing Propeller Boat Company from Sam Botting.

Greavette Boats Ltd. had been established in 1930 when Thomas Greavette,[1] former sales manager at the Ditchburn works, decided to break away and form his own enterprise. During his years at Ditchburn's he had become know to a number of wealthy Muskoka cottagers. He was able to obtain the financial support of some of these influential men, and a few of them also sat on the Board of Directors of the new organization.[2]

In Canada, the production line method of boatbuilding had been initiated before 1920 by the Disappearing Propeller Boat Company in its Port Carling factory. Greavette Boats Ltd. from the beginning used the same revolutionary technique in the manufacture of all its stock lines of watercraft.

After a slow start in 1930 as a Canadian-licensed manufacturer of the popular American "Dart" runabout, Greavette Boats recovered the following year when Tom Greavette, as General Manager, persuaded the company directors to obtain a license to build a line of inboard runabouts of 18 to 26-foot length, designed by the distinguished American naval architect, John L. Hacker of Detroit, Michigan. These craft proved to be more popular and the fortunes of the company gradually improved during difficult economic times. In 1936 the first Hacker design "Streamliner" was built for Mr. R. Burgess, a Muskoka lakes summer resident.

By 1937, Greavette Boats had secured the services of another well-known American designer, Douglas Van Patten of Bay City, Michigan. Boats built to his designs were unusually stylish, with ahead-of-the-times performance.

---

[1] Thomas Greavette, 1881-1958, grew up in the Port Carling area where he worked for several years at the Ditchburn agency, located beside W.J. Johnston's boat livery near the locks. He subsequently worked his way up through the ranks at the Ditchburn Boat Co. His brother Ernest was employed as a planker at the Disappearing Propeller Boat Co. in Port Carling.

[2] Gordon Lefebvre, a senior executive of General Motors of Canada and Muskoka boating enthusiast, served as first president of Greavette Boats Ltd. Other influential backers of the venture were: Sir Ellsworth Flavelle, E.A. Wilson, Col. J.R. Moodie and A.J. Davis.

1936 STREAMLINER, from Boating Magazine, July 1955.

After moving to Gravenhurst in 1937, Van Patten was responsible for the redesigning and continued production of the world-famous Greavette "Streamliner" series. These craft soon placed the company in the forefront of modern inboard runabout design. The "Streamliner" not only had a dazzling performance, but was also an artistically beautiful, glamourously-finished product. It was viewed by many as the epitome of fine marine craftsmanship.

Of equal importance in the company's rise to world acclaim was its involvement in the design and construction of the "Miss Canada" series of custom racing boats for the Wilson family of Ingersoll, Ontario. These boats are a story in themselves, and would require a complete book to present their history properly. Harold Wilson holds a position of honour in the Canadian Sports Hall of Fame for challenging and almost winning the coveted Harmsworth Trophy for Canada in 1949 with the Rolls-Royce Griffon-powered *Miss Canada IV*, designed by Van Patten. In addition, he set a North American official water speed record of 149.292 m.p.h. at Picton, Ontario in this same boat. What a contrast to the Dispro, being produced at Greavette's at the same time, with its top speed of less than 10 m.p.h.!

This, then, was Greavette Boats: a company which during its half-century existence built countless numbers of runabouts, cruisers, hardtops, racing boats, wartime boats, rowboats, sailboats, auxiliary boats, workboats, outboard boats, inboard-outboard and even a folding boat.

Given his wide range of interest in boats, it is not surprising that by 1936 Tom Greavette's attention had turned to the Dispro, a craft which had been most familiar to him through his earlier Port Carling connections.

The motivation behind his interest in acquiring the manufacturing rights to the D.P. is not known, but the profit motive is believed to have been secondary. Certainly by the mid-30s it was well known among boatbuilders that construction of the labour-intensive D.P. boat was, at best, a break-even proposition. It appears, therefore, that Tom Greavette saw the Dispro in much the same light as farmers view maple syrup production; that is, as a fill-in operation during slack periods. He may also have perceived that it would give the company a larger market base from which to draw future customers to other, more deluxe watercraft. And perhaps most important of all, Greavette, like so many others before and since, had a soft spot in his heart for the Dispro.[3]

[3] R. MacNab (Greavette's son-in-law, and later General Manager of Greavette Boats) recalled Greavette's affection for the D.P. boat.

Greavette Boats, however, did not acquire Botting's operation directly; rather, a separate holding company was established to retain the patent rights and trademarks which were still in effect. Tom Greavette enlisted assistance from Bruce P. Davis, a Muskoka summer resident, and on December 18, 1936 the new company was formed with Davis as President, Doris Chadwick as Secretary, and Gordon R. MacNamara as Director. Consequently, in much the same way that Botting's Lindsay Boat Company had built Dispros under contract for Barr's Disappearing Propeller Boat Co. during the late 1920s, Greavettes built boats for the holding company known as the Disappearing Propeller Boat Company (1936) Limited. Thus the serial numbering system used on Greavette-built D.P.s is quite different and distinct from that used in regular Greavette production.

A Greavette 16' rowing skiff built by Tom Cossey. (Courtesy Bruce Wilson)

The first Greavette Dispro is believed to have been built sometime in late 1936 or early 1937 by the fine lapstrake skiff builder, Tom Cossey, who had come to Greavette's from the Keewatin area. Cossey was later joined by another boatbuilder, Dempsey Barnes[4], but these men were not required to build boats untutored. Bert Hurst, who had been employed as a nailer and planker at the old Port Carling factory during its heyday, and who by this time had become foreman of Greavette's Service and Installation departments, provided many helpful hints with regard to the peculiarities of Dispro design and construction.

Greavette Boats had acquired all the hull and device patterns, as well as a considerable stock of old Model E-1 Silent Dis-Pro engine parts from Lindsay, and thus the earliest Greavette D.P.s appear to have been almost carbon copies of the late Lindsay boats.

The tough economic times were still having an effect on advertising budgets. Dispro brochures issued by Greavette's in the years before the Second World War were composed mainly of existing artwork and material from earlier Port Carling and Lindsay catalogues. As a result, they are not reliable sources of information on the actual design features of early Greavette models. The 1939 brochure was printed on common newsprint, a far cry from the elaborate colour catalogues of the early '20s.

---

[4] Dempsey Barnes recalled building as many as 25 Dispros in 1938 (interview with author, 1983). This was accomplished in two month's time, using production methods such as pre-sawn and numbered planking. Some of these boats may have been sold as 1939 models, as no 1938 boats are now known to exist.

Also carried over from Lindsay was the practice of grossly exaggerating D.P. production figures. While the 1936 Lindsay catalogue had stated "over 6,000 now in use," Greavette advertising by 1939 was claiming "7,000 now in use," a figure more than double the total number of D.P.s ever built![5]

In spite of the fact that early Greavette brochures portray the sumptuous "Sport Special" model, lifted directly from earlier Lindsay catalogues, it is believed that the only boats actually produced were 18 foot 6 inch Uncle Sam (Deluxe) models having a modified version of the Sport Special bridge-deck treatment over the engine. This basic design was continued throughout the Greavette era.

Motor Boat Salon at Morgan's in Montreal. (Courtesy Bruce Wilson)

The only known recorded evidence of the true appearance of these first Greavette Dispros is a photograph of the company's display in the Motor Boat Salon at Morgan's in Montreal.[6] The D.P. boat shown bears an uncanny resemblance to late Lindsay-built craft. (Note the price: $555)

[5] See Appendix 3.
[6] The photograph, which is dated 1936, is thought to have actually been taken in 1937, If the 1936 date is correct the boat may, in fact, be Lindsay-built.

Greavette Dispro with centre-mounted rectangular fuel tank. (Courtesy Bruce Wilson)

Another rare pre-war Dispro photograph, showing an interesting variation from the normal front-mounted, triangular-shaped fuel tank, was taken inside the Greavette plant. Here the boat has a rectangular fuel tank mounted under the bridge deck on the starboard side of the engine compartment. This arrangement is thought to have been soon abandoned for safety reasons.

Production records for the Disappearing Propellor Boat Company (1936) Limited, as for all previous operations, have long since disappeared. This, coupled with the almost complete lack of surviving boats and of photographic evidence, makes the first two years of Greavette production a period of considerable conjecture.

One pre-war Greavette brochure advertised D.P.'s as having keels of either cypress, clear pine or spruce and planking of either edge-grain British Columbia cedar or Ontario cedar. Whether or not boats were actually built with such a variety of woods is unsubstantiated, as nearly all surviving Greavette Dispros have B.C. cedar keels and planking.[7]

It is known, however, that former Lindsay engineer, Fred Tillcock, was transferred to Greavette's and that through his efforts the old Model E-1 Silent Dis-Pro engine was revived and updated. It appears that all Greavette D.P.s produced until 1945 were fitted with these modified copper-jacketed engines, made up by Tillcock on a selective-fit basis largely of leftover spare parts from earlier E-1s. After machining the parts about six at a time for economy reasons, he would then assemble the best-matching components into complete engines, ready for testing. Device housings and related parts were machined and assembled by Tillcock in a similar manner.

Renamed "Dispro Specials", these Greavette-built engines were somewhat changed from the original 1922 models: the elliptical serial number plate on the copper jacket was replaced by a Greavette hull decal; the aluminum crank case castings were considerably strengthened, and in 1938 the old E-1 timer brush and brush holder were lengthened.

[7] At least one postwar D.P. was planked in cypress.

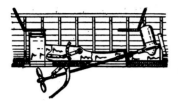  

Run over all obstructions with automatic
Propeller Protection

Your Ignition Troubles Are Over

THE FIRST TIME DISPRO MOTORS EVER OFFERED WITH THIS NEW AND REVOLUTIONARY SYSTEM

1939
Special

Greavette Engineers have created this smartest, cleanest, most fool-proof ignition system to bring your DisPro Motor right up to date.

Features of this new ignition are as follows:

1. Eliminates old fashioned coil and employs new non-vibrating type of coil similar to those in use on modern motor cars.

2. Contact points are isolated from grease or dirt and require less attention.

3. Absence of missing at high speeds due to the point of action being the same at all times.

4. The system is very accessible for examination or adjustment.

5. Improved construction permits movement of timer lever from full advance to full retard in one half the previous movement necessary.

6. Battery consumption less than in any previous type of ignition.

This new ignition system can be attached to your standard timer lever at small cost. Write for information.

LET US KNOW YOUR BOAT NEEDS
WE INVITE YOUR INQUIRIES

Under able management and expert supervision Greavette Boats Limited are building better boats than ever before. There is a great demand for these marvellous boats.

Nothing has yet been devised to equal the Disappearing Propeller boat for FISHING. Full control at all speeds.

We guarantee QUALITY BOATS and reasonable prices.

Just the Boat to Round Out Your Summer Vacation.

NEW TYPE BRUSH HOLDER ASSEMBLY FOR MODEL E1

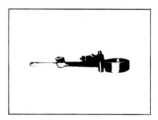

The timer lever and brush holder shown here, which is standard equipment for 1938, will be of special interest to all DisPro owners and prospects, as we have incorporated a remarkable improvement and have made the ignition practically foolproof. The brush holder itself is substantially longer, using a much longer brush, of high grade copper.

To present DisPro owners this brush holder, brush, and insulating washers are available at a very low cost, and it takes only a few moments to change over.

FLYWHEEL MAGNETO
THE LATEST IN DISPRO IGNITION

The magneto flywheel shown here is available for any Model E1 DisPro motor, and is optional equipment for 1938 at a slight additional cost. This equipment needs no coil or battery and is a high grade product, thoroughly guaranteed.

Both highly recommended for
"THE GREATEST LITTLE MOTOR BOAT AFLOAT"

From 1938 brochure.

Replacement Parts

HAVING ACQUIRED THE SOLE MANUFACTURING RIGHTS FOR DISAPPEARING PROPELLER BOATS AND PARTS IN CANADA, INCLUDING TAPS, DIES, JIGS, ETC., WE ARE THE ONLY SOURCE FOR GENUINE PARTS. A FULL LINE OF REPLACEMENT PARTS ALWAYS KEPT IN STOCK. YOUR ORDERS WILL BE FILLED THE DAY RECEIVED.

Greavette brochure, 1939.

Even the paintwork was changed from black to red. The same year, an optional magneto ignition system was offered which utilized a stock outboard motor flywheel and related components. In tests, it was really quite successful, but the old story of cost increases versus sales killed the idea. Only the prototype was sold, and it was said to work well for the owner for several years.[8]

As the Depression years drew to a close, Dispro sales began to show a modest upswing and the 1939 models sported an improved ignition system. "Your ignition troubles are over," ran the headline in the 1939 brochure. "The first time Dis-Pro motors ever offered with the new and revolutionary system ... Greavette engineers have created this smartest, cleanest, most fool-proof ignition system to bring your Dis-Pro motor right up to date." This revolutionary system, also designed by Fred Tillcock, was appropriately known as the "F-T" timer. It consisted of a special plate fitted with automotive points and condenser attached to the old Model E timer lever. A flat spot ground on the flywheel hub actuated the points, and a standard 6-volt automotive coil was mounted nearby, on a special cast bronze bracket attached to the induction pipe. Greavette's believed that the substitution of these modern components in place of the archaic wooden vibrator coil and timer arrangement would forever end the constant ignition problems that had previously plagued all D.P. owners.

As it turned out, the ignition troubles were not over, after all. Eventually, grease escaping from the front main crankshaft bearing would be thrown onto the points, and the engine would stop. Nevertheless, the "F-T" timer did function quite well, particularly so when the engine was new and grease leakage from the bearings was minimal. It was the standard ignition offered on all Dispro Special engines from 1939 until 1945.

The final modification to the copper-jacketed engine was made by Tillcock about 1940. An electric starting system was fitted, using such automotive components as a 6-volt storage battery, flywheel ring gear and Ford starting motor, in place of the former pull-starter arrangement. It is believed that almost all Dispros built by Greavette's from this time on were equipped with electric starting as standard equipment.

All "Dispro Special" engine installations used a brass dashboard and controls almost identical to the earlier Port Carling units, the electric start engines having a starter button mounted nearby instead of the former pull-starter handle. However, to simplify the priming procedure, Greavette's eliminated the use of the earlier priming rod and 3-position priming cock on the engine cylinder, substituting instead a simple tee fitting and check valve attached by a tube to the dashboard primer. An auxiliary manual priming cup was provided in case of primer failure; nevertheless, the new system seemed to work very well.

During the Lindsay period the use of cypress for planking had gradually diminished in favour of edge-grain cedar from British Columbia, a material which may not have been as long-lasting but was, nonetheless, cheaper and much easier to work with. Few Greavette Dispros were planked in cypress. Cedar is much lighter in weight; consequently, cedar-planked boats tend to ride higher and be a trifle faster than earlier models made of cypress.

Thought by some to contribute to an easier-running craft is a distinct "rocker" or curvature built into the keel of all Greavette D.P.s.[9] Greavette device housings were manufactured with a fore-to-aft curve along the mounting flange so that they would conform to the new keel design.

In many respects the so-called "pre-war" Greavette Dispro hulls, that is those built up to and including 1942, were similar in construction to earlier Lindsay and Port Carling models. Although Greavette's admittedly weakened their hulls by eliminating the labour-intensive reinforcing knees and permanently fixed seat bottoms which had acted as thwarts

[8] R. MacNab, interview with author.
[9] See page 139.

on earlier D.P.s, they nevertheless continued the use of the four inch rib spacing, alternating strip-deck treatment, and laminated splash boards with spray-deflecting curve underneath. Skilled labour during these post-depression and early war years was still relatively cheap, so the old time-consuming methods of boatbuilding were still practicable. This was a situation which was soon to change.

Doug Wilson in a Greavette Dispro with striped deck. (Courtesy Bruce Wilson)

THE POSTWAR DISPRO, 1945-1950

Greavette Boats Ltd., like most other boat manufacturers in Muskoka, became heavily involved in war contract work in the early 1940s; thus no Dispros are known to have been built in 1943 or 1944. When the war appeared to be drawing to a close late in 1944, planning was already underway for the production of new postwar D.P.s.[10]

Faced with rising labour and material costs Greavettes, from this time onward, began to simplify or eliminate some of the labour-intensive aspects of earlier models. For example, the simple expedient of changing the former four inch rib spacing to six inches[11] produced a saving in time and materials, although the hulls were somewhat weakened as a result. The complex light and dark strip-deck treatment was eliminated in favour of solid 3/8 inch mahogany, and the graceful spray-deflecting curve underneath the laminated splash boards was discontinued.

---

[10] The first postwar D.P.s were built by Greavette's layout man and master craftsman, Pete Miller.
[11] Nailing was still retained on two-inch centres, as before.

As the years passed, more ways had to be found to cut production costs. Most of these changes were either hidden from view or were done in such a way as to enhance the craft's attractiveness to prospective buyers. Greavettes were aware that the average purchaser judged a boat mainly on the basis of appearance, that is, beautiful wood grain and a shiny varnish job, and that time was better spent on these visual aspects of a boat than on unseen structural detail. It must not be forgotten that competitive small-craft design had moved onward and the labour-intensive Dispro had been an anachronism for some time. It can also be argued that it was due to Tom Greavette's personal affection for the craft, and his determination to postpone its demise as long as possible, that he was willing to make compromises. Such compromises were, sadly essential if the Dispro were to survive in the so-called "Jet Age".

The postwar models, that is those boats built from 1945 to 1950, were slightly wider than their prewar sisters, and had less sheer or upward sweep at each end. Several variations in the use of materials and in hull design have been noted in boats from this era, suggesting that it was a time of experimentation. For example, many pre-1949 models appear to have less moulded depth or freeboard and a noticeably lower arch to the decks than later boats. Some D.P.s were made with Philippine mahogany sheer planks, while others from the same production run had sheer strakes of B.C. cedar.[12] After 1947 the use of solid mahogany for decks was discontinued in favour of various kinds of ¼ inch marine plywood. Some of these plywood decks were very light in colour, although the majority were a darker red mahogany.

The 1945 models were still powered with the 3 h.p. Dispro Special but the device housing was now cast in aluminum, thereby reducing the weight of the unit by almost half. Aluminum was seen to offer several advantages over cast-iron in addition to weight: it was much easier to machine, easier to transport and handle, and would not rust.[13] It was probably cost-competitive with cast-iron as well, all factors being considered. The new aluminum housings were still made from the same patterns that had been used to make the former cast-iron devices, so the embossed lettering "DISAPPEARING PROPELLER PAT. MARCH 16 1915 OTHER PATS. PEND" was retained, although the patents had in fact expired by 1940. Perhaps it was felt that leaving this information on the castings might act as a deterrent to persons seeking to copy the design.

The new aluminum device housings were originally cast by the Toronto Brass Machine and Foundry Co., but later the work was done by Clarke Brass in Toronto and the Callander Foundry Mfg. Ltd., of Guelph, Ontario. Although all Dispros manufactured from 1945 on were equipped with aluminum housings there is some evidence to suggest that by customer's request the occasional boat was fitted at the factory with an old cast-iron device removed from the customer's derelict Port Carling or Lindsay model.

The year 1946 saw the adoption of the St. Lawrence XAE electric-start engine, built in Brockville, Ontario, as standard equipment, and the Dispro Special was discontinued. The similar XA series of pull-start St. Lawrence engines had been previously used with success by Botting's Lindsay Disappearing Propeller Boat Co. and had been very popular as replacements in earlier Dispros, particularly the troublesome Caron-equipped models. The new electric-start XAE engines produced more power than the old copper-jacket types, and fitted with 3-blade 10-inch diameter by 18-inch pitch propellers, provided a considerable increase in speed.

---

[12] Ron MacNab suggested that the mahogany sheer planks were tried in an attempt to strengthen the hull, weakened by the elimination of some ribs, against torsional movement. An alternative explanation is that it was done to improve appearance.

[13] Ironically, after many seasons of immersion in water, many of the aluminum devices have corroded by electrolysis.

The Ideal Boat

The electric starting, improved high speed St. Lawrence engine for Disappearing Propeller Boats

Single Cylinder
Developing 3 h.p.
at 900 r.p.m.

These motors are fitted with aluminum pistons and light steel connecting rods and are free of vibration at all times.

From 1946 brochure.

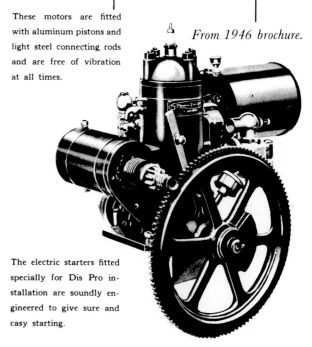

The electric starters fitted specially for Dis Pro installation are soundly engineered to give sure and easy starting.

This line of one-cylinder, two-stroke marine engines dated back, essentially unchanged, to the earliest days of the St. Lawrence Engine Company, in 1905. In many respects the XAE engine with its archaic vibrator coil ignition was itself an outdated design by the late 1940s, and yet it proved to be unquestionably the most rugged and durable power plant ever used in D.P. boats. Except for a tendency to "pound" and a proclivity for mangling its starter, it was a most satisfactory and dependable unit. About half of all D.P.s manufactured by Greavettes from 1937 to 1958 were built during the six-year period immediately following the Second World War and except for 1945 production, all boats of this group were fitted with St. Lawrence engines as standard equipment.

Dashboard controls for the St. Lawrence engines were at first made up by simply hacksawing appropriate sections out of earlier brass dash plates and then installing the pieces in various spots on the midship bulkhead. By 1947, however, black plastic plates had been adopted which were reminiscent of the old brass units but which had a suitable rearrangement of controls. These were mounted on the midship bulkhead, directly above the device housing, rather than on the starboard side of the bulkhead, as previously.

Most of these XAE engine installations were fitted with choke controls on the Schebler carburetors. Although chokes were not factory equipment, they were ingeniously made up and installed by Greavette engineers, using throttles removed from old Silent Dis-Pro Kingston carburetors. These chokes worked with varying degrees of success; therefore many owners resorted in defeat to the traditional use of the brass priming cup mounted on the cylinder head, a primitive method perhaps, but one which rarely failed to work.

The return of economic prosperity during the latter 1940s resulted in an increased demand for Dispros, so much so that in 1947 alone, close to 60 boats were built, a production figure unmatched since the mid-1920s. The new Greavette models with their more modern appearance, electric starting, and increased speed capabilities rekindled the interest of boaters, and for a few years the fortunes of this little motorboat were once again on the rise. Many of the new customers were those whose 25-year old D.P.s were understandably requiring major work by this time, and who chose to purchase new boats rather than attempting to repair their old ones.

Around 1949, a prolonged strike at the Schebler carburetor plant in Flint, Michigan apparently forced the St. Lawrence Engine Co. to substitute a different carburetor on their 1950 single-cylinder engines. The Model D Schebler, designed in 1902 when engine speeds were low, was particularly well-suited to the characteristics of the St. Lawrence. The replacement Zenith carburetor, whose design was at least a quarter-century more recent, had been designed for more modern high speed applications. It required some modification to make it function on the St. Lawrence. An ingenious auxiliary air-valve mechanism was made up in Brockville and installed on each Zenith carburetor, but even this addition did not adequately recreate the performance of the old Schebler. Consequently, the 1950 D.P. boats which used these engines were less satisfactory than previous Schebler-equipped models.

A gradual downturn in Dispro sales, coupled with the aggravating carburetor problems encountered in 1950, was undoubtedly the major factor in Greavette's decision to discontinue use of the St. Lawrence engine in favour of a more up-to-date replacement. As it turned out, the 1950 D.P.s were to be the last of the old-style one-cylinder "putters" and subsequent models were to be very different indeed in both function and temperament.

THE FINAL YEARS: THE COVENTRY VICTOR DISPROS, 1951-1958

The D.P. boat underwent its final major change when the four-stroke, twin-cylinder, horizontally-opposed Coventry Victor "Midget" engine was adopted as standard equipment.

The Coventry Victor Motor Co. Ltd. had been founded in Coventry, England in 1911, but only entered the internal combustion engine field in 1919 when it began manufacturing motorcycle engines. After a period of building three-wheelers, Coventry Victor started to build industrial engines and throughout the Second World War both the "Midget" and the "Neptune" engines were supplied in considerable quantities to His Majesty's Forces, where they were used extensively in British landing craft and assault boats. The engine now to be chosen for use in the Dispro was manufactured under fundamental design patents of Mr. Weaver, the company's founder, and it had already proven its capabilities in many different applications.

Gordon Trent & Co. Ltd.[14] of Toronto, Ontario became distributor for Coventry Victor engines in 1948. Available in either hand-start or electric-start versions, the "Midgets" were at first imported for use mainly as auxiliaries in sailboats and other small craft.

In 1950, when Greavettes were searching for a suitable replacement for the St. Lawrence, the electric-start "Midget" was chosen to be the successor. Largely through the efforts of James G. Perrin, of Gordon Trent & Co. Ltd., the stock MW1 "Midget" engine was modified somewhat to suit the special requirements of the Dispro, and the first boats so equipped appeared in 1951.

The Coventry Victor "Midget" had a 285 c.c. (17.4 cu. in.) displacement and could develop 6½ h.p. at its full rated r.p.m. of 3300. When installed in Greavette D.P.s, however, it was fitted with a propeller which prevented it from achieving a speed anywhere near its maximum capability. As a result, only about 4½ h.p. was available at full throttle. This may have been done for three reasons: to improve fuel consumption, to reduce noise and vibration, and to ease the burden on the universal joint and device mechanism, which was ill-equipped in its "stock" condition to withstand such high rotative speeds and forces.

---

[14] Later known as Trent & Perrin Ltd.

The new bigger and faster DISPRO
with the COVENTRY VICTOR ENGINE

Here is what you have been looking for . . .

The Boat with the Disappearing Propeller is right up to the last minute now with a compact 4 cycle power plant that makes the Dis-Pro as slick as your new convertible or your fast runabout.

The British built Coventry Victor MW engine, a horizontally opposed, vibrationless twin with a 6-volt electric starter, water cooled and oil pressure system, developing 6-8 h.p. is now standard equipment for Dis-Pro boats.

Top speed of 14 m.p.h. is now obtainable with the Victor engine and for trolling she is a fisherman's dream.

There is nothing like the Greavette Dis-Pro for all round family safety and fishing. An 18-footer that will go anywhere under power in water that will float a skiff, she's the perfect answer to the cottager's prayer. Sandbars, sunken logs, weeds and rocks can not damage her disappearing propeller.

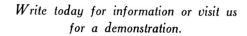

Write today for information or visit us for a demonstration.

Greavette
BOATS LIMITED
Gravenhurst, Ontario,   Canada

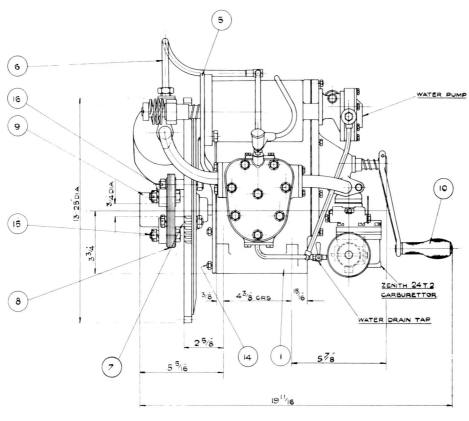

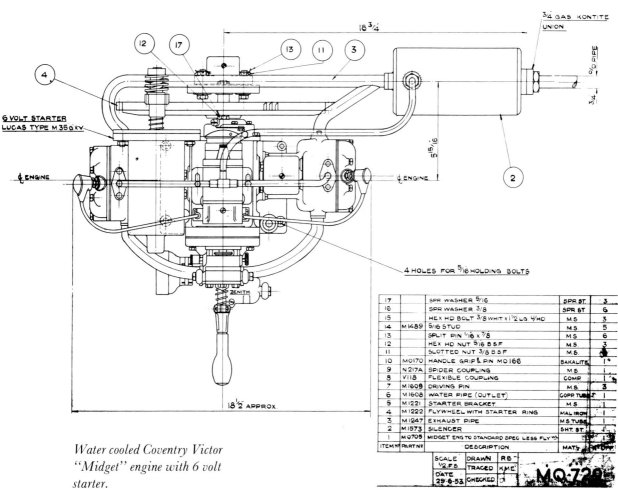

Water cooled Coventry Victor "Midget" engine with 6 volt starter.

ITEM Nº	PART Nº	DESCRIPTION	MAT'L	Nº OFF
17		SPR WASHER 5/16	SPR. ST.	3
16		SPR WASHER 3/8	SPR. ST.	6
15	M 1489	HEX HD BOLT 3/8 WHIT x 1 1/2 LG 4/HD	M.S.	3
14	M 1489	5/16 STUD	M.S.	5
13		SPLIT PIN 1/16 x 7/8	M.S.	6
12		HEX HD NUT 5/16 B.S.F.	M.S.	3
11		SLOTTED NUT 3/8 B.S.F.	M.S.	3
10	M0170	HANDLE GRIP & PIN M0166	BAKALITE	1*
9	N 217A	SPIDER COUPLING	M.S.	1
8	V 118	FLEXIBLE COUPLING	COMP.	1
7	M 1609	DRIVING PIN	M.S.	3
6	M 1608	WATER PIPE (OUTLET)	COPP TUBE	1
5	M 1221	STARTER BRACKET	M.S.	1
4	M 1222	FLYWHEEL WITH STARTER RING	MAL.IRON	1
3	M 1247	EXHAUST PIPE	M.S TUBE	1
2	M 1573	SILENCER	SHT. ST.	1
1	MQ705	MIDGET ENG TO STANDARD SPEC LESS FLY WL		1

SCALE 1/2.F.S	DRAWN R.B.	
	TRACED K.M.E	
DATE 29.6.53	CHECKED	MQ.729

Nevertheless, the Coventry Victor Midget soon proved its worth in the 1951 Dispros. Speeds as high as 14 m.p.h. and an 8 h.p. rating were claimed in advertising, although these figures were yet further examples of Dippy ad-writer's exaggeration. The twin-cylinder opposed arrangement was inherently vibration-free, a distinct improvement over the former St. Lawrence. Magneto ignition with fixed timing provided trouble-free spark, and for the first time ever Dispro owners were not required to comprehend the intricacies of manual spark advance and retard. Some disgruntled observers noted that the boats no longer sounded like D.P.s and many purists lamented the passing of the old "one-lungers". But times were changing and that perennial menace, the outboard motor, with its convenience and speed capabilities, was offering ever-increasing competition to the D.P.

Now that the Dispro was able to achieve speeds well beyond anything previously attained it was felt that the narrow fine lines of the craft might be sacrificed somewhat in order to provide better lateral stability. Therefore, hull dimensions were once again altered to produce a flatter, wider bottom much like the old John Bulls. The result was a roomier craft, and one which had less tendency to roll from side to side when passengers were getting in or out.

Coincidental with the introduction of the Coventry Victor, Greavettes sought to revive waning interest in the D.P. by dressing up its appearance. Now workmen were instructed to sort through incoming shipments for extra-wide mahogany planks, and to use them for making up the one-piece seat backs and bottoms. Some boats of this era have been seen with mahogany stems and sternposts as well. With the addition of mahogany bulkheads and dark mahogany plywood decks, and occasionally even mahogany floorboards, the new Dispro had an impressively solid and rich appearance, which undoubtedly did much to boost sales.

The former dashboard plates were discontinued and the new oil pressure gauge and engine controls were mounted directly in holes drilled in the midship mahogany bulkhead.

Even the aluminum device housings underwent one final change. The former raised area above the universal joint was removed and the embossed lettering changed to GREAVETTE BOATS GRAVENHURST ONT.

The old bronze propeller shaft stuffing boxes were eliminated, and a packing gland mounted on a flexible hose was substituted instead. This was not entirely an economic consideration; the poorly designed engine beds provided for the Coventry Victor Midget, resulted in serious propeller shaft alignment problems, and the new flexible stuffing box was much more forgiving of inaccuracies than the former solid units. These rubber hose arrangements, because of their flexibility, were often the source of annoying and occasionally violent harmonic vibrations in the propeller shafts.

The "modernized" Greavette Dispro, with its rich mahogany appearance and much improved speed, was an instant success, although annual production was, at best, never more than half of the record 1947 figure. For a time it looked as though the D.P. might go on forever. Some owners of earlier Dippies were attracted by the convenience of the electric starting and the speed capabilities of the "Midget" engines, creating such a demand that repowering of old Dispros developed into a popular service at Greavette's during the 1950s.[15]

An optional reverse gear was offered, for the first time in the history of the D.P. boat, in 1954. Known as the Coventry Victor "Perfecta", this unit is said to have been first installed in a Dispro built for a Mr. Wade, of Canton, Ohio, for use at his summer home near North Bay. The additional cost of the "Perfecta" gearbox was almost the cost of the engine itself, and its installation involved some fundamental changes, as in device location and

---

[15] *Margie* (see next page) is an example of an older model upgraded at Greavettes by the installation of a Coventry Victor Midget. Several Port Carling-built Dispros are known to have been converted as well.

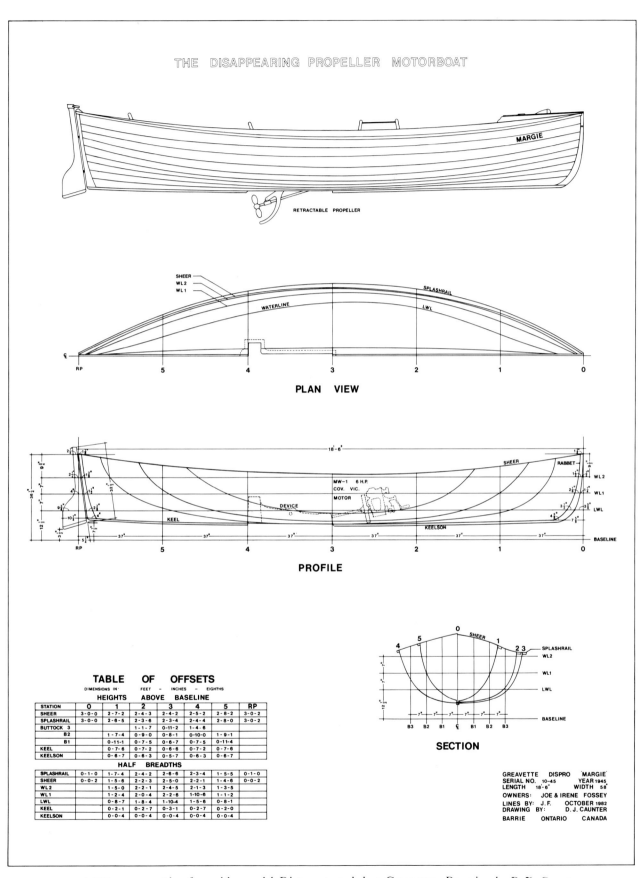

PLAN VIEW

PROFILE

SECTION

TABLE OF OFFSETS

DIMENSIONS IN FEET - INCHES - EIGHTHS

HEIGHTS ABOVE BASELINE

STATION	0	1	2	3	4	5	RP
SHEER	3-0-0	2-7-2	2-4-3	2-4-2	2-5-2	2-8-2	3-0-2
SPLASHRAIL	3-0-0	2-6-5	2-3-6	2-3-4	2-4-4	2-8-0	3-0-2
BUTTOCK 3			1-1-7	0-11-2	1-4-6		
B2		1-7-4	0-9-0	0-8-1	0-10-0	1-9-1	
B1		0-11-1	0-7-5	0-6-7	0-7-5	0-11-4	
KEEL		0-7-6	0-7-2	0-6-6	0-7-2	0-7-6	
KEELSON		0-6-7	0-6-3	0-5-7	0-6-3	0-6-7	

HALF BREADTHS

STATION	0	1	2	3	4	5	RP
SPLASHRAIL	0-1-0	1-7-4	2-4-2	2-6-6	2-3-4	1-5-5	0-1-0
SHEER	0-0-2	1-5-6	2-2-3	2-5-0	2-2-1	1-4-6	0-0-2
WL2		1-5-0	2-2-1	2-4-5	2-1-3	1-3-5	
WL1		1-2-4	2-0-4	2-2-6	1-10-6	1-1-2	
LWL		0-8-7	1-8-4	1-10-4	1-5-6	0-8-1	
KEEL		0-2-1	0-2-7	0-3-1	0-2-7	0-2-0	
KEELSON		0-0-4	0-0-4	0-0-4	0-0-4	0-0-4	

GREAVETTE DISPRO 'MARGIE'
SERIAL NO. 10-45   YEAR 1945
LENGTH 18'-6"   WIDTH 58"
OWNERS: JOE & IRENE FOSSEY
LINES BY: J.F.   OCTOBER 1982
DRAWING BY: D.J. CAUNTER
BARRIE   ONTARIO   CANADA

MARGIE, an example of an older model Dispro upgraded at Greavettes. Drawing by D.J. Caunter.

engine bed design. Largely because correct propeller shaft alignment proved to be virtually impossible to achieve and maintain with this unit, considerable drag was produced, with a resultant top speed reduction. The Dispro would not respond well to the stern hung rudder when operating in reverse. For these reasons, the reverse gear was an unpopular option and only about four Dispros were so equipped.

During these last years of production there were a few customized models made up on special order. In 1953, for instance, a Dispro hull, number 3-53, was purchased by an inventive American who wished to experiment with a battery-operated electric propulsion system. The engine compartment contained the large storage batteries to supply power to an electric motor which was outboard mounted on a gunwale bracket at the bow. Although the boat had no Disappearing Propeller device, and therefore is not, strictly speaking, a Dispro, it is nevertheless an intriguing and unusual craft. It is said to have worked well.

Another customer ordered a Dispro in 1956 which was fitted with a twin-cylinder Kermath engine, a manilla rope fender inset in a special groove in the gunwhales, and several other unsual features, such as a cigarette lighter. The total cost of this custom model came to $1628.50. In one or two other cases unusual engines were installed in new D.P.s on special order.

The factory price of a 1954 Greavette D.P. (without reverse gear) was $1125.00. Extra-cost accessories were listed as: navy top, $110; canvas cover, $37.50; and side steerer tiller $10.00. By 1956, continually rising material and labour costs had driven the price up to $1232.00 for the boat alone. In spite of Greavette's policy of simplifying and cheapening the craft while at the same time making it as attractive in appearance as possible, the competition from modern boats of moulded plywood, aluminum, and now fibreglass-reinforced plastics was inexorably luring more and more customers away. After 1954 rapidly declining sales were an indicator than the venerable Dispro could not survive much longer.

Greavette's built only about ten D.P.s in 1956 and probably none in 1957. It is rumoured that the ten or so boats produced in 1958 were built mainly to please Tom Greavette.

Install this new light Navy Top on your Dis-Pro and enjoy your outing rain or shine.

Navy Top down and up.
Boating Magazine, June 1952.

140

Tom Greavette (left) and Ron MacNab (right). From Boating Magazine, July 1955.
(Celebrating Greavette's 25th Anniversary)

It seems likely that the real reason for the survival of the Dispro into the Space Age was Tom Geavette's special affection for the craft, an affection which was not by this time shared by others in the company. So, when he passed away in August of 1958 at 77 years of age, the Dispro really died with him.

It seems somehow appropriate that the building of the last production D.P.s should coincide closely with the discontinuance of the old 285 c.c. Coventry Victor MW1 engines. Manufacture of this sweetly-running little twin, which had helped to extend the production life of the Dispro far beyond its time, was now ended by the Coventry Victor Motor Co. in favour of a redesigned MW2 model of larger displacement and horsepower.[16]

One former Greavette salesman recalled that the final 1958 production run of D.P. boats proved difficult to sell. For three years afterwards, Greavette Boats displayed one of these craft at the annual Boat Show in Toronto, and at best only three Dispros were sold there per year.

The outboard motor, now mounted on the transom of a fibreglass-reinforced plastic runabout replete with gaudy tailfins had, at last, triumphed over the antique little Dippy. All the Dispro jigs, moulds and plank patterns are said to have been disposed of following Greavette's death, and in October, 1962 the charter of the Disappearing Propeller Boat Company (1936) Limited was cancelled. By strange coincidence, the original Disappearing Propeller Boat Company Limited, which had been established nearly a half-century earlier, on May 2, 1916, but which had remained dormant since its financial collapse in 1924, was also dissolved in 1962, on April 30.

Over a period of 22 years, roughly 380 to 400 D.P.s had taken shape in the Greavette plant on Bay St. in Gravenhurst. And although the Dispro's passing was mourned by many boating enthusiasts, this admiration had not always been shared by the craftsmen who made them for a living. It is only human nature that the construction of a 150 m.p.h. Miss Cana'da Harmsworth racer should make the adrenalin flow faster than the routine of building seemingly endless numbers of slow, small Dippies. Some Greavette workers interviewed actually seemed to resent having had to build them, but then, as now, a workman may not always choose his assignments. Dippies were viewed by some workers as being obsolete even before they were built, and yet others still own and use them with loving pride.

And so, after 40-odd years of production, years of both triumph and despair, Billy Johnston's Disappearing Propeller Boat quietly chugged off into her place in Canadian boating history. Her quiet and simple, yet elegant design will probably never again be matched.

[16] An updated Mark III version of the 340 c.c. Midget MW2 engine is still being manufactured by A.N. Weaver (Coventry Victor) Ltd. in Coventry, England. Of the various manufacturers who supplied engines for use in D.P.s this is the sole survivor.

Being a True Story
of an *Adventurous*
Cruise of Exploration

Reprinted from June, 1922, issue of
MoToR BoatinG

COMPLIMENTS OF

DISAPPEARING PROPELLER BOAT CORPORATION
OF NEW YORK
NORTH TONAWANDA, N. Y.

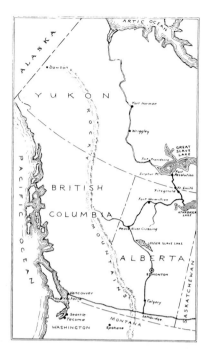

Fifteen Hundred Miles in the Canadian Wilds

An Adventurous Cruise of Exploration to the Fort Norman Oil Fields on Rivers and Inland Seas

By W. G. Ogilvie

WE were assembled at Peace River Crossing, some three hundred miles northwest of Edmonton, fit, in every way, for our 1,500-mile cruise to Fort Norman, in the Mackenzie River District. Only two years before, it had been a peaceful, fur-trading land, and now it was on the verge of an oil boom, a bonanza perhaps, of the first magnitude.

Our party consisted of three: Bill Dyer, of the Geological Staff of the University of Toronto; Rex Henderson, and myself, representing a Toronto syndicate, formed for the express purpose of participating in the claim staking at the Norman field.

Our equipment, or better our means of travel, consisted of a 16-foot Disappearing Propellor Boat, powered by a single cylinder, 3-h.p. engine. It was just one of those boats, that in summer-resorts are termed putt-putts, and very often, more or less sarcastically.

As food in that vast northland is none too plentiful in the early springtime, we were forced to carry a supply sufficient for at least two months, until the first steamboat of the fur-trading companies, should bring down a further supply. Furthermore, all gasoline for the trip, had to be taken from the starting point. Our tiny motor boat could not with any degree of safety or comfort, carry our supply of food and fuel. So an 18-foot Chestnut freight canoe, and a 15-foot Peterboro freight model canoe were brought into requisition.

We figured that 80 gallons of gasoline, with 4 gallons of Polarine, would be sufficient for the trip. Our supply of grub, and it was a generous one, weighed close on to 800 pounds. With our bed-rolls, kits, and our surveying, and

W. G. OGILVIE

camping equipment, the total weight which our three boats should have to carry, and which our little engine should have to shove along, came approximately to 2,400 pounds. To the reader this may not seem a very large load, but to the party setting out on a 1,500-mile journey, down rivers that are of an average width of two miles, and across a vast inland sea, whose sudden squalls are sufficient to put a wholesome fear in the hearts of the sturdy pilots, and captains, who yearly ply these waters, in their large flat-bottomed paddle-wheel steamers, our four inches of free-board seemed none too much to us, when we cast off from the ferry landing at Peace River Crossing.

With the help of a seven-mile current, and with our engine doing her best, the picturesque, little western town of Peace River, dropped out of sight. We were off at last, on our long cruise. I cannot define what our feelings were like, but I fancy they ran along similar lines to those of some adventurous explorer, as he bids good-bye to the last point of civilization, although in our case, we were not saying good-bye to civilization, for we should find it to a certain degree, in the fur-trading posts along the way, but we were bidding farewell to what seemed very precious to us just then, and that was the end of steel, and the countless things it means in that out-of-the-way land. But the nostalgia, if such it was, passed, and we were forced to enjoy the glorious vista spread out before us. The river here narrowed to a width of half a mile, with banks averaging 500 feet in height, banks that were high and rolling, with here, and there, large patches of grass merging into dense groups of poplar, spruce, and birch, all clothed in their fresh spring

21

Memories of a Dispro Salesman

by William G. Ogilvie

It was 1919, after returning from overseas, when I was enjoying a few weeks of camping at Stoney Lake, that I saw my first Dispro. My companions owned an Evinrude outboard motor and while it ran it was fine but there were many times when no amount of coaxing could make that motor come to life. Other times, with one pull of the starter cord, it would run like a top. The owner of the Dispro seemed, in comparison, to have a much more dependable craft. It started at the first flip or two of the flywheel and though our 8 horsepower motor could run rings around the Dispro, we could never be certain that it would start.

It was later on, in the next year or two, that I joined a syndicate to stake oil claims in the Fort Norman area on the lower Mackenzie River. I was asked by the leader of the expedition Dr. William S. Dyer, a geologist, to recommend a safe boat for the trip which would start from the Peace River Crossing, travel down that river and the Slave, across Great Slave Lake and down the Mackenzie. I recommended the Dispro on more than one account but especially because of its dependability. I was also impressed with its seaworthiness due to its double-ended design ideal in a following sea, and the location of the propeller slightly aft of amidships. There the propeller was not likely ever to be spinning out of the water, no matter how high the waves. Not least of the boats recommendations was its ability to make from twenty-five to thirty miles to the gallon. Compared to this performance the outboards, the only other choice, were far too undependable to even consider.

So it was that Dr. Dyer, Rex Henderson and I set forth on the 17th of May, 1921 to navigate the rough and turbulent waters of those far northern rivers and lakes. That little Dispro didn't fail us once. So it was not surprising that later on during 1923 or 1924 that I threw in my lot with that of the Disappearing Propeller Boat Company which then was based in a fine showroom at 92 King Street West, Toronto.

Under Billy Johnston's able guidance the factory was still putting out several hundred boats annually which the Toronto sales staff under the sales manager Judd Wight, a cousin of Mr. Hodgson from Syracuse, managed to find a market for in Canada and abroad. News of the excellence and reliability of the little craft had filtered to the corners of the world and orders came from such far off places as the Amazon River and another from somewhere up in the Andes, where the carburetor had to be changed to use kerosene in place of gasoline because of the rarefied atmosphere. But it was becoming increasingly difficult to sell all the boats the factory produced. Outboard motors became increasingly popular and with their greater horsepower and consequent increased speeds, they were gradually eating into Dispro sales.

Each year the struggle to sell all the boats became greater. More salesmen were taken on and more and more advertising space was used with less satisfactory results. The tempers of the personnel at both factory and sales office often flared. The sales office would blame the factory for slowness of delivery of various models, orders which had been placed months before and the factory employees would blame the slowness and falling off of sales on the sales staff and each year's business would diminish a shade from last year's.

However, no one was greatly alarmed. Sales and production were still sufficient to keep the company in a sound financial position and able to maintain the expensive showroom at 92 King West. It was a good location in the downtown heart of Toronto. In the window was a cut-out model of a half section of the Dis-Pro engine. The 3 h.p. model showed the piston and cylinder moving up and down together with the bronze skeg and the shaft with its propeller and the universal joint. It was an eye-catcher and there would usually be a few window-gazers. Further back in the showroom the three Dispro models were on display, while back of them was the stock and spare parts department. Alongside were the offices for the president, sales manager and office staff.

The sales staff was made up mostly of university boys in medicine and law who were given one day a week to sell from the showroom floor. The rest of the time they followed up leads handed to them. They were on a straight ten percent commission and two or three of them did very well and were able to pay their way through university. At the time I was the only full-time salesman, sometimes on salary for showroom duty and the sale of spare parts. Spare parts were quite a lucrative part of the business. Ordinary wear and tear accounted for the replacement of countless worn out bearings and despite the protection afforded by the skeg and propeller housing a great number of shafts and propellers also needed to be replaced. Because of their safety features users of Dispro boats took all sorts of unnecessary risks and they didn't always escape damage to their propellers. By an unlucky chance the protecting skeg could just miss a sharp projecting rock which would nip off a propeller blade or crumple it up beyond straightening.

Once, shortly after joining the company, I was taken up to see the factory at Port Carling by Judd Wight, the sales manager. There I met Billy Johnston for the first time. He was tall and somewhat angular with a pleasant countenance. The workmen I met appeared to be a congenial group and what I saw of their workmanship impressed me. It was good honest work, nothing shoddy, only the best of materials went into the boats. The workmen took a pride in their skill and accomplishments. It was to be two or three years before I was to revisit the plant and then under different circumstances.

The three horsepower Dis-Pro motor was now manufactured specially for the company by the Automotive Products Co. whose factory was on King Street East not far from the Don River. Here they built the complete engine, several hundred at a time under the supervision of H.R. Astridge. The President of the company was Harry W. Knight who many years later became a mining and financial magnate. But in those Dispro days when I was a junior salesman on floor duty I could not help but observe how J.R.C Hodgson and Harry W. Knight sparred and wrangled away for hours, while fumes from their cigar smoke billowed out over the low partition which separated their office from the showroom and finally all would quieten down and they would leave the office to go out for a belated lunch, after finally settling how many Dis-Pro engines Harry Knight's Automotive Products Plant would build for the season and how much the Disappearing Propeller Company would be paying for them. I suppose it was a very important transaction and the cost of the engines and other machined parts supplied would run into quite a sum of money, though I thought at the time, what a lot of palaver. I think the two men enjoyed their battle of wits and probably each one thought that he had outwitted the other.

It was at times interesting doing floor duty in that first year with the firm. One day a white bearded, elderly gentleman strolled in and almost immediately, when I approached him, told me that he wanted to order a new boat for fishing, but it had to be built wider than any of the three models on the floor. I wrote out the order, but had to leave the price blank as I was not too certain that the company would even unbend sufficiently from the standard production line to build the several inch wider and flatter bottomed craft which he was ordering to be shipped to his summer place on Sturgeon Point. His signature Joseph Flavelle on the order form did not mean anything to me, a fairly recent newcomer to the city, until Miss O'Connor the bookeeper told me that that was Sir Joseph Flavelle and that she was sure that the company would go all out to build him a special wide fishing Dispro.

Plenty of other interesting characters would be fascinated by the moving display in the window and peer into the showroom and finally come in sometimes only to chat. One chap, after looking at the various models for a prospecting trip he had in mind recounted his earlier trip to the Yukon where on climbing up the Chilkoot Pass he had caught up with a fellow traveller struggling up those grueling heights with a piano on his back. I had heard plenty of tall tales and that might have been one. Another would-be-client came and spent a long time sizing up the boats with respect to taking one down through the Colorado canyon. Neither he nor the Yukon character purchased a boat though they were interesting and helped to pass the sometime monotony of being confined to showroom duty.

So far as I can recall the plant remained closed during the winter of 1925 while the newly formed group from Lindsay attempted to set things back in motion. I continued to sell on commission until the spring and was then engaged by Tom Hodgson, the new president, to go up to Port Carling to look after the office and sale of boats and service at the plant. It was a pleasant change, a chance to enjoy a summer in beautiful Muskoka, and I went gladly. Mr. Astridge, who had served for many years as superintendent of the Automotive Products Company building the Dis-Pro motors was engaged to replace Billy Johnston as superintendent of the Port Carling plant.

Mr. Astridge and I arrived at Port Carling about the same time and he immediately hired workmen to clear the decks preparatory to starting production. There was quite a bit of work to be done. The boiler had to be cleaned, saws sharpened and machines oiled and greased, belts mended and a host of minor things to be put back in shape before the wheels could be ready to run again. But Astridge thought of it as a challenge and was enjoying it. He was considerably shaken, though, when he discovered that there wasn't a drawing or even a blueprint of any of the three models of the famous Disappearing Propeller boats and, so far as he could find out from some of the older workmen he had engaged, there never had been any. The boats were built mainly on bare frame moulds and the plank and rib fitting was done by the old fashioned rule of thumb. Astridge, machinist foreman that he was, was aghast at such sloppy methods. No wonder the boats varied in dimensions. Not much, it is true, but here and there there would usually be a discrepancy of an inch or two in length or beam. It didn't really matter too much in that style of boat but to an engineering man like Astridge, who lived with a slide rule in his hand and thought in terms of decimal equivalents through most of his working life, such a way of building boats was nothing short of sacrilege.

Shortly after he had the plant operating to his satisfaction and he found some time to spare on a Sunday, Astridge made his way into the plant and set about drawing up plans. He was determined that from now on they were going to be built to his plans and to proper specifications. No more basket building as he called it. He had blueprints made from his drawings and pinned them up for the workmen to consult. I don't know how closely they adhered to them while Mr. Astridge remained as plant manager, though I do know that after he left the workmen disregarded them completely and followed their old methods.

Sales had continued to fall as summer progressed and management began to cut back on expenditures. Mr. Astridge, a highly paid foreman, was the first to go. He had set up the shop and the forty men that he had hired were performing well and boats were being turned out at a good speed. Comparing the time sheets of the last year made Billy Johnston's practised hands and the four or five of the key men he had under him, present production scale suffered in comparison. Our men took a few hours more to produce a finished craft, but then they were not drawing the higher wages that the former employees had received. The wages ran from forty-five cents an hour for helpers up to the top of seventy-five cents for plankers and finishers. They were content to get the work.

I was now the plant manager as well as continuing on with my other duties. But that new job was a sinecure, the plant ran itself; each man knew his job and did it as well as he could. The only cloud in that summer sky was the knowledge that the supply of orders would soon run out and I would be obliged to lay some of the men off a task far from my liking.

By the end of September production had ceased and all the men let go, except the night watchman and myself, who were to stay on for another month or two. Money was obviously getting scarce and the Lindsay Group were not too eager to invest more that fall.

I was not too certain of my future occupation and had entertained thoughts of seeking more reliable employment elsewhere. It was not hard to leave Muskoka in November, all the tourists had gone, the steamers had ceased to transport their hordes of summer passengers and Port Carling had returned to its normal small village quietness.

I went home to Lakefield to spend Christmas with my family. Tom Hodgson wrote to ask if I would continue to sell for them during the spring. I was not too anxious to go back but I finally wrote to say that I would if they would pay a commission of twenty percent instead of the usual ten. I was almost certain that I wouldn't hear any more from them and I was just as glad, as I could see that they were not going to restore the company to its former prestigious position. They didn't wish to risk putting any more capital in the company and without some better financial backing I couldn't see how it was going to get better. Perhaps it was too much to expect, especially with the outboards offering such powerful competition.

However, they were willing to take me on again, on my terms. I had plenty of incentive with twenty percent commission and good fortune was with me. After I had broken the ice with one or two sales and some of the commission was in my pocket I was closing orders for three or four boats a week.

The company had hired Neil Wilson as Sales Manager. Neil had been Sales Manager of the Tonawanda plant and he had returned to his home town of Toronto after having spent three or four years in the States. He was considerably older than I was and certainly far more experienced in selling. He was a very likeable type and was doing his best to put the company back on its feet with the limited resources put at his disposal.

He had outlined to the management what he required in the way of advertising and when I arrived, he was immersed in sending out a great pile of form letters to a large list of cottage owners, applauding the merits of the "GREATEST LITTLE MOTOR BOAT AFLOAT." I don't know how many thousand form letters he sent out. No doubt they did their job of acquainting the cottager with the good qualities of the Dispros but they were not bringing in many sales and the management was not too happy about the large sums that were being spent in this direction without any visible results.

My sales totalled some sixty orders for the various Dispro models, while less than a dozen orders had come into the office as a result of a barrage of advertising letters.

By early May there was a backlog of close to a hundred orders. Some of these orders stipulated a late May or early June delivery. I was beginning to worry about what was going to be done about them and I dreaded the thoughts of their being cancelled. So far there had been nothing definite from the management as to just when they would be re-opening the factory. Perhaps they weren't going to open it. If not, I could probably kiss the rest of my hard-earned commission money goodbye.

But there was surprising news when I came back to the office after a few day's absence. Neil Wilson had either resigned or had been let go and I was to be appointed not only Sales Manager in his place, but General Manager as well. This was quite a shot in the arm for me. I was still pretty young for a position of that responsibility. I would have little time for any selling now. I had to order sufficient lumber to take care of building the boats, go up and open the plant, take on the forty or fifty men necessary and start producing boats as fast as possible so as to make delivery on the designated dates.

But my first need was to buy a car. I had never owned a car nor indeed driven one and I sauntered into Avenue Road Motors and fell in love with a 1926 Pontiac coupé which had less than eight thousand miles on it. The salesman pointed out a few of the extras that were included, especially the horn which had a beautiful tone. The salesman didn't have to work hard for his commission as I didn't need much persuading before I said that I would take it. After signing the necessary papers the salesman took me for a short drive to familiarize me with the controls and then turned over the wheel to me. I drove up Avenue Road along Davenport and back to the car showroom to drop off the salesman. That was my only driving tuition. One didn't have to pass any driving tests in those days and in a few days of practising I was ready to take on the trip to Port Carling. But first I had to order the lumber.

One of the directors of the company was John Crewe of the Crewe Lumber Company and while his firm didn't stock the cyress we used for planking, they supplied the oak for the ribs. Mr. Crewe extended a letter of credit for twenty thousand feet of first grade cypress lumber and I made arrangements to go to Detroit to hand-pick the lumber before it was shipped. The reason for my concern was that I had noticed a tremendous amount of sappy cypress lumber in last season's shipment. Well over thirty percent had been discarded as not being suitable for boat planking. First class cypress was light and clear grained, very similar to cedar. Boards which were sappy were heavy and liable to turn green or black in the water and rot within a few months. Much of the discarded lumber could be used for seatbacks but definitely not for planking. I had from time to time seen some of the results of a bad and sappy plank having missed the planker's eye. You could actually shove your finger through the worst spots. I arrived at the Detroit Lumber Company and at first I let the men load the lumber into the car. Then I hefted one or two planks and found that some that they were about to let pass as first class was the same heavy, sappy lumber that I had seen cast away on the dock at the plant as not fit for planking. Not trusting the men to pick and choose, I ended up hefting practically every piece of that twenty thousand feet of lumber before it was placed in the car and sealed up for shipment. I know that I saved the company considerable money and I also know that there ought to have been some easier way of accomplishing the saving. I was pretty well worn out when I finally got back to my hotel and I didn't have any energy left to see the sights that the big city offered. I did have the satisfaction later on that summer, after the lumber had arrived at the Port Carling plant and was sorted for planing and cutting into planking, to find that the waste was cut down to about ten percent which could be nicely absorbed into useful lumber for seatbacks.

My first trip to Port Carling via my own car was an experience I will never forget as the roads into Port Carling at certain seasons of the year were pretty hopeless. Anything more than a speed of five miles an hour would have shaken the car to pieces. The steep little rocky inclines didn't give the engine much of a chance to climb them and down the next side was usually a pool of mud, the slough of despond in miniature, I thought, as I sadly forced that once beautiful shining new car of mine through the mire. Somehow I made it to the factory determined that I would try the other road via Bracebridge when I returned. The lumber arrived in due time and I could now take on the full complement of workmen and really get going on producing boats to fill the waiting delivery dates. We didn't do too badly thanks to the honest workmanship of the men.

I still had to make my weekly trips to Toronto to supervise that part of my dominion. I was very concerned about sales. While the university boys were handing in a few orders they were not producing nearly as many sales as in former years and were losing heart to some extent. I could see the writing on the wall (as the fall approached) and it would soon be laying off time again unless sales picked up. I would have to spend more time at the Head Office seeking ways of bolstering up sales.

Meanwhile I made preparations to show a slightly altered model at the Canadian National Exhibition. The company had been in the habit of having a display of their three models at the C.N.E. and they had been very fruitful in both securing some immediate sales and a great number of leads for the sales staff to follow up during the coming winter months.

The slight change I wanted to make in the eighteen-foot Deluxe model which I planned to exhibit at the Ex incorporated a flush deck over the engine compartment in place of the former box with folding lid. Even that small innovation met with some opposition from the working staff who didn't like the idea of changing anything. However, I prevailed and the new deck was put over the motor with a small access hatch, an improvement I thought made the boat look a little less like the 'glorified rowboat' it was often termed.

Exhibition time came. The model was displayed in the only space available — among the washing machines. Not a very good location—though that was where they had been displayed for the past several years and the prospective customers would know where to look. The display did not meet with success, though we did manage to secure a good log of customers' names and addresses for future sales efforts. This was a disappointment to me as I knew that the Lindsay Group of directors would not see much value in a bunch of leads. Of course these leads had to be followed up by a salesman but when a visitor to our booth was good enough to leave his name and address, it meant that he was a serious prospect and wanted the salesman to call on him and discuss the matter. But the Lindsay Group placed little value on these things. Shortly after the Exhibition was over they informed me that they planned to close down, showroom, plant and everything, and put the business up for sale.

Strange as it may seem this famous little craft which had passed through so many troubled seas has had a rebirth. A new and younger generation have taken a fancy to the old Dispro. Stored away in some old barn or tumbledown shed or boat storage place they have found a boat, covered in inches of dust, battered and forlorn. With loving hands these seekers after the old, the out of date, the antique, ease it out from where it has lain, put it on their trailers and carry it away, caring little or nothing of what that will cost in either effort or money.

Three or four years ago I was able to attend an antique boat show held at Gravenhurst. There had been numerous other shows held at various places before and I had somehow missed them. But at Gravenhurst I wandered about taking in the splendid sights of ancient craft that had been restored to even better condition than when they had left their builders hands. Beautiful Minett runabouts dazzling with their several coats of hand rubbed spar varnish and chrome polished to the 'nth degree — Ditchburns too and Sea-Birds, as well as a Billy Johnston Dispro. It was a "Scout" model, similar to the one in which I and my two companions had travelled down the Mackenzie River away back in 1921. When I learned of the years that the proud owner of that "Scout" had spent resurrecting a wreck to its present pristine condition, I thought how Billy Johnston would have been pleased to see this boat, his first love, made so much of.

Dippy Anecdotes & Apocryphal Tales
as compiled by Paul Dodington

Hugh MacLennan, who for many years was a mechanic in the Port Carling Boat Works, recalls seeing a vintage Dippy piloted by two rather ancient white-haired ladies, heading at a snail's pace for the town dock one calm summer's day. In fact, the boat moved so slowly that the last quarter mile took almost two hours. When they finally arrived, the ladies said to Hugh:

"We think there must be something wrong with the boat. It seems to be rather slower than ususal."

Upon inspection, Hugh discovered that the universal joint had broken, and the propeller and shaft were dangling straight down from the skeg.

"The only reason the boat moved at all," he maintains, "Is that the engine exhaust was puffing against the water!"

The usual group of half-dozen elderly former Dispro owners was gathered at the government dock at Pointe-au-Baril station. The recently-arrived flotilla of four restored Dispros was taking on extra supplies for an extended voyage on Georgian Bay and, while the various tins of beans were being carefully stowed away in the respective bilges, the misty-eyed onlookers regaled the voyageurs with tales of untold happy hours spent so long ago, cruising the 30,000 islands.

One old codger stood listening in the background, but did not come forward until the others had departed. He had once owned a Dippy too, he said, and remembered it very well. And, like the others, he had had one particularly happy experience concerning the boat that he wanted to relate.

"The very best thing I ever did with my Dippy happened the day I bought my new bulldozer," he recalled. "I pulled that boat up on the shore and ran the bulldozer back and forth over it dozens of times until there was absolutely nothing left of it. I don't think I've ever enjoyed anything quite as much as getting back at that cursed Dispro for all the dirty tricks it pulled on me!"

Harry Greening, the owner of the legendary Gold Cup Class Ditchburn, *Rainbow IV*, which set an all-time distance record in 1925 on Lake Rosseau by covering 1218.88 miles in 24 hours, owned a Dippy as well. Its name? *Little Rainbow*, of course!

During the 1920s there lived at Hanlan's Island on Toronto Bay a very precise Englishman, named Fred Hedgeman, who had a quaint sense of humour. He owned a Dippy to get back and forth to the city and attached special boards, with the boat's name in large brass letters, on either side of the bow. With a twinkle in his eye he would explain, "She's the *Aquascopia*, the smallest ship of the Cunard Line."

It is a well-known fact among Dippy aficionados that the old "one-lungers" were at times capable of driving even the most patient of owners to the very brink of insanity.

A certain doctor, who had a clinic in the town of Parry Sound, spent his summers at a cottage several miles out in Georgian Bay and each day, he would make the long trip back and forth in an old one-cylinder D.P.

One morning, when he had failed to show up at the office, a rescue boat was despatched to his aid. He was found drifting about half-way between the cottage and the town and it was obvious that he had been attempting vainly to re-start the engine for quite some time. The lifeless Dippy was taken in tow, but the exasperated doctor insisted in continuing his surgery on the engine.

By the time the boats arrived at the town dock, roughly three-quarters of an hour later, the smoke was beginning to come out of the doctor's ears. He grabbed an enormous sledgehammer from his tool box and proceeded in a fit of rage to smash the spark plug right down through the top of the cylinder. That operation being swiftly completed to his satisfaction, he then sauntered off uptown to his waiting patients.

A lady at Key Harbour tells the story of two fishermen in a John Bull who spied a bear swimming between islands in Georgian Bay, near the mouth of the Pickerel River. One of the men, who had a camera, kept urging the other, who was operating the boat, to get closer and closer to the bear so that it could be photographed at close range. As the Dippy drew up alongside the bear, the animal proceeded to climb into the boat and the astonished fishermen were obliged to jump overboard.

The John Bull continued merrily on its way with the bear at the helm.

"Slower than the hour hand of eternity" is a favourite phrase used by Hugh MacLennan to describe the speed characteristics of the more venerable models.

Few authors have been capable of capturing the true essence of a boat's personality in words. The following hilarious passage, quoted from the book entitled, *Ojibway Melody*, published in 1946, written by Harry Symons of Pointe-au-Baril, is a notable exception.

"Now, unless you have known and enjoyed the many unexplainable eccentricities of the earlier vintage models of D.P. it is absolutely beyond the power of any presently known manner of speech to describe their vagaries and whimsies to you..."They are, in our case, definitely a one man contrivance. Let two people try to run them (the vintage models, we refer to throughout) and it all rapidly became very discouraging. If any engine ever coughed or backfired more than ours, we have yet to hear of it. It is, we think, the long distance cougher and backfirer of all time. And we are doubtful if we have ever seen so small an engine that can throw around quite so much oil and grease and gasoline. We do not exaggerate when we state that more of these ingredients go into the bottom of the boat than into the engine itself. And from the bottom of the boat it is not time at all, as you may imagine, before they are all over our clothes, our hands, our face, and even in our hair! And when it comes to getting in the hair, we prefer to revert to outboards, or be left to swim home on our own

"The advantage of the D.P., supposedly, is that it's just a nice homey, comfortable, large-sized rowboat, with this presumable docile and quietly behaved engine in its midriff. And that it can, and will go anywhere a rowboat ordinarily can and will go...because its propeller has a skeg, or metal guard underneath it, which, when hit by some solid body, such as a shoal, or a case of ale, will retract on a hinge-like device, which swings the propeller shaft and propeller upward and safely out of the way, into a cosy little metal box that appears in the after part of the craft, well back of the funnel.

"Having made all its advantages so interesting and so clear to you, we invite you without further delay, and politely, mind, to just jump in and come for a happy, happy spin in what we laughingly refer to as our 'Harmsworth Trophy'.

"It's too bad you slipped and fell as you stepped on the grease on that seat. We thought you knew about that grease. We hope you haven't fractured your pelvis. On the other hand, if it's only a matter of a rib, or a severe strain, we must say you're very lucky. Because the average beginner usually gets something much worse than that, you know.

"Now, would you mind sculling us out clear of the boathouse? Thanks very much, that's nice of you. In the meantime we'll get down on our knees and start dulcet overtures to the engine. Now what's wrong? O, you've bumped your head on the boathouse door overhead? We thought we heard a light crash. Goodness knows we should have warned you. Three people hit it last week. Can we rub it for you? There, how's that? Feeling better?

"O never mind about the oar you've broken while sculling. We still have one, anyway. That's not a bad average is it? One out of two? Now sit down, and relax, and just let yourself drift off into dreams. We won't be any time at all with the engine. It's going to start any minute now. It really can't help itself but start, because we've tugged on every wire, and opened every valve, and closed all the switches, and primed it every place we can think of and ...BANG...!!...BANG...BANG...CRASH...BANG...!!...

"You swim quite well with your clothes on, don't you, all things considered? It's not far, anyway, to the dock. We should make it, if we're lucky. But you'll have to keep swimming, you know. You can't climb up on top of us like that. That won't do any good. No good at all. We'll both of us s-s-s---sink. Why we...we are s-s-sinking! Per--per--perhapsas...well...!

"And that's what we think, too, about our very rare museum piece. Our vintage D.P. Our Harmsworth Trophy. She's a dream in some ways. A perfect dream. And in others...well, we can't say it aloud, without retiring around to the back of the chemical toilet, in case somebody hears us."

One of the most hotly-contested events at the annual Port Carling Regatta back in the '20s and '30s was the Dippy race. Each entrant would strip his boat of seats, toolboxes, lifejackets and any other excess impedimenta so that it would be as light as possible. The contestants, two to a boat, would line their craft up facing outwards along the government dock, engines running full speed, propellers down, each with a third assistant on the dock holding on to the rudder. At the firing of the starter's pistol, each assistant would release his rudder and the boats would go chugging off on their three-mile course up the winding Indian River into Lake Rosseau. The Dippies were to go out around Baker's Island and then return by the same route to the starting point.

To the chagrin of the other contestants, a certain team managed to capture the laurels several seasons in a row by waiting until they had rounded Echo Point in the river, out of sight of the judges, and then one man would get out the oars and row while the other steered. By the time the pair had made their way back to Echo Point, they would be well ahead of the rest and they would ship the oars and complete the home stretch under engine power alone.

Justice finally prevailed, however. The contestants were lined up as usual, awaiting the signal, with engines racing and propellers flailing. Whether by accident or design, the starter's pistol was suddenly fired off behind the dockside assistant of the defenders of the title. He thereupon leaped up in fright, yanking the rudder right off the boat. Legend has it that the rudderless Dippy was last seen careering uncontrollably downstream, amid a jubilant chorus of jeers and catcalls.

Dippies became very popular work boats on the Muskoka Lakes during the Depression, partly because a well-used one could be had for around ten dollars but mainly because, like Model T's, they seemed to be able to carry on in spite of the most incredible abuse.

One day, many years ago, Edwin Rogers, George Hall and Frank Curtis were heading from Port Sandfield out into Lake Rosseau in their work boat, a rather ancient and decrepit John Bull. On this particular occasion they were making pretty slow headway because they were towing a scow which was laden right down with a heavy load of sand. A strong north wind was blowing and, as the craft headed out into open water, huge waves further impeded their slow progress. Suddenly, the Dippy stopped moving altogether, as though an anchor had been dropped overboard. Rogers glanced back just in time to see the scow and the load of sand disappearing beneath the waves. For a moment, it looked as though the D.P. was about to follow the scow stern-first to a watery grave but Rogers hastily grabbed an axe and brought it down with a mighty crash on the after deck, severing the tow line. The John Bull popped back up like a cork, and continued unconcernedly upon its way.

One pitch-black night, just before the second war, a Dippy-load of cottagers was returning home from the Temple Bros. Motion Picture Theatre in Port Carling. As they entered the narrow canoe cut, the operator raised the propeller in order to safely navigate the shallow channel. They had progressed only part way through the cut, which was not much wider than a Dippy in those days, when a dim shape stepped into the boat, walked across the curved engine cover, and jumped out on the other side. Had it not been for the faint additional aroma which mingled with the exhaust fumes, few of the passengers would ever have known that they had just provided Mr. Skunk with a safe dry passage across the cut.

The ill-fated 1917 Water-Ford in which Rev. T.W. Bucklee later lost his life. The lad on the right, Leonard Amey, was in later years night watchman in the defunct D.P. factory. (Courtesy Rev. Stephen Gilbert)

On the morning of December 9, 1923 the Reverend T.W. Bucklee, incumbent of the Anglican Parish of Port Carling, Gregory and Port Sandfield, was on his way to a service at Christ Church, Gregory. The lakes had remained open late that season, so Mr. Bucklee was still making his rounds in the Water-Ford model which had been donated to the parish by the Brough sisters back in 1917.

The temperature had dropped well below freezing the previous night, and a thin sheet of ice had formed in the more sheltered areas of Lake Rosseau. As he neared his destination, the Reverend Bucklee found that the ice extended far out from shore, but being of a rather impetuous nature he forged ahead regardless.

As the little Dippy pushed bravely onward, the razor-sharp edges of the ice cut deeper and deeper into the thin cypress planking. In a short time the bottom was cut completely out of the craft and she quickly went down. Mr. Bucklee lost his life in the chilly waters of Lake Rosseau and thus became the only person known to have been lost at sea in a Dispro. His remains are buried in the little churchyard at Gregory.

```
             IN   LOVING   MEMORY
                    of
          THOMAS WILLIAM BUCKLEE

  Incumbent of Port Carling Nov.1921 to Dec 1923.

            Accidently drowned Dec 9th 1923.

  Absent in the flesh--------Present with the Lord.
```

Memorial to Rev. T.W. Bucklee, lost at sea in a Dispro. (From Port Carling Church of England Magazine, Dec. 1930. Courtesy Port Carling Pioneer Museum)

A quaint couple was often seen in the early days, touring the many lagoons of the Toronto Islands in a Dippy named *Edelweiss*. The boat was equipped with a canopy top and the gentleman, who had a curled-up moustache, was always seen wearing a waistcoat and yachting cap.

About 1920 a number of the factory employees formed an organization sponsored by the Disappearing Propeller Boat Co., known as the Port Carling Amusement Club. Membership fees were 25¢ per month and meetings were held in the old Port Carling Town Hall. At the end of the first season, after paying for coffee, sandwiches and hall rent, there was apparently enough left in the kitty to purchase a secondhand piano! Coffee was made in an old-fashioned boiler about three feet long over a box stove burning 3-foot hardwood sticks.

Almost everyone in the village would turn out every Saturday night to enjoy round and square dancing, all provided by volunteer entertainers. Once a year during the Christmas festive season a really mammoth affair was held and a special band was brought up from Toronto. The band was led by Bert Campton, then Superintendent of Knight Metal Products, who was an expert banjo player. Others played the fiddle, guitar and so forth. For years it was the gala event of the season and in order to pay accommodation and meal expenses for the music makers, there was an admission charge of one dollar!

"People were very honest in those days, and I can remember, on a bet, putting a five dollar bill on the little dock between the main D.P. building and the warehouse, with a small stone over it, and leaving it there for an hour, from five to six o'clock. I went back at six and it was still there."

(G. Tassie, 1974)

"Around 1950 I spent a portion of a summer in Muskoka with my rather frail and elderly aunt. As an impressionable young boy I soon gained great respect for her prowess in handling her "putter", an Uncle Sam, which by that time had seen many summers and was in much the same condition as she.

In those days Dippy owners took it as a matter of proper seamanship always to pass on the wrong side of every buoy, and my aunt was no exception. On a trip to Port Carling one sunny day, we were heading over a very shallow sandy area in the Indian River, on the wrong side of the markers as usual, when the large 750-ton passenger steamer *Sagamo* passed by. For a brief moment, the ship drew all the water out from beneath our little Dippy, and there we were, sitting high and dry on the sand, with the propeller thrashing about up in its housing. In a silent panic, I glanced at my aunt to see what she would do in this terrible predicament. A second or two later, when the wash returned, we were gently floated off the sand and my aunt, with an air of utter nonchalance, shoved the device handle firmly back down again with her foot. Had she been Sir Malcolm Campbell himself, I doubt that I would have been any more impressed."

(Paul Dodington)

Epilogue

by Ron Hill

According to the chart the Dispro era was over in 1958. An idea whose time had come lingered and finally faded into the past. But forgotten? Not on your life! Soon after the last Greavette Dispro was produced a 1922 John Bull was painstakingly restored by Doug McConnan and Ed Stanger at the former's cottage near Port Carling. The boats had been built for so long that only a year after production ceased and the patterns were burnt enthusiasts were restoring earlier models.

Paul Dodington, still a young man, was so impressed with McConnan's and Stanger's work and the fact that a thirty-five year old wooden boat could be made almost like new that he decided to restore his aunt's Dispro, *Wharerah*. This was a formidable task as Hurricane Hazel had sent it to the bottom of the lake in 1954. There it remained until Paul retrieved it in the summer of 1955. Thinking that its gray and incomplete hull was beyond hope he purchased a sound 1921 Dispro named *Pinafore* to replace *Wharerah*. But after seeing McConnan's *Tiddley Jazz* he set about the now familiar routine of removing varnish (safety glasses, gloves, hat and old jeans), sanding, sanding, sanding, replacing missing ribs and planks, renailing and varnishing, varnishing, varnishing.

These three boats, together with a couple of others, were the nucleus of the Dispro Club. Early activities centred on short day trips on the Muskoka lakes, tinkering with engines, and what was called "The Battle of Jutland." The half-dozen restored Dispros and other vintage craft would recreate the famous World War I battle. Those who lived on the east side of Lake Rosseau were the 'Germans,' those on the west side the 'British.' Small fireworks were used as ammunition. The battle would take place after dark and neither side would know exactly where the enemy was lurking. There were many close calls but surprisingly no boats were burnt or sunk and no lives lost. Nevertheless, mounting fears of damage to the carefully renovated boats brought these confrontations to an end in the early seventies.

What remained was the realization that owning and running a vintage Dispro was not only possible but fun. So out of the Battle of Jutland an *ad hoc* Dippy owners' association was formed. The early members were Doug McConnan and *Tiddley Jazz*, Ron Whitehouse and *Helena*, Paul Gockel and *Idle Hour*, Paul and John Dodington and *Pinafore* and *Wharerah*, Tom Wood and *Victoria*, and Ron Hill and *Emily*. The first regatta was planned for August 11-12, 1973 at Woodington House, a rambling, rundown resort on Lake Rosseau. The dining room tables were surrounded by old highbacked, spindled

First Dippy Regatta, Woodington House, Muskoka, August 1973.

presswood chairs which seemed fitting for the Dispro group. There were races — slow and fast (if that is a term you can use with a Dispro), good meals, speeches, a moonlight cruise to Clevelands House and back, and attendance plaques — a memorable event which set the pattern followed to this day. One might add that Woodington House closed down forever on the same Sunday evening that the six little Dispros faded into the twilight heading back to Port Carling.

The first camping trip was in July of 1975. The boats started at Georgian Bay and worked their way through the locks on the Trent River System to Lake Couchiching and back. Another regatta was held on September 10-11, 1977 at the home of Ron Whitehouse at the north end of Lake Rosseau. The annual two week Georgian Bay trips from Port Severn to Manitoulin Island and back started in 1978.

Interest now was intense. Articles appeared in newspapers and magazines, a Dispro was added to the permanent collection of the museum at Port Carling; there was even a Dippy found in the Lake District in England. Dispros were being invited to antique boat regattas in Port Carling, Beaumaris and Gravenhurst. Ron Hill received from the mayor of Gravenhurst two bronze plaques for his *Emily*, one for the best Dispro and the other for best in show under twenty-five feet. Many people were scouring the countryside to find a D.P. to renovate. Both Paul Dodington and Joe Fossey were doing extensive research into the Dispro's history.

The time was now ripe for a formal Dispro Owners Association to be established. Credit must go to Joe Fossey (helped by his wife Irene and Dr. Jim Smith) who after much preparation called the inaugural meeting at the Continental Inn in Barrie on April 29, 1979. The group was a success from the start. Joe became its first president, a position he held for two years, and Jim Smith became secretary-treasurer. The Continental Inn is still used for the annual April meeting although membership is increasing to the point where a new venue will have to be considered. One of the most recent members is The Honourable John Aird, Lieutenant-Governor of Ontario. He purchased the most unbelievably mint-condition Lindsay Dispro yet discovered. It belonged to Howard Fox of 20th Century Fox fame who had a retreat in the Laurentian Mountains north of Montreal.

Dispro Owners Regatta, Pineland's Lodge near Port Sandfield (photo courtesy Laura Rosen).

In September of 1979 and every year since then the club regatta and social weekend has taken place at Pineland's Lodge on Lake Rosseau. This lovely old turreted resort is graciously presided over by Alan and Queenie Reville who are very tolerant of the unusual needs of Dispro owners. The location is perfect for the association because there is a long, gentle sloping beach where more than thirty Dippys can be pulled up for all to see. The beach has even been known to provide easy access for engine repairs. On Sunday morning comes the highlight of the weekend. Some twenty odd Dispros, facing more or less in the same direction and with most engines running, put off for a tour of Lake Rosseau and Lake Joseph. After a sumptuous lunch at the lodge and the presentation of attendance plaques members take their unique craft back home to prepare them for a long winter's rest. Another exciting Dispro season has come to a close.

Port Carling Dispros have become rarer and rarer in recent years. Enthusiasts have been attracted to wrecks in the most advanced state of decomposition. There have been restorations that were hitherto thought impossible. Roger Dyment's *Maigret* is one example of a drastic restoration beautifully and faithfully done.

SARAH, 1979. "Needs work mind you."

Ron Hill's *Sarah* was the first Dispro to be completely disassembled. The original was purchased from Paul Gockel who had abandoned it as a hopeless case years before. What chiefly rendered the boat useless for renovation, other than general rot, abuse and neglect, was a huge hole four planks and a keel wide where the device should have been. This hole was brutally boxed in up to the level of the splash boards so that — believe it or not — an outboard motor could be dropped in. This abomination was removed as well as all ribs, seats, dashboard and what was left of the deck. The boat was then completely reribbed without nails. This ensured that the exact shape would be duplicated. The keel stem and sternpost were removed and replaced with new ones.

SARAH, 1981. "Fifteen minutes after christening and still afloat."

Now each plank, starting with the garboards (next to the keel), was removed, used as a pattern on new cypress and resawed. This permitted each plank on starboard to be matched to its opposite number on portside. This procedure continued for all nine planks, finishing with the sheer plank. The boat now was turned upright and the ribs nailed in permanently, using the original style of copper clout nails. All information regarding plank sizes, bevels, number, size and position of nails, kinds of joints, kinds of wood, etc. was recorded. The only original pieces of wood in their original position were the skyboard (rear deck) and two bulkheads under the captain's seat. All the thicker wood from the original, such as the seats, was planed down to make floor boards and the stern seat.

Most Dispros were made of tidewater cypress which is a terrible wood to work with but beautiful to look at after it is varnished. A blue sun-dappled lake caressing the glistening tawny strakes of a classic Dispro creates a perfect harmony. This cypress is also a wood of astounding decay-resistant properties. There would be few Dippys extant today had they been made of some other wood. A serious fault, however, is that it splits easily. This occurs if the boat is left out of the water too long and dries out and shrinks, or when it is rolled over for winter protection. Split planks are hard to repair and of course leak badly if they are below the water line.

One such boat belongs to Stephen Gilbert who is being the most fanatical of all in his adherence to original design as he does his restoration. Each plank has been removed and the many split ones are glued back together before being replaced in their original position.

It is unlikely that Billy Johnston could have foreseen such exceptional love and devotion being put into his cherished Disappearing Propeller Boat nearly three-quarters of a century after its appearance. He would have been amazed but certainly pleased and gratified.

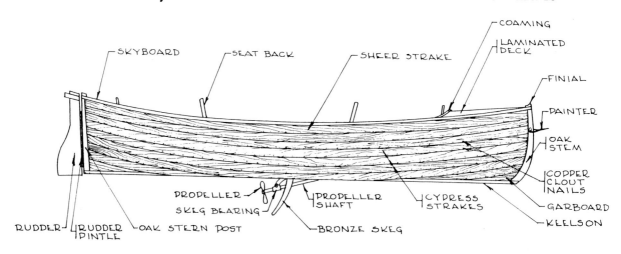

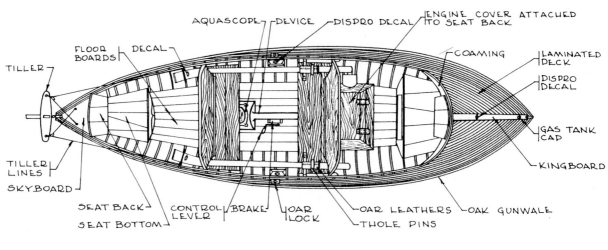

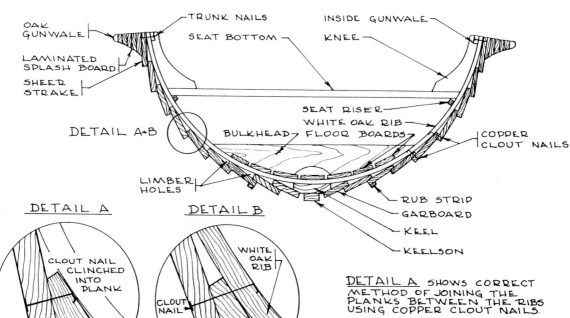

DETAIL A SHOWS CORRECT METHOD OF JOINING THE PLANKS BETWEEN THE RIBS USING COPPER CLOUT NAILS.

DETAIL B SHOWS CORRECT METHOD OF JOINING THE PLANKS TO THE RIB USING COPPER CLOUT NAILS.

APPENDIX 2   D.P. DRAMATIS PERSONAE

The following is a list of persons who are known to have been employed by the Disappearing Propeller Boat Co. Ltd. between 1916 and 1926. An asterisk (*) next to someone's name signifies that this person later went to Lindsay to help establish the D.P. facilities there. Those individuals referred to here as "engineers" were not graduate engineers, but were involved in the engine and device installation. They were known in factory operations as engineers.

PORT CARLING

Amey,* Charles F.: planker. Later: Ditchburn's & Port Carling Boat Works.
Amey, C.J. (father of C.F.): part-time varnisher; installed oar leathers.
Anderson, Alf: varnisher. Later: Ditchburn's.
Anderson, Peter: helped Tassie tow boats to Bala.
Aull, Vera: corporate director.
Batten, Duncan: engineer, blacksmith.
Bradshaw, Charles: night watchman; had pet toad in boiler shed.
Britton, A.H.: company secretary.
Brown, Leslie: operated woodworking machinery.
Campton*, Bert: engineer (Toronto); pioneered dashboard idea.
Carter, (?): chore boy.
Clark, Harold: engineer.
Cooper, Harold: engineer.
Croucher, Alf: planker.
Croucher, Bill: engineer.
Croucher, Don: part-time chore boy.
Croucher, Max (Alf's son): chore boy.
Croucher, Tom: planker; favorite expression: "By gorrie".
Duke, Art: finisher; oversaw construction of storage shed.
Duke, C.J.: planker. Later: Ditchburn's.
Duke, Toby: finisher with Art Duke.
Duncan, Andy: machinery maintenance; from West Gravenhurst.
Eade*, Tom: finisher; had worked at Lindsay coffin factory.
Ennis, Bob: night watchman.
Erichsen-Brown, Frank: company solicitor.
Greavette, Ernie: fastest planker in the plant... when he worked.

Harris, Bud: engineer.
Harris, George: planker.
Harris, Vern: finisher.
Henry, G. Morton: finisher.
Hodgson, John Robinson Clair: President 1916-1924.
Hodgson, Tom: President 1925-1926.
Hurst, Bert: nailer; nicknamed, "Fog Horn".
Johnston*, Johnny: sawyer.
Johnston, William James Jr.: plant manager and inventor.
Johnston, W.J. Sr.: oars; "Uncle Billy Wagtail".
Kaye, Albert: part-time varnisher.
Massey, Clifford (Tip): chore boy; died young.
Massey, Garnet: part-time varnisher.
Massey, Wm.: owned *Vedette, Priscilla* & barges.
McCulley, Charles: factory office manager, 1922-1925.
Milner, Cam: finisher.
Milner, Doug: planker.
Minchinton, Harry: treasurer.
Nott, Art: operated sanding machine.
Ogilvie, William G.: salesman, factory manager, general manager.
Parmenter, Graydon: salesman; Port Carling.
Riddiford, Bert: rudder, engine box maker, nailer, bench work.
Sharpe, Hubert: chore boy.
Stephen*, Eric: planker.
Stephen*, Reginald: head of varnish department.
Sweet, Wm.: cut stem rabbets.
Tassie, Garth: factory office manager, assistant factory manager, salesman.
Wight, G.R.W.: director, sales manager.
Wilson, Neil: secretary.

LINDSAY

Amey*, Charles: planker.
Botting, Sam: plant manager.
Brown, Bill: chore boy.
Campton*, Bert: engineer, machine shop.
Cope, Lionel: nailer.
Eade*, Thomas: helped Johnny Johnston, finisher.
Eberts, Lloyd (Ike): finishing, ribbing, planking.
Griffiths, Bill: engineer.
Hawkes, Bert: designer.

Johnston*, Johnny: millwork, sawyer.
Milburn, John: (?).
Saunders, Pat: finisher.
Shine, Frank: maintenance man.
Smith, Ross: machine shop.
Stephen*, Eric: planker.
Stephen*, Reg: varnisher.
Thompson, George: machine shop.
Tillcock, Fred: engineer.

GRAVENHURST

Barnes, Dempsey: boatbuilder, Dispro Bldr.
Borneman, Murray: built last 10 D.P.s.
Cossey, Tom: built 1st Dispro.
Greavette, Ernie: boatbuilder, D.P. Boat Co.
Hawker, Bert: designer.
Hayton, Ike.: engineer. Copper jacket & St. Law.
Hurst, Bert: motor mechanic & installer, D.P. Boat, foreman.

Miller, Pete: boatbuilder.
MacNab, Ron: general mgr.
Robinson, Vince: engine installer.
Scheel, Cecil: finisher.
Scheel, Wes: finisher
Thrift, Jim: boatbuilder.
Tillcock, Fred: machinist, Lindsay.

161

APPENDIX 3 by Paul Dodington

GUIDE TO IDENTIFICATION AND DATING OF DISPRO BOATS — 1916-1958

LOCATION OF SERIAL NUMBERS

The serial numbers on a Dispro boat are found both on the hull and under seats and back rests. Engine numbers bear no relation whatever to the actual boat serial numbers.

On Port Carling models built up to the end of 1921, numbers were pencilled onto the planking, generally about the third or fourth round up from the keel, usually in the vicinity of the bow or stern seat. Sometimes the planker signed his name here too. Seat bottoms and backs were numbered as well, this being done to keep the proper seats with each hull at the factory. There was considerable variation in hull dimensions and this system helped to keep the seats from being mixed up.

Starting at about #2760, in early 1922, the numbers were stamped into the woodwork, although there appears to have been a sporadic use of pencil numbers after this time.

Before the liquidation in the spring of 1925, serial numbers were stamped on the after face of the sternpost, usually near the top.

In 1925 and 1926 they were stamped on the inside of the sternpost, about halfway up from the keel. Of course, all seats and backs were stamped as well. An occasional boat has been seen having the serial number stamped into the keel, just ahead of the engine.

At Lindsay the numbers were once again stamped on the outside of the sternpost, near the top, and on seats as previously.

Boats built after 1936 at Greavettes generally have the number stamped onto the forward face of the stern deck as well as on seats, backs and often under floorboards. Some 1947 models have been seen with pencilled numbers.

Boats have often been found with two or more different serial numbers. There are several explanations for this. As the seats were usually kept separate from the boats in the factory warehouses, sometimes the first set of seats that fitted properly were installed in the boat when it was sold. Many boats have had damaged seats replaced with seats from other derelict boats over the years. And it is known that some Greavette boats were originally sold with seats and floorboards from other Greavette boats built in different years.

Therefore, the only way to be absolutely sure of the number of a Dippy is to locate it somewhere on the hull itself.

DISPRO SERIAL NUMBERING SYSTEMS

PORT CARLING 1916-26

Until 1919 a block numbering system was used. For example, all 1916 models were in the 100 series; 1917 models were in the 200 series and so on.

In 1919 the same system was continued except that the first two digits were to indicate the year, while the last two digits were the actual boat serial number for the year. The serial numbers thus became four-digit numbers, and numbers of this type continued through to the end of 1936 production by the Lindsay Disappearing Propeller Boat Company.

However, production in the year 1919 increased so rapidly that over 100 boats had been built part way through the season, and thus, the entire 1900 series had been used up. From this time on numbering was continued serially. It is believed, therefore, that during the year 1919 the serial numbers went up to approximately 2100.

By the end of Port Carling production in September 1926, numbers had reached as high as about 3785. Total Port Carling production was approximately 2025 boats.

TONAWANDA 1921-23

Tonawanda production can be identified by a prefix "A" before the number. Insufficient quantities of Tonawanda-built boats are known to have survived to give a clear picture of the numbering system used, however it appears that numbers may have started at 1, or possibly 100, and ran serially from there. Total production is not known but is estimated roughly at 500.

LINDSAY 1927-36

There were actually two companies operating out of Lindsay. The first, still known as the Disappearing Propeller Boat Company, was really a continuation of the old Port Carling operation and it functioned until about 1931, when it went bankrupt.

This company continued the same system used at Port Carling and all the boats known to have been built by this outfit, save one, are in the 3800 series. The only square stern deluxe dippy known to have survived is #3928. Total production was approximately 130 boats.

The second company was formed in 1932 by Sam Botting and George Thompson and was called the "Lindsay Disappearing Propeller Boat Company," to differentiate from the previous operation under C.J. Barr. Boats built by this company have serial numbers in the 4000 series, the highest known presently being 4031. Total production is thought to be approximately 40 boats.

GRAVENHURST 1937-58

Dispros built by Greavette Boats in Gravenhurst, Ontario were actually built for a separate holding company called the "Disappearing Propeller Boat Co., 1936, Ltd." and thus they are not numbered in regular Greavette production.

The numbering system which had been in use for nearly 20 years was abandoned, and a new one introduced. Starting with first Greavette production in 1937, a double-barrelled number was used, with a space or a dash between the two numbers. In the beginning the boat number came first, then the year; for example, 7-37 was the seventh boat built in 1937. The numbers did not run serially, however, as the following year, the boat numbers started all over again at 1. Thus 1938 production would be numbered 1-38, 2-38 etc.

In 1941, someone began reversing the sequence of the numbers and the year came first. Thus, the first boat built in 1941 was 41-1. During subsequent years the numbers were reversed at random, sometimes within the same year. It is therefore possible that two Greavette-built Dispros may appear to have identical serial numbers. In the odd case it is difficult to establish the exact year of manufacture with any degree of certainty. As there was considerable change in both hull and mechanical design during the Greavette period, questionable serial numbers can usually be decoded fairly readily by someone having a good knowledge of these changes.

Both stamped and pencilled numbers have been seen on Greavettes, the latter particularly in 1947.

No production figures are available, but it is estimated that a total of about 380 to 400 Dispros were built at Greavettes during this period. None appear to have been built during 1943, 1944, or 1957.

As no original factory records are known to exist this serial number listing is intended only as a rough dating guide. It is constantly subject to revision as more information comes to light. The Lindsay period 1927-36 is particularly nebulous.

The following list has been compiled from an exhaustive study of surviving D.P.'s rather than relying on original advertising claims. During all periods of production there were wildly exaggerated estimates of quantities of boats produced annually.

1916	100 series	
1917	200 series	Disappearing Propeller Boat Co. under W.J. Johnston and
1918	300 series	J.R.C. Hodgson, Port Carling, Ontario
1919	1901 to 2100	
1920	2101 to 2375	
1921	2376 to 2725	1921 to 1923
1922	2726 to 3050	Tonawanda Production: insufficient data available.
1923	3051 to 3350	able. All boats seen have a prefix "A" before the
1924	3351 to 3580	three-digit serial number.
1925	3581 to 3640	Disappearing Propeller Boat Co. in Liquidation, Port Carling
1925	3641 to 3700	Disappearing Propeller Boat Co. under Tom Hodgson,
1926	3701 to 3785	Port Carling, Ontario
1927	3800 to 3835	
1928	3836 to 3870	Disappearing Propeller Boat Co. under C.J. Barr at Sam
1929	3871 to 3905	Botting's shop, Lindsay, Ontario
1930	3906 to 3930	
1933	4000 to 4010	
1934	4011 to 4020	Lindsay Disappearing Propeller Boat Co., under Sam Botting
1935	4021 to 4030	
1936	4031 to 4040	

1937 to 1958

All Greavette boats have a two-part serial number indicating the year and the boat number within that year. For example, No. 47-2 is the second boat built in 1947. Sometimes the year comes before the boat number, and sometimes vice versa. There is no standardization of numbering, even within model years.

Port Carling Total Production Approx. 2025
Tonawanda Total Production Approx. 500
Lindsay Total Production Approx. 170
Greavette Total Production Approx. 400
TOTAL ENTIRE PRODUCTION APPROX. 3100 BOATS

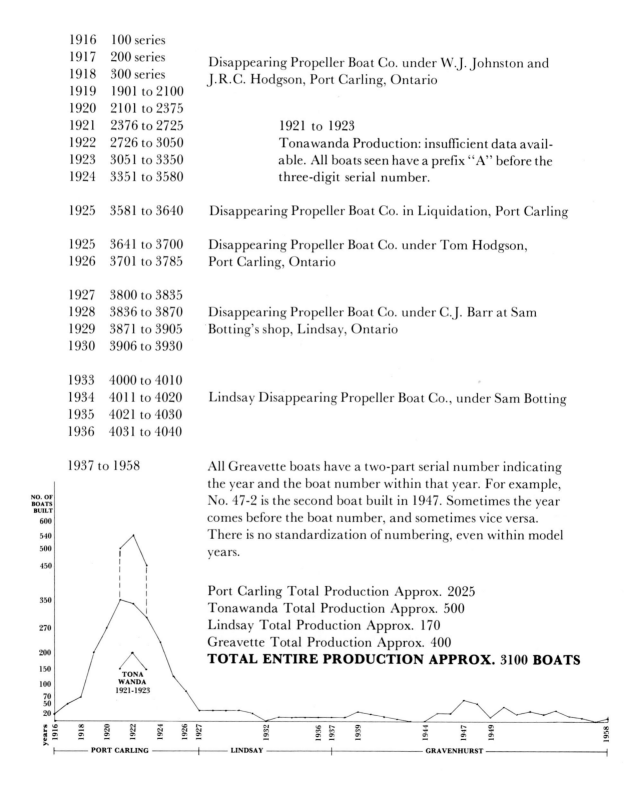

APPENDIX 4 by Paul Dodington

ENGINE SPECIFICATION CHART

ENGINE NAME	MANUFACTURER	MODEL	YEARS USED	ESTIMATED[1] ENGINE SER. # GROUPINGS	# OF CYLINDERS	STARTING	ENGINE WT. (w. muffler) IN LBS.	BORE	STROKE	DISPLACEMENT (cu.in. unless specified)	H.P.	TYPE OF IGNITION	PROPELLERS # OF BLADES	DIA.	PITCH	ROTATION
Waterman	Waterman Motor Co. Detroit, Mich. (1915-16) Arrow Machine and Motor Co., N.Y. (1917)	K1	1915-17	16000	1	HAND CRANK	40	2¾"	3"	17¾	2	Vibrator coil and 6v dry cell battery	2	10"	14"	L.H.
Kingfisher	A.D. Fisher Co. Toronto, Ont.	A1	1918	18000 - 18200	1	HAND CRANK	40	2¾"	3"	17¾	2	Vibrator coil and 6v dry cell battery	2	10"	14"	L.H.
Kingfisher	A.D. Fisher Co. Toronto, Ont.	A2	1919	20500 - 20700	1	HAND CRANK	42	2¾"	3"	17¾	2½	Vibrator coil and 6v dry cell battery	2	10"	14"	L.H.
Waterman	Arrow Machine and Motor Co. N.Y.	K2	1918-19	16200	2	HAND CRANK	65	2¾"	3"	35½	4 @ 800 rpm	2 vibr. coils and 6v dry cell battery	4	10"	14"	L.H.
Silent Dis-Pro	Knight Metal Products, Toronto	D1	1920-21	2000 - 2900	1	HAND CRANK	55	2⅞"	3"	19½	3 @ 906 rpm	Vibrator coil and 6v dry cell battery	2	10"	14"	L.H.
Silent Dis-Pro	Knight Metal Products, Toronto	D2	1920-1928?	4000 - 4125	2	Hand Crank Treadle, or Recoil	83	2⅞"	3"	39	6	2 vibr. coils and 6v dry cell battery	4	10"	14"	L.H.
Silent Dis-Pro	Automotive Products Ltd. (Clear Vision Pump Co.) (Service Station Equip.) Tor	E1	1922-1926 1932-36	3000 - 5550	1	RECOIL	60	2⅞"	3"	19½	3 @ 906 rpm	See Footnote 6	2	10"	14"	L.H.
Caron[2]	Caron Bros. Sales Corp., Montreal	S	1926-30(?)	500 - 630	1	RECOIL	75	3"	2¼"	15.89	3-4	Vibrator coil and 6v dry cell battery	3	9"	7¾"	L.H.
Caron[2]	Caron Bros. Sales Corp., Montreal	M	1927-1930	500 - 630	1	RECOIL	125	3½"	3"	38½	5-6	Vibrator coil and 6v dry cell battery	3	10"	12"	L.H.
St. Lawrence	St. Lawrence Engine Co., Brockville, Ont.	XA	1934-1936	6500	1	RECOIL	105	3¼"	3½"	29	3-4 @ 750-900 rpm	Vibrator coil and 6v dry cell battery	3	10"	18"	L.H.
Dispro Special	Greavette Boats Gravenhurst, Ont.	Modified E1 E39T	1937-45	See Footnote 4	1	See Footnote 5	55-75	2⅞"	3"	19½	3 @ 906 rpm	See Footnote 7	2	10"	14"	L.H.
St. Lawrence	St. Lawrence Engine Co., Brockville, Ont.	XAE	1946-50	7540 - 7950	1	ELEC TRIC	132	3¼"	3½"	29	3-5 @ 750-900 rpm	Vibrator coil and 6v storage battery	3	10"	18"	R.H.
Midget[3]	Coventry Victor Motor Co., Coventry, England	PMW1 MW1	1951-58	25220 - 30600	2	ELEC TRIC	105	55 mm	60 mm	285cc	4 @ 2000 6½ @ 3300	Magneto (B.T.H. or Lucas)	2	8"	5"	L.H.

[1] These serial number groupings have been estimated from a study of existing boats, and are accurate to the best of present knowledge.
[2] Most Caron engines became troublesome, and were later replaced with St. Lawrence engines.
[3] Only one Dispro is known to have been factory equipped with a non-standard engine: #56-8 had a 2-cylinder Kermath #111055.
[4] No numbers before 1940. 1940-45 electric start models in 500 series.
[5] 1937-40 Recoil; 1940-45 Electric.
[6] Vibrator coil and 7½ volt dry cell battery (some with magneto 1934-36).
[7] A) 1937-8 vibrator coil and dry battery, B) 1938 flywheel magneto (optional), C) 1939-45 Delco coil wet or dry 6 volt battery.

BIBLIOGRAPHY

BOOKS & PERIODICALS

Murray, Florence B., *Muskoka and Haliburton 1615-1875*, (University of Toronto Press, 1963)

Cope, Leila M., *A History of the Village of Port Carling*, (Herald-Gazette Press, Bracebridge, 1956)

Rogers, John, *Muskoka Lakes Blue Book Directory and Chart*, (Capt. John Rogers, Port Sandfield, Muskoka, 1915)

Rogers, John, *Muskoka Lakes Blue Book Directory and Chart*, (Capt. John Rogers, Port Sandfield, Muskoka, 1918)

Beach, S.M., et al, *1921 Port Carling Ripple*, (Young People's Union, Port Carling, 1921); (reprinted by Port Carling Pioneer Museum, 1979)

Disappearing Propeller Boat Co. Ltd., *Instructions for Disappearing Propeller Boat Owners*, circa 1922, (D.P. Boat Co., 92 King St. West, Toronto)

Kallman, Potvin & Winters, *Encyclopedia of Music in Canada* (University of Toronto Press, 1981)

Symons, Harry, *Ojibway Melody*, (Harry Symons, Pointe-au-Baril, 1946)

Carding, Rev. A.E., *Port Carling Church of England Magazine*, (Port Carling, December, 1930)

Guide to the Northern Lakes of Canada, (Williamson & Co., Toronto, 1888)

Stern, P. Van D., *Tin Lizzie*, (Simon & Schuster, 1955)

Ogilvie, W.G., *Fifteen Hundred Miles in the Canadian Wilds*, (Disappearing Propeller Boat Corp. of N.Y., North Tonawanda, N.Y., 1922)

Toronto City Directories, 1915, 1919, 1920, 1921, 1922, 1923, 1924, 1925, 1929

Caron Bros. Sales Corp., *Instructions for the Operation of the Caron Marine Engine*, (Montreal 1926)

D.P. Boat Co. Ltd., *Instructions for the Operation of the Caron Motor*, Toronto 1926

North Tonawanda Directory, 1922

Sorenson, Charles E., *My Forty Years with Ford*, (Macmillan, N.Y. 1956)

ADVERTISEMENTS AND MAGAZINE ARTICLES

Canadian Motor Boat magazine, *Disappearing Propeller Boat Co. Ltd. Advertisement*, August 1917

Maclean's magazine, *McMullen & Lee advertisement*, May 1918

Canadian Motor Boat magazine, *Unique Power Boats Traverse the Waters of Hudson Bay*, circa 1918

Popular Mechanics, 1913, (exact date unknown) *Power Driven Catamaran*

Popular Mechanics, circa 1913, *New Shallow Water Boat For Explorers*

UNPUBLISHED MANUSCRIPTS

Tassie, J.S.G., *A sketch of the Boat Building Industry at Port Carling*, circa 1938, (Author's collection)

Vincent, Tom, (Pseudonym of Thompson, Gordon V.), *Come Take a Trip in My Dippy-Dip-Dip*, Toronto, circa 1922, (Author's collection)

Sanford Women's Institute, *Tweedsmuir History Book*, 1952-1956, (Port Carling Public Library)

CATALOGUES

Arrow Motor & Machine Co. *Catalogue*, 1917, (30 Church St., New York)

T. Eaton Co. Ltd. *Spring and Summer Catalogue*, 1927, (Toronto)

Disappearing Propeller Boat Co. Ltd. *Catalogue*, 1919, (69 Bay St., Toronto)

Disappearing Propeller Boat Co. Ltd. *Catalogue*, 1920, (92 King St. West, Toronto, Ontario)

Disappearing Propeller Boat Co. Ltd. *Catalogue*, 1921, (92 King St. West, Toronto, Ontario)

Disappearing Propeller Boat Corporation of New York *Catalogue*, 1922 (North Tonawanda, N.Y.)

Port Carling Boat Works Ltd. *Catalogue*, 1926, (Port Carling, Ontario)

Disappearing Propeller Boat Co. Ltd. *Catalogue*, 1925-26, (92 King St. West, Toronto, Ontario)

A.R. Williams Machinery Co. *Catalogue*, circa 1924, (Toronto, Ontario)

Johnson Motor Co. *Catalogue*, 1922 (South Bend, Indiana, U.S.A.)

LETTERS PATENT — DISPRO DEVICE

161,292 Canada, (to W.J. Johnston Jr. and R.A. Shields), issued March 16, 1915

1,151,107 United States, (to W.J. Johnston Jr. and R.A. Shields), issued August 24, 1915

170,381 Canada, (to W.J. Johnston Jr. and J.R.C. Hodgson), issued June 27, 1916

1,225,252 United States, (to W.J. Johnston Jr. and J.R.C. Hodgson), issued May 8, 1917

104,178 United Kingdom and Isle of Man, (to W.J. Johnston Jr. and J.R.C. Hodgson), issued Jan. 3, 1918
225,945 Canada, (to H.R. Astridge, assignor to D.P. Boat Co), issued Nov 14, 1922
1,434,581 United States, (to H.R. Astridge, assignor to D.P. Boat Co.) issued Nov. 7, 1922
484640 France, (to W.J. Johnston Jr. and J.R.C. Hodgson), date of issue unknown
2986/17 India, (to W.J. Johnston and J.R.C. Hodgson), date of issue unknown
468/17 Italy, (to W.J. Johnston and J.R.C. Hodgson) date of issue unknown
254 Newfoundland, (to W.J. Johnston and J.R.C. Hodgson) date of issue unknown
3223/17 Australia, (to W.J. Johnston and J.R.C. Hodgson), date of issue unknown
7939 Holland, (to W.J. Johnston and J.R.C. Hodgson) date of issue unknown

LETTERS PATENT — CARON ENGINE

210323 Canada, (to W.O. Lavallée, Montreal), issued April 12, 1921
224820 Canada, (to Caron Brothers, Montreal), issued Oct. 17, 1922
1,437,428 United States, (to W.O. Lavallée, Montreal), issued Dec. 5, 1922

LEGAL CITATIONS

Johnston vs. Hodgson, Supreme Court of Ontario #578-25
Disappearing Propeller Boat Co. Ltd. vs. Bank of Nova Scotia, Supreme Court of Ontario #1927-24
Disappearing Propeller Boat Co. Ltd. vs. J.R.C. Hodgson, Second Divisional Court #2914-24, Archives of Ontario
Crown vs. J.R.C. Hodgson, 1924, York County Judge's Criminal Court
William Joseph Johnston and William James Johnston, notarized agreement re Port Sandfield Boat Livery, Nov. 22, 1910

NEWSPAPER CLIPPINGS (FROM TORONTO PAPERS)

"Notice of Judicial Sale of Assets", April, 1925, (undated), (Publisher Unidentified)
"Twenty-Seven Theft Counts", Dec. 7, 1924, (publisher unidentified)
"Boat Company in Tangle", (undated), (publisher unidentified)
"Bank Manager Testifies" (undated), (publisher unidentified)
"Twenty-Six Charges Proved Against Late President", Mar. 11, 1925, (publisher unidentified)
"He's for Speedy Trials", (undated), (publisher unidentified)
"Goes to Trial Judge", (undated), (publisher unidentified)
"Company Owns Patents", (undated), (publisher unidentified)
"Action Against Promoter", March 7, 1925, (The Evening Telegram, Toronto)
"President of Boat Company Liable for Commissions", April 24, 1925, (publisher unidentified)

LETTERS

W.G. Ogilvie, (Mgr., D.P. Boat Co.) to C. Amey, Sept 20, 1926 (letter of reference)
Weston Farmer to Joe Fossey, April 21, 1981
J.R.C. Hodgson to W.J. Johnston Jr., March 8, 1916
J.R.C. Hodgson to W.J. Johnston Jr., Mar. 2, 1922
W.J. Johnston Jr. to R.H. Parmenter K.C., Sept. 8, 1924
J.S.G. Tassie to Furniture Manufacturers Assoc., Toronto, June 5, 1925
W.J. Johnston Jr. to R.H. Parmenter K.C., Sept 2, 1924
T. Hodgson to W.J. Johnston Jr., May 26, 1926
W.G. Ogilvie, letter of reference for C. Amey, Sept. 20, 1926
C.W. Farrar to J.P. Dodington, April 28, 1980
W.J. Johnston to Dr. R.J. Hutchinson, April 27, 1925
R.H. Parmenter K.C. to W.J. Johnston, Aug. 19, 1924
R.H. Parmenter K.C. to W.J. Johnston, Aug. 30, 1924
W.J. Johnston to R.H. Parmenter K.C., August 25, 1924
R.H. Parmenter K.C. to W.J. Johnston, Sept. 4, 1924

DRAWINGS, PROSPECTI AND COLLECTIONS

Dory Shaft Haul-Up, Atlantic Bridge Co. Ltd. Lunenburg, N.S.

File #23792, Ontario Department of Provincial Secretary, (Collection of Documents re. Affairs of
D.P. Boat Co. Ltd.)

Prospectus, D.P. Boat Co. of Delaware, U.S.A., Feb 25, 1922

Installation Plan of Dory Shaft Haul-Up, Lunenburg Foundry and Engineering Co., N.S., Nov. 1918.

PERSONAL INTERVIEWS AND TAPE RECORDINGS

Amey, Charles F., series of personal interviews, 1977-1983, Port Carling, with J.P. Dodington
and P.W. Gockel

Amey, Leonard, personal interview, Feb. 1982, with J.P. Dodington

Cope, Russell, personal interview, Feb. 1980, Bala, with P.W. Gockel

Croucher, William, personal interview, Feb. 1983, Port Carling, with J.P. Dodington

Dixon, John, taped interview, January, 1983, Port Carling, with J.P. Dodington

Johnston, W.J. Jr., personal interview, July 1967, Port Carling, with J.P. Dodington

McCulley, C.J., series of personal discussions, 1965-1982, various occasions Port Carling, with
J.P. Dodington

Milner, Douglas, personal interview, July, 1974, Port Carling, with J.P. Dodington

Ogilvie, W.G., series of personal interviews, 1980 to 1982, Lakefield, Ontario, with J.P. Dodington
and P.W. Gockel, plus 2 tape-recorded interviews, 1981 and 1982.

Riddiford, Bert, taped interview, December, 1981, Port Carling, with J.P. Dodington and P.W.
Gockel

Schreiber, Parry, personal interview, April, 1982, Port Carling, with J.P. Dodington

Stephen, Eric, personal interview, Dec. 1982, Port Carling, with J.P. Dodington and P.W. Gockel

Stephen, Reginald, series of personal interviews, 1965-1979, Port Carling with J.P. Dodington
and P.W. Gockel

Tassie, J.S.G., series of personal interviews, 1970-1977, Port Carling, with J.P. Dodington; also
taped interview with Audrey Duke, December, 1974

*Aerial view of Port Carling as it appeared about the mid-1960s. At lower right can be seen the large
Duke storage shed which was built during the 1930s on the cribs of the old D.P. warehouse. Immediately
to the right is W.J. Johnston Jr.'s Boat Works, (the lower level of the former D.P. factory) and to the
left of Duke's storage shed is the boathouse of the cruiser VEDETTE, located almost exactly on the spot of
W.J. Johnston Sr.'s original Boat Works. (Courtesy H.R. Oakman)*